THE NATURAL HISTORY OF GAME

THE
NATURAL HISTORY
OF GAME

JOHN MARCHINGTON

THE BOYDELL PRESS

First published 1984
by the Boydell Press
an imprint of Boydell & Brewer Ltd
PO Box 9 Woodbridge Suffolk IP12 3DF

British Library Cataloguing in Publication Data

Marchington, John
The natural history of game.
1. Game and game-birds—Great Britain
2. Birds—Great Britain
I. Title
598.2941   QL696.G2
ISBN 0-85115-196-5

TO MY DAUGHTERS
SALLY AND JOANNE

Contents

List of illustrations   vii
Introduction   1

PART I   GAME BIRDS

1   The Red Grouse   7
2   The Grey Partridge   27
3   The Red-legged Partridge   39
4   The Pheasant   46
5   The Ptarmigan   62
     Introduction to the Woodland Grouse   69
6   The Black Grouse   71
7   The Capercaillie   79

PART II   VARIOUS

8   The Woodcock   89
9   The Common Snipe   100
10   The Golden Plover   107
11   The Brown Hare   111
12   The Mountain Hare   125
13   The Wood-Pigeon   130
14   The Rabbit   146

PART III   WILDFOWL

Introduction to the Wildfowl   161
Introduction to the Anatini (Dabbling Ducks)   165

15	The Mallard	167
16	The Wigeon	173
17	The Teal	177
18	The Pintail	181
	Introduction to the Anserini (Swans and true geese)	185
19	The Pink-footed Goose	189
20	The Greylag Goose	193
21	The White-fronted Goose	196
22	The Canada Goose	200
	Conversion tables	205
	Bibliography	207
	Index	213

Illustrations

Colour Plates

			facing p.
I.	Red Grouse	(*Lagopus lagopus scoticus*)	24
II.	Grey partridge	(*Perdix perdix*)	25
III.	Pheasant	(*Phasianus colchicus*)	54
IV.	Blackcock	(*Lyrurus tetrix*)	55
V.	Capercaillie	(*Tetras urogallus*)	88
VI.	Woodcock	(*Scolopax rusticola*)	89
VII.	Wigeon	(*Anas penelope*)	184
VIII.	Teal	(*Anas crecca*)	185

Plates I and II are from John Gould, *Birds of Great Britain* (courtesy of British Museum, Natural History).
Plates III, IV, V, VII are by Maurice Pledger, from *Game Birds*, published by Dragon's World Ltd (courtesy of Linden Artists).
Plate VI is © Trevor Boyer/Lindens, London.

Black and white illustrations
(All photographs are by the author)

1	Due to their low flight grouse are rarely viewed from below. When they are, the full extent of the under-wing white feathering is revealed.	9
2	When flushed, grouse often head downhill to gather speed, but their preference is to follow the contours.	18
3	Colouring varies considerably with sex, location and season.	18
4	Winter wastage in severe conditions can be high.	28
5	Grey partridges in flight.	33
6	Hedgerows provide safer nesting sites than crops but are more vulnerable to predation.	33
7	Red-legs are relatively easily bred.	42
8	At this age partridge chicks are very vulnerable to wet and cold.	42
9	Cock pheasant along a Hebridean estuary.	47
10	Hen pheasant.	56
11	Newly hatched pheasant chicks.	56
12	A well-marked cock pheasant.	60
13	Ptarmigan in full winter plumage.	64

14   Ptarmigan midway between winter and summer plumage—
     photographed in early April.   64
15   Photographs of woodcock in flight are rare.   94
16   The photograph vividly illustrates the size of the bill in
     proportion to the head.   103
17   A snipe springing.   103
18   The black tips to the ears of the brown hare are prominent.   113
19   Hares at dawn in Cambridgeshire.   113
20   Leverets will freeze at the approach of danger rather than
     run.   119
21   Keen sight and powerful legs are the hare's main defences.   119
22   At close quarters the previously dull grey bird reveals a
     myriad of subtle shades.   133
23   A small flock dropping into a clover ley.   137
24   In the spring, when natural food is scarce, buds are
     favoured.   137
25   Few birds can out-fly the wood-pigeon.   141
26   Even at rest rabbits remain alert.   149
27   Wild rabbit of approximately three weeks.   149
28   Caught in mid-leap.   155
29   Severe myxomatosis.   155
30   The mallard is not given the credit it deserves for the beauty
     of its colouring and feathering.   164
31   Duck mallard—we take it for granted that all birds retract
     their 'undercarriage'.   164
32   A healthy brood of mallard.   171
33   Mallard dropping in with undercarriages down.   171
34   Drake wigeon.   175
35   Drake wigeon displaying.   175
36   Drake pintail drinking.   183
37   Drake and duck pintail.   183
38   Pinkfeet and whitefront geese.   188
39   Pinkfoot goose grazing.   192
40   White-front geese overhead.   197
41   White-fronts alarmed.   198
42   Canada goose.   200

Introduction

The last book to be published on the subject of British game appeared, so far as I can trace, in 1946. Written by Brian Vesey-Fitzgerald, and published by Collins in their New Naturalist series, it was an excellent work but is now very much out of date. Nearly forty years have elapsed since its appearance and in that time science has made enormous strides in our knowledge of the natural world. At the same time, the environment in which wild creatures live has changed considerably: in some ways for the better, but mainly for the worse.

The time is ripe, then, for another book on the natural history of British game, but I present the work which follows with a measure of humility. A century ago any naturalist/sportsman could write from his personal observations and produce a book which, if not opening fresh horizons, would at least contain a few tit-bits of new information. For many species, knowledge was limited to merely a scattering of basic details and such facts as the dependence of partridge chicks on insects, or that two distinct races of whitefront geese winter in Britain, were quite unknown. Now there are scientists who have devoted the whole of their careers to studying just one or two species and who could readily fill a complete book on just one aspect of one animal. You will, therefore, appreciate the feeling of humility with which I, a layman, venture to cover such a wide range of mammals and birds.

It may cross your mind to query whether, knowing less of the subject than an impressive array of scientists, I am justified in writing this book at all but, in this area, I stand on firmer ground. A vast range of natural history knowledge now exists but it is widely scattered and, in some cases, is not easy to obtain. For example, anyone interested in learning more of the red grouse could not readily put his, or her, hand on *Maternal Nutrition and Breeding Success in Red Grouse* by Messrs Moss, Watson and Parr, or G. R. Miller's paper on *Burning of Heather Moorland for Red Grouse*, and *Ticks, Louping Ill and Red Grouse on moors in Speyside* by J. S. Duncan and others. My task has been to ascertain those areas in which significant advances have been made; to track down the various papers, books and reports; and then to abstract, condense and present the information in them which is both relevant and interesting for the sportsman. And I hope that this book will not be read just by sportsmen, for the interests of the shooting community and the naturalist run parallel.

Such a combination of interests was not always the case. The sporting literature of the eighteenth and nineteenth centuries was, in the main, concerned with successfully bagging the quarry; and even such a famed sportsman as Colonel Peter Hawker had only a rudimentary knowledge of natural history. It was not until the closing years of the nineteenth century, with the books of Abel Chapman, that we find the combination of an enthusiastic sportsman/naturalist who was also very concerned to see fair play for the quarry. Since then, shooting men have become increasingly interested in the natural history of their quarries and the ethics of the sport. Evidence of this modern philosophy is abundant. The important scientific work of the Game Conservancy is almost entirely funded by the shooting community and the change of name of the old Wildfowlers' Association to the British Association for Sport and Conservation is significant. One point to emerge time after time from my research was that it is not shooting which is the threat to wildlife, but the actions of man in changing or destroying habitats. Shooting, in fact, creates positive conservation by putting in money for habitat conservation or creation where otherwise there might have been only good intentions. And this shooting habitat is invariably good for other, non-sporting species. A wise man once wrote that if quail flew like partridge and tasted like woodcock they would exist in England in abundance. Difficult though it may be for those hostile to shooting to accept, a ban on the sport of shooting would be to the detriment of the countryside generally.

A comparison with the contents of Vesey-Fitzgerald's book will show that time has made changes necessary in both content and coverage. Some species, for example, curlew, jack snipe and eider duck, are now protected and some activities, for example, punt-gunning and gamekeeping, have no place in a book on natural history. Additionally, the economics of space have made it impossible to give full coverage to every species and a degree of rationing has been necessary. This I have done in accordance with the importance of individual species as quarries and, also, the extent of new knowledge.

I have not covered deer, for this is a book for users of shotguns rather than rifles; and in any case, so much more is now known of deer that they warrant a book in their own right.

To a modest degree, and where appropriate, I have dealt with the management techniques applicable to individual species. In most cases considerably more detailed advice is available from The Game Conservancy, at Fordingbridge, Hampshire. This is an appropriate point to commend the work of the Conservancy which for many years—in recent times under the directorship of Charles Cole and for the last few years under Richard Van Oss—has been responsible for many of the advances in our knowledge of the natural history of partridge, pheasant, woodcock, grouse, hare and other species. As with most research, progress comes in slow, painstaking and small steps, which rarely make sufficient impact to generate the increased support the Conservancy badly needs.

Apart from a rare intrusion or so, all measurements and weights are given in the metric scale, which is now used exclusively by the scientific world. For those who still think and judge in Imperial terms, there is a conversion scale at the end of the book, on page 205.

I am grateful to various people for their help, but I am particularly anxious to record my thanks to Dr Richard Potts and Dr Stephen Tapper of The Game Conservancy; Charles Coles, until recently and for some twenty years, Director of The Game Conservancy; Dr David Jenkins of the Institute of Terrestrial Ecology; Dr Tim Lovell and Keith Howman of The World Pheasant Association; Dr Harry V. Thompson, the originator, and until lately director, of The Worplesdon Laboratory of the Ministry of Agriculture, Fisheries and Food; Dr John Harradine, Research Co-ordinator of The British Association for Shooting and Conservation, and Dr M. A. Ogilvie of The Wildfowl Trust.

Additionally, it would be very unjust not to pay tribute to the great assistance I have gained from the Volumes I and II of the *Handbook of the Birds of Europe, the Middle East and North Africa*. Published by the Oxford University Press and with Stanley Cramp as the Chief Editor, this most comprehensive work has been at my elbow throughout.

Finally, my thanks go to Jennifer Sutton for typing the manuscript with such patience and accuracy.

I very much hope that this book gives as much pleasure to its readers as I have derived from writing it.

Mayes Court, Surrey.   JOHN MARCHINGTON
January, 1984

PART I

GAME BIRDS

1

The Red Grouse

It can be argued that the grouse provides more pleasure for the sportsman than any other quarry. Whether or not a curling pheasant in January, sliding down the face of the South Downs on set wings, is a more testing target than a grouse with a gale in its tail appearing over a short horizon in October, is a question of individual assessment. Personally, if I had to shoot for my life I would pick the pheasant, but the truth is unimportant. What matters is that the two provide far more game shooting than all the other game species added together. However, I suggest sportsmen view the two species rather differently: we esteem the pheasant for the sport it provides, but we love the grouse for itself and the surroundings to which it takes us. Read the literature of shooting over the last two centuries, and observe how author after author deals objectively with pheasant shooting, and then waxes lyrical when his attention moves northwards to the moors. Is it just the marvellous surroundings that affect us so? If the two species were transposed, would we feel the same affection for the pheasant in the heather and less for the grouse in its lowland covert? I think not: the pheasant, I suspect, is a little too gaudy for the British. Fine chap though he is, he leads a relatively easy life and our hearts go out to the hardy red-brown grouse who survives atrocious conditions unaided.

The red grouse is one of the family *tetraonidae* which is of the order *Galliformes*. For many years it was thought to be a full species and we were proud of the fact that it could be found nowhere else in the world. Indeed no less an authority than the British Ornithologists' Union granted it full species status as recently as 1952, but now it is accepted that the red grouse is simply one of the sixteen races of the willow grouse spread around the Northern Hemisphere. The sole special distinction of 'our' red grouse is that, unlike its fifteen relatives, it does not go white in winter and, as a result of its demotion, its scientific name becomes *Lagopus lagopus scoticus*.

Whatever the rights or wrongs of its species claim, the red grouse has been a native of these islands for a very long time. James Fisher advanced the theory that the first arrivals came from the north, having been pushed south by the beginning of the last Ice Age. Certainly many grouse remains have been found from the Early and Middle Upper Pleistocene age, that is to say some 150,000 years ago, and the first humans to take grouse were probably Stone Age hunters.

The shooting season begins on August 12, an occasion marked by ridiculous media reporting and publicity stunts, and finishes on December 10. After the pheasant, it is the most important quarry species in Britain and wealthy sportsmen travel from the world over to shoot driven grouse. It is an important provider of work in many a remote Scottish area which would otherwise remain isolated and poorer.

Duncan Macdonald, writing in 1883 in his book *Grouse Disease*, gives some excellent evidence of the effect of the growth in popularity of grouse shooting on moor rents. In 1836 the shootings of Glen Urquhart were let for £100 per year: by 1881 the rent had risen to £2,000. In the same time span the Glen Morison moors rose from £100 to nearly £3,000 per year. Even more dramatic rises occurred with the shootings of Erchless Castle and Fasnakyle, where the rents increased more than twenty times in as many years. And I note with interest that the Macdonald estates on Skye fetched an aggregate of £1,250, for I write these words in a cottage on the very ground. There is also a reference to what may have been the first sporting agent, a Mr Snowie of Inverness who published his first list of shootings to let in 1836, which contained only eight offers. By 1883 his sons were producing three or four large lists every year.

Nowadays the grouse moors of east Scotland cover between two and three million acres, and England and Wales have another million. All this ground is primarily managed for grouse shooting, which gives some idea of the importance of the sport to a substantial part of our wilder areas. Ireland has a further million acres of heathery moorland and west and southern Scotland add a few million more. However, grouse densities on these areas are poor and the shooting takes second place to other uses, usually sheep.

Nor does the value of the grouse end with its value as a target, for it is a prized culinary item. Given a young grouse, properly cooked, this confidence is well placed; but an old male grouse, bagged in some desolate peat hags, could well shatter the confidence of some aspiring young cook.

To describe a grouse as a brown cannon-ball is not wildly inaccurate, for it is of a rotund shape and when hurtling towards one's butt, the description fits well. It has a small head, and relatively short tail and wings. Short or not, the grouse manages to fly very quickly with bursts of rapid wing-beats followed by gliding. Grouse in flight tend to follow the contour lines, rarely rising to any height and often ground hopping at only a few feet. When walked up, they are adept at flitting behind the nearest obstacle to place themselves out of sight at the earliest possible moment. When alarmed, they often move on foot before bursting into flight and usually walk, often slowly but sometimes quickly, uphill, presumably to assist in gaining maximum speed quickly when they flush.

Attempts to describe the appearance of grouse are more difficult than first thoughts suggest, for the plumage patterns vary with race and season. Basically the male is deep vinaceous-brown and the female tawny-brown. Both have black tail feathers which are more obvious in flight. There are two plumages worn during the year, the male displaying the rather curious practice of only wearing his breeding plumage from late spring when the breeding season is over. Having at last achieved his best looks, he retains them until late summer, which explains why we shoot so many handsome cocks. The female very sensibly assumes her breeding plumage in March or April and again retains it until the late summer.

At one time naturalists made great study of grouse skins, dividing them into various types of male and female and, in turn, attributing these types to various areas. Anyone interested in following this line of thought should obtain an original copy of the *Report of the Grouse Disease Committee* 1911 (to which magnificent publication we will return) which has a bewildering array of excellent illustrations of grouse skins. Ogilvie-Grant divided males into three types, females into five and said that, generally speaking, the types depended on the locality. Vesey-FitzGerald poured polite scorn on this and gave personal examples in confirmation of his doubts. My own grouse shooting having been limited to three main areas, I do not feel qualified to give a view; but I am satisfied that there are wide variations on a single moor, never mind an area. I am attracted to the general observations given in the Game Conservancy booklet on *Grouse Management*, in which Adam Watson and G. R. Miller say grouse in north and east Scotland and north-east England are darker, and have more white on their legs and bellies than birds from Wales, Ireland and the western seaboard of Scotland. The reason, they say, is that the latter birds have more yellow barring in the winter plumage which makes them look lighter.

Although both male and female have moulted most of their feathers by the end of August, they continue moulting at a slower pace. By the depths of the winter the grouse of north-east Scotland have virtually stopped moulting. In all areas, the winter plumage is darker than the breeding plumage as the feathering of the latter contains wide yellowish bars. As a final complication, the darker hens are slightly darker than the lightest cocks.

Fortunately we are not obliged to comment when the bag is examined at the end of the day, but the more adventurous might like to bear in mind that in addition to the cocks *usually* being darker, the hens have smaller, pink combs. Old cocks have big red combs and old hens have a paler plumage than their mates. The individual body feathers of a hen are heavily barred, whereas a cock's are finely grained with spots and thinner lines. There is often no difference between the comb colours of young cocks and hens in

1. Due to their low flight grouse are rarely viewed from below. When they are, the full extent of the under-wing white feathering is revealed.

August, but the cock's chin and throat feathers are chestnut and the hen's more yellowish with black bars.

One can avoid commenting on the above aspects without appearing too uninformed, but the ability to separate young from old is essential if face is not to be lost. In mid-August many young are distinguishable just by size; but this guideline is absent with a well-grown covey or after the first few weeks of the season. The three well-known tests for a young bird are that the third primary feather is shorter than its neighbours: that the lower jaw will not hold the weight of the bird without breaking: and that the skull is easily crushed by the thumb. These tests are sound as long as one or more applies, but they suffer the drawback that as the bird develops so the tests fail. Certainly by October few young birds can be detected in this fashion, and many well-grown youngsters will present a puzzle in early September. The more reliable method is to compare the shape of the tips of the two outmost primaries with the remainder. Pointed tips, sometimes with gingery spots, show a young bird and more rounded tips an old one. There are other pointers. A shedding toe nail in August or September indicates an old bird, as does a still growing outermost primary feather and a fully grown third primary. The claws of young grouse are long, smooth and sharp, whereas those of old birds are thicker and blunter.

However, it is the bursa test which is most likely to impress one's fellow guns. This is a short pouch which is sited just inside the vent and leads inwards towards the abdominal cavity. It is present in a young bird and has a depth of some 8–18 mm but is absent in old birds. A primary quill makes an excellent probe.

As we will find on examining other birds of the grouse family later, there is an orange, kidney-shaped, patch over the eye and a crown of a dark red comb. Both are more prominent in the male than the female. The bill is dark brown, the claws horn-brown, and both shed a horny sheath which peels off in summer.

The male red grouse is about 5% larger than the female and the largest are little smaller than the female black grouse. Red grouse are some 37–42 cm long, of which the tail takes some 8–9 cm, and have a wing span of 55–66 cm. They are about 10% larger than ptarmigan. At the start of the shooting season, and including the crop contents, a study gave an average weight for males of 680 g and females 586 g.

Interestingly, while the tarsus and toes are permanently feathered, this feathering is both longer and denser in winter. The explanation of the scientist who discovered this fact is that it assists in walking on snow, but the simpler explanation to cross my mind is that heavier feathering will help to prevent cold feet. (Before readers comment that birds do not suffer from cold feet, may I point to the mention in the chapter on black grouse of their habit of standing on their own droppings to insulate their feet in winter.)

The various racial forms of the willow grouse *Lagopus lagopus* encircle the Northern Hemisphere. In the Western Paleartic, and in addition to Britain, it is found throughout most of Scandinavia, Finland and the northern USSR to 60°N. There have been numerous attempts at introductions, including Denmark, West Germany and Poland. One of the few to succeed was into south-west England in 1915–16, after several failures in the early 1820s.

On the best British moors, which in Scotland means the eastern half of the country, the populations are still at a very high level but elsewhere, both in this country and abroad, there has been a decline. In Ireland numbers have fallen drastically from 1920, and a less dramatic fall began in Britain in the 1930s. In 1976 the total number of breeding pairs in both countries was estimated at half a million. Finland and many areas in the USSR report substantial falls, the former blaming it on excessive hunting. The grouse population in any given area is subject to large fluctuations and much effort has gone into discovering both the reasons and the remedies. It is a subject to be touched on at length later in this chapter.

It is a mistake to think that the red grouse and its close relatives live only on heather moors. In Britain the development of farming has left the red grouse little choice but in wilder, northern areas the willow grouse exists on treeless tundra, bogs, moors, heaths, open wetlands and dunelands in arctic, subarctic, boreal and marginally temperate zones. The ptarmigan apart, the red and willow grouse are the hardiest of their family and will survive in very severe conditions subject only to a food supply. Heather is, obviously, favoured, but many other food plants suffice and in the USSR willow grouse often feed on willow and dwarf birch.

As we will see later, the quality of heather is critical for the red grouse, not just for food but shelter. In particular old heather, of poor nutritious value, is essential for nesting cover and shelter and it is a mistake to burn off all such heather. Feeding grouse rarely move more than 15 m away from tall heather and cocks seeking territories will not consider ground unless at least some of the heather reaches 150 mm. From June to August old heather is also much in demand by moulting grouse. This explains why large moor fires are so detrimental for, while on badly managed moors they clear away large areas of wiry old heather, they render the ground unsuitable for grouse for several years.

The initial effect of tree planting on moorland is often to increase the grouse stocks, particularly where there was previously heavy grazing by sheep. The stock are fenced out, the ground is fertilised and lush, good quality heather develops unchecked. For a few years grouse numbers increase, although shooting over dogs is usually rendered very difficult by the deep, ploughed, drainage ditches half hidden in the heather. However, after the trees have reached a height of about 3 m the grouse desert the woods, irrespective of the quality of the food supply.

Even where heather conditions are good it is noticeable that grouse do not like flat, featureless, areas of moor. Their preference is for broken ground of small hillocks or peat hags, often giving depressions of only a few feet but providing adequate shelter from the winds which are an almost permanent feature of their habitat. In the infinite variety of forms which make up a moor there are small pockets which have a grouse 'feel' to them and the experienced rough shooter after grouse will recognise these areas as surely as a salmon fisher, faced with a new river, will identify potential lies. As confirmation, there are areas on the ground I know well where, in most years, I have found grouse almost irrespective of the changing ages of the heather. A clear impression is found that the liking of the birds for these spots is such that they favour them even in thc ycars of lcsscr hcather quality.

As far as behaviour patterns are concerned, red grouse can be both gregarious and solitary, depending on the time of year, the weather and the social status of the individual. After the family coveys break up in early autumn, they frequently gather into large packs, much to the distress of shoot owners who see most of the population of their moor stream over two butts in a few seconds. As the winter progresses the males become increasingly concerned with establishing and defending individual territories, leaving the females and the non-territory seeking males in small flocks. These flocks feed in non-territorial areas or in territorial areas in the late morning or afternoon when the male owners cease defending them. In hard weather flock sizes increase, with the territory holding males being the last to join.

Red grouse form monogamous pair-bonds, usually from October but sometimes earlier. There is usually an excess of cocks to hens, so while a cock without territory has no chance of a mate, even some territory holding cocks may fail to find a hen. Virtually all the hens pair in the first year but the cocks only if they establish a territory. A 'marriage' may last two or more years but only if the male holds onto his territory. If he fails the relationship breaks up—yet another example of the similarity between human and animal behaviour. Both cock and hen guard and protect the young but the hen alone carries out the incubation and brooding. However, if the hen dies the cock, in keeping with our high regard for him, will take charge of the brood even if very young.

The older cocks are the first to begin establishing their territories each autumn, usually with the ground they occupied in the previous year. Next the young cocks seek unoccupied ground and if there is no suitable territory they challenge the older cocks for theirs. The density of the breeding population each spring appears to be determined by the number of males taking up territories. This might be fairly obvious, except that some cocks are unsuccessful in obtaining territories. The unfortunates who fail disappear over the winter and, as no adjacent moors see an influx of single cocks, the presumption is that they die; and this has been determined in Scottish studies. Having been forced by the competition of their physical superiors into the poorer habitats, they are prey to starvation, disease and predation, although a few survive to take over territories left vacant by the death of the previous owners.

In general terms, then, the population of a moor is limited by territorial behaviour and it is on the territories that the pairs court, copulate, nest and feed. Courting, copulating and nesting can take place in a very small area, so the size of the territory is largely determined by the quality of the food supply upon it. The critical relationship between heather quality and the grouse population now becomes clear, for the better the heather the smaller the area required for each territory and the more territories can be established on a moor. However, the position is not quite so simple, for spring stocks are determined by the territorial behaviour of the cocks in the previous autumn and their aggressiveness is not dependent upon heather quality alone. There is evidence that after a poor breeding season young cocks are more aggressive and take larger territories than older cocks and, conversely, after a good breeding season young cocks are less demanding. The degree of spring stock fluctuations appears to vary from moor to moor, some ranging widely and others being relatively even. In the latter class is a moor on upper Deeside, reported by Adam Watson, where over fifteen years the extremes varied only between 33 and 63 birds per 100 acres. Conversely an Aberdeen moor went from 29 to 2 birds per 100 acres in two years.

This general picture relates to good grouse habitat, where stocks are relatively high and predation is relatively unimportant, as there are more grouse than available territories. Research shows that 7 out of every 8 grouse taken by predators are birds without territories who would be in poorer condition. Such birds also cover a far wider area than territorial grouse and, lacking the same high level of experience of the dangers, escape routes and shelter cover, would be more vulnerable. Even if a bird with territory is killed, it rarely has much effect on the breeding stock as its place is filled by one of the surplus birds. However, the picture is different on marginal ground, in West Scotland and Ireland, where grouse are scarce and predation can severely deplete the breeding stock. The main predators are foxes, hen harriers and golden eagles, with lesser threats coming from peregrines, sparrow hawks, buzzards, cats and stoats.

During the winter most red grouse are communal roosters, often selecting some shelter in the form of a hillock or vegetation and positioning themselves about half a metre apart. A few pairs roost together on their territories in the winter, and nearly all pairs do so in the spring. Roosting commences just after dusk until just before dawn and in the spring the first songs are heard an hour or so before sunrise. In snow, grouse scratch out a hollow and roost facing the wind.

Although cock red grouse are frequently hostile to their own kind and sex, most hostile behaviour occurs in territorial defence. In such confrontations the subordinate bird normally flees or behaves submissively, but if neither gives way they face one another with combs erect, heads forward and wings flicking. The heads are then lowered in unison to the ground and raised again quickly. If the dispute escalates further the cocks then peck at each other, with one or both swivelling and leaping to gain a better position. At its severest the birds strike with the bill and front edge of the wings, sometimes rolling over and over or jumping into the air.

There are numerous other variations of stereotyped performances, all devoted to the one fundamental purpose of holding on to the individual bird's territory and occasionally this can so motivate a cock grouse that it will threaten both humans and vehicles.

To those of us who love the hills, the call of the grouse is one of the most evocative of sounds. The familiar, 'Go-back, Go-back', is better described as 'koh WA-koh WA-koh WA', and is used on landing after the flight song and as an attack call, particularly when displaying at the edge of its territory. There are separate calls for a flight-song (which is also used in an abbreviated form when flushed); a perch-song; flight-intention; chase-call; warning-call; hawk-alarm; sexual-call; assembly call; defence-call; and several others. Many readers will be familiar with the distress call of the young; a shrill cheep, so distinctive that in many areas young grouse are invariably known as cheepers.

Grouse are essentially residents and only move far under duress. In one experiment 818 young grouse were ringed in June and July, over several consecutive years, and recovered in the shooting seasons which followed. Ninety-five per cent of them had moved less than a mile and only two per cent had travelled more than two miles.

There are many reports of large packs of grouse migrating large distances, but no firm evidence. An eagle or harrier will cause most of the birds on a moor to travel a mile or more (and ruin a drive in the process). Grouse will also travel at least half a mile in front of the beaters. However, all these birds will return very quickly, whereas if deep snow covers the heather grouse have little choice but to move downhill until the thaw. This may take them some distance and owners often fear these losses are permanent, but all investigations show they return as soon as the thinning snows expose their food sources.

Of course, the knowledge that grouse rarely move more than a mile is of little consolation to the owner of a small moor where even half a mile will take them over the boundary. The only advice one can give is the old farming adage to, 'tether them by their teeth', which is to say, manage the heather so that the birds have every incentive to stay. There is also the consolation that birds can arrive as well as depart.

Throughout much of the range of the various races of the willow grouse the ground vegetation is under snow cover for much of the winter and the birds live on willow and birch, taking catkins, buds and twigs. Willow is the first preference and, although I cannot find an author to confirm the point, this is obviously the derivation of their name.

In Britain and Ireland the shoots and flowers of heather form most of their diet in summer and practically all of it in winter. This large intake of heather appears to reflect availability rather than preference, for in Sweden heather, although plentiful, is ignored in favour of dwarf shrubs. Certainly, when alternatives are available in summer red grouse take them, particularly the stalks and leaves of blackberry, bilberry and whortleberry, the flowers and shoots of cotton-grass, and the seeds of the heath rush and other grasses. Whether they would feed exclusively on these alternatives, abandoning heather completely, if there was an adequate supply is hard to say. The suggestion cannot be disproved by saying that in high summer red grouse could live entirely without heather but choose not to, for to do so would require greater movement to find the less abundant plants than the plentiful heather. This would take more energy, more time and cause greater exposure to predators. Although one authority states that grouse do not take the actual blaeberries until autumn, eating just the stalks and leaves until then, my own experience is that August grouse frequently have crops stuffed with the berries.

There is growing evidence that insects are of much greater importance for grouse chicks than adults. At the beginning of the century one of the entomologists of the Committee of Enquiry on Grouse Disease found that, 'the food of young grouse is largely made up of insects'. Little further work was done until 1977 when John Savory at the Institute of Terrestrial Ecology examined the crop contents of 100 chicks from moors in the north-east of Scotland. However, this merely showed that insects formed a small proportion by weight of the chicks' diet, and it was not until 1983 that more conclusive evidence came from the Game Conservancy's study areas in northern England.

The results showed that the survival rate of the broods was significantly better when the diet contained more insects. Grouse chicks select heather shoots rich in nitrogen and phosphorus, but to obtain sufficient of these nutrients from heather alone requires eating unreasonably large quantities. An intake of only 10% of insects in a chick's diet could improve nitrogen intake by 50% more than an all-heather diet. Insects are also an excellent source of the 'first-limiting' amino-acids, methionine and lysine.

Brood movements seemed to confirm the preference of the young for insects, as 12 out of 15 broods studied stayed close to the nest for the first two days of life, then moved to damp areas where insect life was abundant. Damp areas, with much sphagnum moss, can produce five times more insects than mature heather and eighteen times more than either burnt or young heather. This is a fact which should be pondered by moor owners contemplating drainage schemes.

It may be more than coincidence that the peak of the cranefly hatch occurs when most grouse chicks are less than two weeks old.

As we saw when considering territorial behaviour, grouse are conscious of heather quality, which leads to the vital fact that heather varies considerably according to management, the soil and the climate. Heather does not like excessively heavy rainfall, which is why the moors of Ireland, Wales and western Scotland have sparser heather and fewer grouse. In the drier climate of eastern Scotland the heather is denser and, if properly managed, sustains larger grouse populations.

The soil is also very important, for good soil grows heather with a higher percentage of nitrogen, phosphorus, potassium and mineral trace elements than poor soil. Moors on limestone, basalt, gabbro and dolerite are usually of good soil while, at the other extreme, moors on granite, quartzite and millstone grit are poor. However, the quality of a moor cannot be judged by merely looking at a geological map to determine the bedrock for this may have been covered, during the Ice Age, by glacial drifting and the top soil could have had very different origins. Even where the underlying rock and soil is of good quality it is of no help if there is a blanket of thick peat, for the heather's feeding roots will not penetrate below about 150 mm and the plants will have to take their nutrients from the rain.

This latter point explains why one sometimes finds grouse in an apparently unattractive area of broken peat hags. The action of the weather in creating the hags has broken through the peat blanket and the heather in the area is more nutritious.

The daily consumption of heather by wild red grouse in Scotland has been calculated as 50–60 g in winter. Although most authorities are silent on the point, Adam Watson states categorically that grouse drink every day from streams, pools and dewdrops and, in winter, from rime and snow.

Of course, moors with good soil do not produce good quality heather every year; nor does the converse apply with poor moors. The weather plays a major part by frequently damaging large areas through winter browning. This can happen at any time between December and April, but principally in January and February, and is the result of anti-cyclonic weather producing sunshine and low humidity, sometimes accompanied by strong winds during the day, followed by hard frost at night. If unprotected by snow, the heather loses water to the dry air faster than the roots can replace it, particularly if the ground is frozen. Within a few days the heather leaves turn brown and die.

This is a very serious matter, not so much for the adult grouse, who can usually find sufficient nourishment to see them through the winter, but for the outcome of the breeding season. Research shows that the degree of chick survival is partly determined by the quality of the eggs; and this quality depends on the condition of the laying hen. Given good heather-growing weather the previous summer, little winter browning and a mild spring

permitting early new growth, the hens commence the breeding season in good condition, lay good quality eggs and hatch strong chicks which survive well. Good chick survival is vital, for most deaths occur in the first week of life and it is a somewhat startling fact that the population of a moor for the coming season is largely determined by heather quality, before the hens even start to lay.

However lay they must, and we will turn to the beginning of this phase, where we find the happy couple, resident on their territory and indulging in a wide range of courtship displays including tail-fanning, wing-drooping, strutting, waltzing, rapid-stamping, bowing and head-waggling. (All of which suggests that humans need not be quite so embarrassed over their own sexual behaviour.) These displays are self-explanatory and, in due course, the cock jumps on the back of the hen, grasps her crown feathers or skin in his bill, droops his wings, moves his fanned tail up and down and mates.

In exceptionally mild weather laying may occur in February and March but the normal period is the second half of April and the first half of May. The nest is a shallow scrape and is usually positioned so that it is at least partly overhung by heather or other vegetation. Some two-thirds of nests are completely lined with vegetation, and the remainder partially lined. The eggs are oval and glossy, coloured basically yellow with blotching and mottling of dark-brown or red-brown. They measure about 46×32 mm and weigh approximately 25 g. The clutch varies between 6–9 with extremes recorded at either end and a tendency for the mean to be slightly larger on high moors than lower. Eggs are laid every one to two days and if the eggs are lost a replacement clutch will be laid. Incubation is by the female only and takes approximately twenty-two days.

Once hatched the chicks leave the nest as soon as they are dry. They are cared for by both parents but brooded by the hen. The young are largely self-feeding and an analysis of the crop contents of chicks in north-east Scotland showed tips of heather formed at least 75% of their diet and anthropods, mainly craneflies, less than 5%. However, as mentioned earlier, there is good evidence that insects are very important for chicks and these results may have indicated insect availability rather than the preference of the chicks. By three weeks chicks have settled to the normal diet of adult grouse.

The young are capable of short flight at 12–13 days and are fully grown in only 30–35 days. In a year when conditions are good they become independent at two months but in a poor year they are often abandoned at six weeks. This illustration of the unsentimentality of nature is reciprocated by the young as hostility develops between them and the parents at about twelve weeks, resulting in a break-up of the family. Some of the young cocks may evict the father from his territory and some of the young hens treat the mother likewise. During the family period the young will crouch and freeze

2. When flushed, grouse often head downhill to gather speed, but their preference is to follow the contours.

3. Colouring varies considerably with sex, location and season.

in response to the warning-call from a parent—a single 'kok' increasing in volume and frequency as the danger intensifies.

Exhaustive statistics exist on breeding success rates, based on work by Jenkins, in 1963, and Watson and Miller in 1971. Of 395 clutches observed, 326 (82.5%) hatched. Of 2,603 eggs laid, 5.4% were predated, 15% were deserted by the hens or failed to hatch, and 79.6% hatched. Chick deaths, as mentioned earlier, were mainly in the first week. In the period 1957–61, the August brood sizes varied between annual means of 1.0–5.2. In the poor years only 10–26% of pairs reared four or more young and in the good years 48–74% achieved this.

Once the young hatch, it is quite common for the family to leave their territory, sometimes moving only a few hundred yards, but often considerably further. As mentioned previously these local migrations are usually made to damp areas with high insect populations but movement also takes place to areas where plant alternatives to heather are temporarily abundant and these limited migrations can explain why a moor which had a promising density of pairs in the spring has only a few birds, many of them single cocks, when shooting begins in August. Normally, however, they return in the early autumn.

Regrettably, even if the birds remain staunchly at home, we will not enjoy their presence for long, as they have a short life-span. In fact, on average, and on good moors where there is a large population, 65% die each year whether shot by sportsmen or not. Until recently it was believed that this high mortality rate was due to the lack of sufficient territories and the near certainty of death for a bird failing to obtain one. However, as I will show shortly, some doubt now exists over this. Further gloomy statistics come from the results of ringing over 1,200 birds. Only 5% lived over three years and only one attained eight years. Most hens only nest once.

So far, in this consideration of the life of the red grouse, we have looked at straightforward and factual matters; but now we consider an aspect which has troubled sportsmen and moor-owners for years. Grouse numbers fluctuate. So do the numbers of numerous other species, but grouse numbers can vary from year to year to a very much greater degree than most other animals. An increase or decrease by five or ten fold is by no means uncommon and a moor which gave excellent sport in one season, and was left with what everyone agreed was a sensible level of breeding stock, can have so few grouse by next August that shooting is cancelled. Obviously with the high value of grouse shooting such fluctations create major loss, not just to the moor-owner or shooting tenant but the many others involved on the periphery, and over many years a number of excellent scientists have tried to solve the problem.

There is ample evidence to show that major population changes have existed for years, and disease has often been blamed. I mentioned earlier

D. G. F. Macdonald's book, *Grouse Disease—its cause and remedies*, which was published in 1883, and in this he wrote, 'It is now eighty years since the alarm of grouse disease was raised in this country.' He goes on to state that many rival theories have been advanced from time to time but, and, indebted though I am to the scientific world, I cannot resist quoting: 'Unfortunately, most of these contributions are from scientists, not from sportsmen, naturalists and keepers. Hence they are not of much practical value.'

Macdonald was by no means the first to record the major declines in grouse populations and lay the blame on disease. *The Zoologist* of 1887 listed a severe outbreak in Sutherland in 1815, and Speedy, whose book *Sport in the Highlands and Lowlands of Scotland* remains fixed in my mind not for the content but the sad dedication to his son lost in the First World War, wrote: 'The first time "Grouse Disease" attracted special attention was 1838. Prior to that date it was not unknown in Scotland but it had not assumed the proportions of a malignant epidemic.' J. G. Millais, in 1894, in his *Game Birds and Shooting-Sketches* said: '. . . the disease once started, it spreads so rapidly that the estate may be decimated in a week, and it may extend its ravages over a whole country'. 'Human powers', he lamented, 'are at present unable to cope with it', to which one might comment that the position remains unchanged.

Not long into the twentieth century a major effort was launched to investigate the so-called grouse disease and a Grouse Disease Committee was formed in 1904. As so often happens in Britain, it was a happy blend of laymen, scientists and administrators, mostly honorary workers and funded by public subscription. The total cost, over six years, was £4,366 and the principal field observer was Edward A. Wilson, who resigned in the autumn of 1910 to join Captain Scott's Antarctic Expedition on the *Terra Nova*. The outcome was two volumes, running into 663 pages, which identified the thread worm *Trichostrongylostenvis*, known as the strongyle, as playing a major part in the problem. However far from viewing their work triumphantly, the Committee concluded, '. . . the present Inquiry has scarcely crossed the threshold of the investigation into the general pathology of birds'.

One popular explanation is that the cause is not disease but that grouse, like many other creatures, have population cycles—that is to say, the fluctuations in numbers are repeated at intervals which are more regular than would be expected by chance. In 1952 J. M. D. Mackenzie and P. A. P. Moran analysed bag records from various Scottish estates for over a century. Their conclusions were that red grouse bag numbers show an oscillatory tendency with a usual period of five to six years. Additionally, bags of all the tetraonids, that is red and black grouse, capercaillie and ptarmigan, are significantly related to one another. Occasionally the bags of the four species move out of phase but then come sharply back into line. And, finally, bags from local populations of red grouse, within a few kilometres of each other, will sometimes drift out of phase but always return.

These conclusions were confirmed by Adam Watson and Robert Moss, of the Institute of Terrestrial Ecology, in a paper *Population cycles in Tetraonidae*, 1979. In this they pointed out that by no means all red grouse populations moved in cycles—some were relatively stable. For reasons of space it is impossible to follow the arguments of this, or indeed any of the other works on the subject of grouse population fluctuations, in any detail. However, a main plank of their argument was that when different populations and species of tetraonids fluctuate, at least partly, in phase over large geographical areas, then there must be some large-scale aspect of the birds' environment which is responsible for this synchronisation. Extrinsic factors such as climate and weather and intrinsic, including food, predation, disease and parasites, together with the interaction of all factors were examined in depth. Put very briefly, their conclusion was that the most likely explanation for cycles is that they are caused by changes in spacing behaviour which occur at high density.

Food quality was ruled out, as the authors had established the possibility of improving heather quality by applying fertilizer. In some experiments this had had the anticipated result of improving heather quality and with it breeding success. However, this treatment failed to halt a large decline in numbers which was part of a cyclic trend.

A paper by D. Chitty in 1967 suggested that when animals are at a very high density the more aggressive individuals enjoy an advantage, and that such aggressors cause great mutual interference. As a result a decline in numbers begins and this lessening population contains a high proportion of aggressive members. Therefore, the decline continues further than it otherwise would and a low population results. At this point there is no longer any advantage in being aggressive and so numbers climb again. The application to this hypothesis in the case of red grouse is that the aggressive birds cause great disturbance to the territorial system and the breeding success rate falls abruptly.

In 1980 the same two authors published a paper setting out their latest conclusions, *Advances in our understanding of population dynamics of red grouse*. Among the contents was a specific rejection that predation was the cause of cyclic declines and also confirmation of their earlier conclusion that 'cycles result from changes in spacing behaviour which occur in response to relatively high densities'.

So we have the view of the two acknowledged experts on the subject, formed after years of investigation, and we should be pleased that an explanation for, as distinct from a solution to, grouse fluctuations has been evolved. However, far from the problem being solved, a large question mark has been thrown over the whole matter by the work of the North of England Grouse Project who, in presenting their thinking up to the beginning of 1982, said: 'These ideas are contrary to some previous research conducted in

Scotland by the Institute of Terrestrial Ecology.' These are, in the very civilised world of scientists, strong words and we had better look at the credentials of the North of England Grouse Project. In fact, it has the impeccable background of the Game Conservancy, who were concerned that, while most of the research on grouse was being carried out in north-east Scotland, different factors might bear on grouse in northern England. The Conservancy held a number of meetings in early 1978 and decided to set up a project to investigate the population, ecology and management of red grouse on the north of England moors. The Earl Peel took the Chairmanship of a steering committee, a main function of which was to raise the finance, and the Director of Research of the Game Conservancy, Dr Richard Potts, took charge of the project, planned to last for seven years. In June 1979 Dr Peter Hudson was appointed the grouse ecologist and since then has worked full time on the project, latterly with an assistant.

Once again, it is impractical to attempt even a review of the investigations, thinking and preliminary conclusions. I can only present the main conclusions in their simplest form. Northern England bag records, analysed on the Game Conservancy computer, demonstrated that fluctuations came in 'quasi-cycles'. this term was used as it was felt the variations were neither pure cycles nor random fluctuations, but were influenced by two factors, one regular and one random. The regular factor is the strongyle worm and the random factor is combination of weather effects, including heather quality and quantity. (This assumes that predators and ticks are effectively controlled and the heather reasonably managed.)

At this point we must look briefly at the strongyle worm. The majority of grouse carry some strongyle worms, which are minute trichostrongyle thread worms, properly visible only through a magnifying glass. A grouse can carry more than 10,000 worms and birds in poor condition usually have more than healthy birds. The worms are carried in the blind gut and in severe cases inflame the wall of the gut, possibly rupturing it and causing internal bleeding and infection. The worms in the gut produce eggs which pass out of the grouse in the caecal droppings (these are the 'melted chocolate' as distinct from the fibrous variety). The eggs hatch and the free-living worm which emerges wriggles up the heather to the growing tip where it is eaten by the grouse. As the eggs do not hatch inside the grouse every worm has to be eaten and, bearing in mind the thousands that a single grouse can hold, the degree of infestation of the heather can be appreciated.

A brief summary of some of the factors contributing to the conclusion that disease is important in cycling is:

1. All cyclic moors had disease present.
2. Non-cyclic moors had relatively low disease levels.
3. Disease levels are related to the density of grouse.

4. Poor breeding success is associated with high worm level.
5. Strongyle worms are picked up by healthy grouse and not as a consequence of stressful conditions.
6. Experiments with the use of anthelmintics have shown significant improvement in breeding success as a result of worm eradication.

The fifth is a particularly important conclusion, for previously most scientists had believed that as worms were present in all grouse they only multiplied and caused death when other factors caused the bird to lose condition. Now the Game Conservancy argues that the uptake of worms occurs in July and early August, before the stress of fighting for territories begins in October.

In essence, therefore, previous thinking had been that disease did not cause the fluctuations but was a consequence of the birds' social behaviour. The Game Conservancy now believes the reverse—that the disease, in combination with the weather, is the cause and not the effect of the quasi-cycles in the population.

If the Game Conservancy's theory is correct our understanding of grouse populations will be clearer and it will be a considerable step in evolving more effective management techniques. As I write, the North of England Grouse Project is devoting much of its resources to test whether strongylosis definitely causes cycles. So far this has involved intensive investigation of radio-marked grouse from which a random sample has been caught and dosed with strongyle worms. Now the intention is to dose grouse on a larger scale.

The outcome may be very significant for the future of the red grouse. It seems that it would be impossible to treat red grouse with preventative medicine in the way we would reared pheasants, but if the strongyle worm is proved to be the villain the attack will switch to investigating the life of the worm to determine how to reduce its numbers. As an example, an initial survey showed that many of the non-cyclic moors, that is moors with relatively stable populations, had significantly lower rainfall than cyclic moors and their worm levels appeared very low. It appears that where rainfall is lower the free-living stages of the worm are less successful. Reducing rainfall on the hills of Britain is hardly a practical proposition, but if we can glean enough facts of this nature it may be possible to evolve practical and economically viable measures to reduce strongyle worm populations.

Before leaving the strongyle worm, I must mention Dr T. Spencer Cobbold, who may be entitled to fame for a prediction he made a century ago. In Mr Macdonald's book of 1883, *Grouse Disease*, which I mentioned in another context earlier, he referred to several views on the cause of grouse disease. Among these he listed a pamphlet by Dr Cobbold and commented, 'The learned doctor believes that grouse disease is caused by a minute

RED GROUSE

Lagopus lagopus scoticus

With the exception of the ptarmigan the red grouse
survives in the most hostile environments to be
found in Britain.

GREY PARTRIDGE

Perdix perdix

In spite of its retiring nature, unassuming plumage
and grating call, the grey, or English, partridge is
much loved by all countrymen.

organism which he calls a strongle. It is to be regretted that he did not pursue the subject further, and inform us what produced the strongle.'

Another, more localised, threat to grouse is louping-ill, a progressive disease of the brain and spinal cord caused by a virus. It is carried by the sheep tick and has been known to affect sheep since at least 1807. Louping-ill was not definitely confirmed in grouse until 1960 but subsequent research shows it can be a major threat in areas carrying a high tick population. A survey in Moray, in the mid-1970s, showed live louping-ill virus or antibodies in about 50% of red grouse chicks and it was calculated that overall survival to August was reduced by no less than 30%. Research with marked chicks showed that the deaths were almost entirely due to louping-ill, for mortality rates were not related to tick numbers but to whether or not the ticks were carrying louping-ill.

Louping-ill is not an overall problem to either grouse or sheep as by no means all areas have heavy populations of ticks. In general the problem is worst in the western Highlands of Scotland, modest in the middle of north Scotland, the lowlands and small areas of England and Wales and low in the extreme north and east of Scotland, northern England and Wales. Tick populations vary partly with the thickness of the mat of semi-decomposed root fibre and litter covering the surface of the moor. Where this mat is less than 1 inch deep ticks are rare, but they increase to the extent that a 3 inch mat has four times the tick population of a 2 inch mat.

The best known remedy against ticks, and with them louping-ill, is adequate and well-planned heather burning, which will lessen the 'mat', but vaccination of sheep, the main carriers of louping-ill, should reduce its effects on grouse. Research at the Game Conservancy is aimed to check whether or not this is the case.

It is the view of Adam Watson and G. R. Miller that, on reasonably well stocked moors, winter predation has little effect on numbers as the birds taken are mainly those without territories. I well recall the uproar of disbelief from the keepering world when this statement was first made some years ago. In their eyes a grouse killed was one bird less on the hill to breed. In fact mortality, particularly in the autumn, is often good for the survivors. If there is insufficient food and territories to see all the population through the winter, some early deaths will improve the chances of survival of the remainder. On the other hand, predation in the nesting season, such as by foxes, can be very serious indeed.

In managing grouse far and away the most important measure is to maintain the heather in the best condition for them. This means burning the right areas, at the right time and in the right way. Ideally the moor needs to be broken up into small patches of heather, all at different stages of growth. Shape is more important than size as grouse will not normally move more than 15 m away from deep heather capable of providing emergency cover. It is better to burn a strip of, say, half a hectare, measuring about 160 m × 25 m, than a square of the same area.

Burning should not be left until the mature stage, but carried out when the plants have numerous woody stems, which are not more than 5–10 mm thick at the base, are 300–400 mm tall and are between ten and twenty years old. Burning requires experience and planning if it is to be done effectively and safely and I can do no better than repeat the advice in the Game Conservancy's Booklet on *Grouse Management*.

1. Avoid burning in unsuitable weather, and stop burning immediately the wind becomes too strong or changes direction dangerously.
2. Have sufficient fire breaks, equipment and men to ensure complete fire control.
3. Burn heather only at the late-building stage when it is 300–380 mm (12–15 inches) tall, has numerous stems less than 5–10 mm (½ inch) thick at the base, and covers the ground densely.
4. Scatter the fires so that many long narrow strips of heather at different stages of growth occur on all parts of the moor.
5. Above all, plan ahead to take every possible opportunity to burn during the lawful burning season.

There is, in my view, little danger for red grouse on the good moors, for the money sportsmen will pay to shoot thereon will continue to make it possible to manage them properly. The position is less happy on the marginal ground where the birds have to look after themselves. The general decline in numbers, both in this country and abroad, shows that red and willow grouse are under pressure and small populations who have clung on precariously for many years may not survive much longer. In particular the less good moors are threatened by increasing sheep densities. Sheep selectively graze heather and high densities eventually result in grassy moors. Grouse populations in some areas of Wales and Derbyshire have been wiped out in this way and moor owners should be aware that in many cases increased sheep numbers will be the end of their grouse.

2

The Grey Partridge

The order *Galliformes* contains an array of colourful and exciting birds many of them traditional sporting quarries of high repute, including the capercaillie, black and red grouse and the pheasant. Tucked away inconspicuously in the family *Phasianidae* is the small, relatively drab, grey partridge, *Perdix perdix*, and an outsider might well dismiss this species as relatively unimportant. In fact, at least among knowledgeable country dwellers and sportsmen, it is a great favourite. Whether we love *Perdix perdix* because his unpretentious nature suits the British character, or because he sets a good example of matrimonial fidelity, or makes a testing shot for even an excellent gun, or, as a little chap coping with a lot of problems, may depend on individual tastes, but love him we do; and his decline is one of the sadder tales of recent years.

Unless specifically stated to the contrary, this chapter deals only with the grey partridge, and bag records suggest there was a major increase in the population beginning in the period 1750–90 and continuing to about 1880. The likely reasons were greatly increased predator control as driven game shooting developed and more gamekeepers were employed, increased nesting cover from enclosures and the additional food supply from legumes used in rotational farming. Numbers settled at a peak from about 1880 to 1914, when the First World War saw a decrease in keepering. In Ireland the decrease began in the nineteenth century and the species was only saved from possible extinction by protection in 1930.

Possibly commencing in the 1920s, but certainly in the 1930s, a widespread and significant decrease began in England, Wales and Scotland and this decline has accelerated since the 1960s. Nor is the decline limited to this country, but occurs over the entire range of the partridge wherever—and this is significant—modern agricultural methods have been introduced. Much of the fall in Eastern Europe has been blamed on the break-up of the large estates, resulting in less predator control, and a reduction in cereal production; but whatever the precise reasons mean population levels have fallen by between 50 to 90 per cent.

4. Winter wastage in severe conditions can be high.

From the time guns were used for sport, the traditional method of partridge shooting had been to walk them up in cover, a technique assisted by the long stubble left by hand reaping. Somewhere about 1845 the new system of driving began, although the credit is disputed between Chippenham in Cambridgeshire and Heveningham in Suffolk. Driven partridge offer superb sport and the practice grew rapidly. In 1797 a bag of eighty partridges had been considered remarkable, but bags of several hundred a day soon became common. In 1887, at The Grange in Hampshire, the bag on October 18 was 1,344 partridges and the following day produced 1,093. The record appears to have been achieved on November 7, 1905 on the Holkham Estate in Norfolk with 1,671 partridges. Nowadays a bag even remotely approaching this magnitude would be frowned on by shooting men as well as the more ardent conservationists; but there is no denying that when the old shooting estates were in their heyday, the future of the partridge was secure.

Now the decline in numbers means that much less driven partridge shooting takes place, and where it does, the ground relies heavily on reared birds. Sadly, rearing tends to be directed at red-legs, for they are much less inclined to stray than the grey. On ground where sufficient rearing is carried out, and particularly where adequate keepering measures are taken to assist the wild stock, reasonable bags are achieved and sportsmen are attracted from abroad. In these areas—Sutton Scotney in Hampshire and the Avon and Airlie shootings in Angus are good examples—a useful volume of local work is generated, both directly and indirectly.

The season begins on September 1 and ends on February 1, but apart from a rough shooter coming to terms occasionally with his residents, no one shoots partridge seriously throughout this period. It is usually mid-September, or later, before birds of the year are adequately strong on the wing and by mid-November partridges are either too wild or too depleted for further shooting. Many shooting men, concerned for the survival of a much-loved quarry, will no longer shoot partridges.

A round head on top of a round body has earned the partridge the description of plump, an impression which is enhanced by the feeding attitude which suggests it has no neck at all. Like the wood pigeon, the true beauty of the colouring is only apparent in the hand. The upper parts are mainly dull brown, including the nape and the crown, the back and rump being barred with chestnut. The under parts are principally grey, and the throat, face and forehead are orange-buff. There is chestnut barring to the flanks and the belly has the dark brown inverted horseshoe which is often regarded as the mark of the male. In fact, the horseshoe often appears on the female but is less obvious. On the wings the scapulars and inner wing-coverts are grey-brown, marked with chestnut blotches and cream streaks. The flight feathers are dark brown and barred ruff. The outer tail-feathers are chestnut-red, and the back and centre brown with chestnut marks.

On the female the orange is duller but the upper parts are darker and browner. The juvenile will not have developed the pattern of the adults and is a yellow-brown with spots and streaks above and thin dark and pale streaks below. The bill of the adult is blue/green and the legs blue/grey. In both areas the juvenile is browner.

Moulting usually starts mid-June to early July and the new feathering to body and tail is complete by mid-August to late September. The new wing feathering lags behind and sometimes the outer few primaries are not complete until early November.

The grey partridge has a wing span of 45 to 48 cm and a length of 29 to 31 cm. A detailed study in the Netherlands showed females to be slightly smaller than males, and juveniles to have a slightly shorter tail than adults. The same study showed weights to vary between a low of 373 g in September to a high of 390 g in December, with the females heaviest shortly before laying.

The grey partridge is found across the whole of the central range of the Western Palaearctic, but has not crossed the Mediterranean to North Africa, nor does it progress northwards much further than the southern tips of Norway and Sweden. In England it is absent from parts of West and

South-west Wales and in Scotland it only creeps across the Caledonian Canal in the north-east. The south-west of Ireland has none and it is patchy in the remainder of the country.

The major problem for the grey partridge is that its preferred habitat makes excellent farmland and it is therefore in constant competition with man. Cool mid-latitude lowlands, moist but not with a high rainfall, are ideal. It avoids deserts and their fringes, rocky areas, swamps and marshes and forests. It seeks fairly short grass or herbage cover interspersed with higher cover such as hedges, rough corners, scrub and woodland verges: in other words, the English countryside as it was before we mechanised agriculture, dug out many of the hedges to enlarge fields and substituted barbed wire. Wise indeed was the man who said the invention of barbed wire had a greater impact on wild life than any other single human act.

The partridge is now in a very difficult ecological position. Its habitat requirements are rarely met on ground which is not farmed; and where such ground is farmed, many of the agricultural practices are harmful.

Heavy clay soils have lower partridge populations than light soils, but the reason is unclear as counts in Suffolk suggested breeding success was the same on both types of soil. However, observations in Hungary showed partridges moving to higher and drier ground to nest.

A final preference is for an area of small hills and undulations which allows a rapid escape by flight, a preference I have also noticed among grouse. Both are low fliers and logically they can be expected to seek surroundings where they can flit out of sight rapidly.

The grey partridge could have been tailor-made for sport. Exploding from the ground in front of a startled rough shooter, or bursting over the hedge as a confusion of brown cannon balls to bewilder the driven game shot who has allowed his concentration to lag, there is nothing to beat the partridge and little to equal it. On the ground it moves nimbly enough and is superb at concealment, even in scanty cover. Its light weight also permits it to flush and gain maximum flying speed faster than a red-leg and considerably more so than heavier birds such as the pheasant. Once in flight it rarely rises more than a few metres and, unless well driven, will avoid any obstacle which requires it to rise. (Oh, to draw the peg by the gap in the tree belt!) Nor does it fly any further than necessary and the old, expert, partridge keepers knew better than to try to drive partridges off their normal territory. Two km is about the maximum and then only under pressure.

Left undisturbed, partridges are residents in their particular area with only restricted dispersals when the coveys break up in February and the pair territories are established. In a Hampshire study, 393 partridges were marked on a study area of 259 ha and only 41 subsequently left this relatively small area (about 570 acres). Continental studies have also confirmed that partridge dispersals are essentially local, except in east Europe where hard weather brings positive movements. Many die in the harder winters and reports suggest that when snow depths exceed 50 to 60 cm in central and east Russia, large southern migrations occur.

By nature the partridge is gregarious, separating into pairs only for the breeding season, then reuniting into flocks from July or early August onwards. These flocks are not always, as is commonly supposed, straightforward family coveys. They may contain one or more unsuccessful breeders, be a combination of two small coveys, or even, in years of high chick mortality, be composed entirely of adults.

Both male and female are sexually mature in their first year and the union is monogamous. (Occasionally a male may take on two females for the first week or two only.) Where both partners survive to the next breeding season they normally reunite once more. Pairing begins up to four months before breeding, with the older birds commencing before the young. Pairing within flocks is usually restricted to those previously paired and the young females leave their flock to associate with others. Both the parents tend the young and parents and young remain together as a covey or part of a larger flock into the winter. After pairing, couples spend a fortnight without establishing a territory, usually frequenting one of the flock areas. Once a territory is established no attempt is made to defend the boundaries and when the young hatch all territorial divisions are abandoned and parents and young move without limitation.

At night partridges roost on the ground either as pairs, coveys or flocks and usually varying the site every night. In snow or rain they may roost under hedges or other shelter but normally they seek the safety of open ground. Any modest shelter from the wind, such as plough furrows, bales, small hollows or tussocks are sought out. Pairs roost side by side, but not always facing in opposite directions, but flocks only roost in a tight bunch in cold weather. At other times they break up into twos and threes, spread over a circle of some 6 to 7 m diameter.

The mating process is complex and involves various acts of aggressive behaviour as flocks approach one another and birds may be seen chasing each other for hours on end. Nor is this aggression always between members of different flocks, for females of the same flock may chase one another to establish dominance and there will even be conflict between parents and children.

Attempts at phonetic descriptions of the call of the partridge are not noticeably successful, with 'Kerr-r-r-r-ik' a good effort. Perhaps the description of a 'rusty gate' is better, this later call being commonly used by the male for self-advertisement and threat. A fairly wide variety of other calls have been recorded and are ascribed to feeding, chick-gathering, ground and aerial predator alarms, and threats.

Adult partridges—and adult must be stressed—live principally on plants.

Feeding activity is greatest after dawn and before sunset and food is taken by picking and only rarely by scratching. Three main types of food are taken: the green leaves of grasses, cereals and clovers, and grain and weed seeds. Insects form some 5 to 10 per cent of the adult diet.

Pairing and mating having taken place, egg-laying begins, in Britain, at the end of April or early May and can continue into August or even September. The nest is a simple shallow depression, lined with leaves and grass, usually sited in a hedgerow or with other overhead cover, but frequently in long grass or crops. The eggs are olive-brown, oval and glossy, weighing about 14.5 g. The clutch size increases from south to north and from south-west to north-east, but in Britain normally ranges from 10 to 20 with an average of about 15. (In south Finland it is 16.9 and in north-west Finland 18.3.) Only the hen incubates and while the eggs can hatch in twenty-three days the norm is just under twenty-five. The male occasionally helps when the eggs are hatching, but not otherwise. The female is at the nest 90 per cent of the time and is never absent at night. Sadly the odds against her at this time, through predation or mowing, are such that she will be fortunate to survive.

The Game Conservancy now estimates that losses due to predation of incubating hens can average 4% *a day* and, even worse, the percentage increases as the density of nests increases. The reason for this increase is doubtless that the thicker nests are on the ground the more worthwhile it is for predators to search. The principal culprits, responsible for about two-thirds of nest losses, are the fox, cat and stoat, and a quick calculation would suggest that at 4% a day and 25 days to hatching all nests would be eliminated. In fact, if one starts with 100 nests and loses 4 in the first day then in the second the loss is only 4% of 96 nests and so on. Towards the end, 4% of a much reduced number of surviving nests represents a much lower daily total. Of course the picture is not as arithmetically clear-cut as this but the general pattern is clear enough.

Adequate keepering will reduce the loss to about 1% a day and prevent an increase among high density nesting, but financial pressures have greatly reduced this aspect of partridge help. There are now considerably fewer keepers than there were in the pre-war days and those there are have usually to concentrate on pheasants. It is sad but true that driven shooting is an expensive sport and it is easier, and more certain, to provide driven pheasants than driven partridge. Consequently, while everyone involved thinks highly of the little partridge, the effort and the money go elsewhere. Once there were many specialist partridge keepers, who tended to regard themselves as a cut above 'ordinary' pheasant keepers: now the partridge keeper is rarer than his subjects.

Pheasant rearing has done more to harm the partridge than merely altering the keepers' priorities—it has also reduced the need for trapping which, although intended to help the wild pheasant, helped the partridge equally. A

5. Grey partridges in flight.

6. Hedgerows provide safer nesting sites than crops but are more vulnerable to predation.

well-keepered area of, say, a thousand acres should carry a hundred traps, but tending these regularly is very time consuming. The majority of keepers are now single-handed and under the pressures of rearing the traps are either reduced or abandoned completely, and particularly so where wild pheasants do not play a significant part. So the ground predators go unchecked and turn their attentions to the unfortunate partridge.

Clutch size and egg fertility are fairly constant, year by year, and records taken over many estates from 1907 to 1978 show remarkable consistency in the mean number of chicks hatched per successful nest. Excluding 1955, when the mean was 12.83 chicks, the figures never dropped below 13 chicks nor reached 15.

When we consider the small size of a newly-hatched partridge chick and the density of cover at the time it is hatched, it is not surprising that little is known of the survival rate. All the evidence is that they are most vulnerable while they are flightless, which is about the first fortnight. At ten days old they can flutter up to 10 m but in so doing they may expose themselves to danger more than by running and crouching. A good example of the problems of assessing the fate of partridge chicks was given by an article in the Game Conservancy Annual Review in 1975 on a report of field work into weasel and stoat predation on partridge chicks. Common sense, doubtless vehemently backed by any keeper one cared to consult, would have suggested weasels preyed heavily on partridge chicks. In the event no gamebird chicks were found in the weasel diet in 1975 and the average proportion of game birds eaten over the last five years had only been 1.6%. The conclusion was that in an average year a weasel would only eat between half and four gamebird chicks and probably most of these would be in poor condition due to cold or food shortage.

Predators, however, are of far less significance to chick survival than an adequate supply of food, and this means an abundance of insects in the cereal crops. A century ago, given reasonable weather in May and early June, the young partridges hatched to a countryside fairly seething in insects. Now the extensive use of pesticides (herbicide, insecticide and fungicide) in agriculture has had its desired effect of crop protection but the side effect of a massive reduction in the availability of insects for partridge chicks.

The importance of insects to partridge chick survival can be seen from a Game Conservancy study of crop contents. Eight grey partridge chicks in the age range up to one week contained a total of 313 insects and just 17 plants or seeds: that is 94.8% animal food and 5.2% plant. In the period one to six weeks this dependence fell to 48.8% animal and 51.2% plant. However, experiments with capitive red-legs showed a strong preference for animal food continuing up to the end of the second week.

In the first week the most common species were beetles (77), followed by aphids (63) and the lucerne flea (61). Sawflies mustered 34, spiders 20, parasites and flies were, in every sense, neck and neck at 18 each and various other species, for example, mites, woodlice, thrips, etc, put in a modest representation. Noticeably there were no ants, but the picture changes dramatically in the next five-week period with 2,565 ants. The next food source, the aphids, provided only 717 and no other species even reached 200. This confirms the wisdom of the old-time keepers who, producing partridge and pheasant foods to their own, often most secret, formulas, always favoured ants and their eggs.

A most interesting comparison was made with a similiar study of chick crop contents carried out in the 1930s. Some of the insect species had varied their order of importance—spiders, for example, were up in the league a little and lucerne fleas down   but these were variations of position only. Essentially all the insects important to chicks half a century ago are just as important today and, noticeably from one week onwards, the ant was top favourite in both eras. The fact that a particular insect species represents a substantial proportion of a chick's food may represent availability rather than preference but this is unlikely to apply to the ant as it was preferred even at a time of wide choice. Availability will also explain why weevils and moth caterpillars were the most important items in the 1930s and weevils and sawflies in the 1970s.

There seems to be no specific age at which chicks turn from an almost complete animal diet to plants. The studies of the 1930s suggested the changeover occurred in the third week but recent research suggests it is less clear-cut. Not only in this country but also abroad there are reports of four- to six-week chicks still living on a diet consisting almost completely of insects.

Most insects in partridge chick crops are coloured either green or yellow and experiments have been carried out in which captive chicks were offered ant cocoons dyed in a variety of colours. The chicks showed strong colour preference, taking far more green, yellow and natural coloured cocoons, even though they were descended through several generations of captive game farm birds.

In the four years commencing 1972 a comparison was made between the five most weedy and the five most weed-free fields in a Sussex area. The total number of insects in the weed-free fields was only 65% of those in the weedy fields. Even more serious was the impact on the insect species most favoured by partridge chicks. The lucerne flea was reduced by 80%, leaf-hoppers by 70%, plant bugs by 68% and weevils by 62%.

If the more favoured insect species are depleted, partridge chicks can, to some extent, switch to alternative species but by 1978 it was estimated that the effect of herbicides had been to reduce the biomass of the preferred food of partridge chicks by no less than two-thirds. The effect, it was calculated, was to reduce chick survival rates by one-third as compared to the 1930s.

As the evidence accumulated the Game Conservancy became increasingly convinced of the threat of insecticide spraying and efforts were made to establish the most important insects. In the event only three groups were found to be essential, and, in order of importance, are:

1. Plant bugs (*Heteroptera*)
   These insects thrive best in weeds and like warm, dry, weather in May. These conditions existed in 1970/71/74/76 and 1980, which were also good years for partridge. The Game Conservancy's knowledge is now so advanced that its scientists state categorically that each heteropteran per square metre of cereal crops adds 1½% to chick survival.

2. Sawfly larvae (*Tenthredinidae*)
   These caterpillar-like insects are to the partridge, for the first week of its life, what sausages are to healthy boys. Although the larvae chew cereal leaves they do not harm the crops and therefore little is known about them. Each sawfly larva per square metre adds, so we are assured, 4% to the chick survival rate of the grey partridge.

3. Leaf beetle (*Chrysomelidae*)
   This is another group of insects which thrives best on weeds. As a result, even chemicals which are not directly harmful to the insect can reduce its numbers by killing the weeds on which it lives. It is believed that if the most important species, *Gastrophysa polygeni*, has one representative per square metre of cereals the chick survival rate increases by 3%.

The great importance of insects becomes clear on learning that, over an eleven-year study period, differences between the abundance of each of the three groups explained no less than 92% of the annual variation of survival rates. In a nutshell, if we reduce the insect populations by the heavy use of insecticides, then the partridge chicks starve to death.

There is, amongst this gloom, a slight glimmer of light in the growing belief that we now spray too many chemicals on our fields and, if we continue, the various animals and plants under attack will develop resistance. In so far as insects harmful to crops are concerned, there is now a school of thought that it would be more effective to encourage the insect predators which prey on them. There are, for example, at least 110 species of spiders in cereal fields, usually in excess of 2 million per ha and all of them hungry. They are reinforced by beetles, beetle larvae, mites, earwigs, centipedes, harvestmen, ladybirds and hoverflies, all anxious to feast on aphids, cabbage root fly, cabbage white butterflies, springtails, wheat bulb flies, fruit flies, wheat blossom midges, wireworms and slugs. In the days before spraying it is easy to imagine a horrific picture of the slaughter of millions of helpless creatures in just a single field.

Work was carried out by the Glasshouse Crops Research Institute to test the importance of predatory insects on aphids by netting in some parts of a test area. In the open areas the aphid population would develop until the predators arrived, when they would quickly disappear. Inside the netted, predator-free area the aphids would increase until reaching nearly 500 per shoot and reducing crop yield by 75%.

The conclusion was that in normal years aphids are controlled within reasonable bounds by insect predators and other natural enemies and it is only when this natural control fails that a major outbreak occurs. Whether there is a future in controlling insects with insects is a fascinating prospect yet to be adequately explored. The knowledge gained so far does, however, pose the question to this particular layman as to whether the loss suffered through a heavy outbreak of aphids, or a similar problem, would be as much as the amount spent on unnecessary spraying in previous years.

Because of the importance of chick survival, much of the research effort has gone into this aspect, and rather less into adult mortality. In Britain (excluding shooting which is not a major factor) winter losses are currently about 45%, with weather conditions having little effect. However, mortality rates with reared birds can be considerably higher with records in this country of up to 73%. Some Continental figures are even worse with reports from Italy of 80%, Czechoslovakia 82%, Denmark 84% and Russia 86%.

Of all the different game species in this country, and very probably in other countries also, none is so desperately in need of prolonged and careful management as the grey partridge. Unfortunately, many of the measures necessary for its welfare run contrary to modern agricultural methods. Farming is very capital intensive and a competitive business and it is difficult for even the keenest shooting man to put his partridges before his farming. Certainly whatever help is given to partridges will come because of the sport of shooting and there is no better illustration of the sportsman's claim that he is also a leading conservationist.

Not all the suggestions which follow will be possible, but every step taken along the right roads will help:

1. Predator control, particularly in the nesting season and in the period leading up to it; and with particular concentration on foxes, stoats and cats.
2. The provision of nesting cover. The ideal hedges are between 1 yard and 2½ yards wide and not so high as to discourage grass growth at the base. No mowing alongside the hedge should take place from mid-March to mid-July. However, any hedge is better than stakes and barbed wire: landowners should only remove hedges if absolutely essential. Fortunately current statistics suggest that, with modern tractor flail cutters, it is cheaper to maintain a hedge than a fence and, hopefully, we may see hedges being created rather than destroyed. Hedges are not the only

nesting cover acceptable to partridges. Any corner, marl pit, power pylon, or similarly relatively useless patch which can be spared to grow wild will help.

3. Pesticides: the damage caused by pesticides can be limited by care. Avoid, if possible, pesticides drifting onto non-tilled areas and hedgerows, for these wild spots are the only reservoirs of insects. It is helpful to spray for couch between hedge and crop, for the alley so formed makes a drying area for chicks after rain. May and June are the vital months, and it is best only to use insecticides when necessary rather than carrying out routine spraying as a precaution.

Well-informed people have been making predictions about the future of the grey partridge for at least the last quarter of a century. Their forecasts have varied but have in common the single fact that all are gloomy. Personally, I am slightly more optimistic, if only because no one ever rallied support for a cause by being despondent. Firstly, compared with a decade or so ago we now know (thanks almost entirely to the Game Conservancy) why the grey partridge has declined and what we must do to help. Whether what needs to be done will be, I cannot say, but knowing the direction one must travel is an essential preliminary to arrival. Next, we have the faint signs of reaction against excessive spraying, hedge removal and prairie farming generally. Lastly, there is the enduring love of all countrymen for the little brown bird.

3

The Red-legged Partridge

As a near relative of the grey partridge the red-leg, *Alectoris rufa*, is also of the order *Galliformes* and the family *Phasianidae*. At first sight, evolution has favoured the red-leg, for with its greater range of colouring it is an altogether more glamorous bird than its relatively dull cousin. However, as so often occurs with the human female, men are not always impressed by glamour and show a preference for the less obtrusive. This preference may be, in part, due to the red-leg also being known as the Frenchman and looking rather a gaudy foreigner, whereas the grey is so obviously a native. There are, however, sounder reasons. The grey is a better sporting bird, more willing to fly, nimbler on the wing and given to rapid changes of direction when it spies danger. Conversely, the red-leg will often run on in front of the beaters until, on heavy ground, its feet can become so clogged that it is incapable of flight. At one time it also had the bad reputation of attacking both nests and young of grey partridges and old-time keepers would destroy its nests. Not because of this preference, but because of pressures of space, I will only list those aspects in which it differs from the grey partridge.

When I wrote *Pugs and Drummers* I found the available evidence on the date of the introduction of the rabbit to Britain both scant and confusing and could make out a good case for the introduction at any time over a range of more than ten thousand years. With the red-leg the evidence is much clearer. We can start with fairly positive evidence as to when it was not here for, about 1667, Sir Thomas Browne wrote, 'Though there be here (Norfolk) very great store of partridges, yet the French red-legged partridge is not to be met with.' And in *Ornithologia*, published in 1676–8, Francis Willugby and John Ray wrote of the red-leg, 'This kind is a stranger to England; howbeit, they say it is found in the isles of Jersey and Guernsey, which are subject to our King.' This position seems to have continued for at least another fifty years, for in 1728 Ephraim Chambers in his *Cyclopaedia* stated, 'The red-legged partridge is not found in England, but is sometimes shot in the islands of Guernsey and Jersey.'

However, an attempt to introduce the red-leg to England was made by

Charles II in 1673, for there exists a letter from the French Ambassador of the time to the keeper at the Chateau de Chambard advising him that the 'Gamekeeper of the King of England' was visiting France to 'procure some red-legged partridges to fill the parks at Windsor and Richmond', and requesting him to provide the same. He goes on: 'Our master (the French King) will not disapprove of your doing him the pleasure', and it is highly probable that a good supply of red-legs were supplied, but the venture seems to have failed for Daniel, in 1801, in *Rural Sports* wrote 'They are supposed to have mostly perished, although some of them, or their descendants, were seen for a few years afterwards.'

Two other early attempts are reported. In November 1682 a brace of 'curious outlandish partridges' were sent to the 9th Earl of Rutland at Belvoir Castle in Leicestershire and between 1712 and 1729 the 2nd Duke of Leeds reared red-legs from eggs on his Wimbledon estate. Unfortunately for the Duke they 'were, after increasing for a time all destroyed by some disobliging neighbour'.

It is clear that about 1770 red-leg eggs were imported from France and hatched out on various sporting estates including, significantly, that of the Earl of Hertford who was Ambassador to France from 1763–5. Other eggs went to Lord Rendlesham in East Suffolk, the Duke of Northumberland at Alnwick Castle and the Earl of Rochford in Essex. We do not have any clear record of how well these individual introductions fared but in 1777 Daniel shot three brace from a covey of fourteen near Colchester and then waited twenty-one years before he shot more—this time at Sudbourne. Again, in *Rural Sports* (1801), he reported that red-legs were common around Oxford and frequently seen near Ipswich.

From then on there are many references to red-legs. In 1874 it was 'quite common' in South Lincolnshire and Norfolk; the first record in Nottingham-shire was made in 1851; a brace were shot between Hull and Grimsby in 1835; in 1865 it was 'breeding very rarely in West Yorkshire'; they were 'resident and becoming common' in Oxfordshire by 1835, equally common in Hertfordshire in 1877 and breeding in Kent by the late 1860s. The red-leg had arrived.

Two attempts were made to introduce the red-leg to Ireland, by a Mr Gildear about 1840 and in Co. Galway, but they failed and I cannot trace any record that the species exists there nowadays.

In spite of its successful introduction it is unlikely that the red-leg would have established a strong position in England were it not for one advantage it possesses over the grey partridge: properly managed it will, as a reared bird, stay in the release area much more willingly than the grey. As a result it is reared by many shoots, a few specialising in partridges but the majority looking for a quarry which will fill the early season gap when the pheasants are still rather immature. By shooting partridges exclusively for, say, the first half of October and then mixing partridges with boundary pheasants, the season can both be extended by several weeks and made more interesting at little cost, for the basic overheads have already been met.

The red-leg is larger and bulkier than the grey by some 10–15%, although it retains the general characteristic appearance and can be surprisingly difficult to distinguish when there are no obvious nearby features to give proportion. The adults are darker than grey partridges, the most obvious distinction being the lack of grey above and the white lines between the flank bars. Once close enough, the bright red of the bill and legs, from which the name is of course derived, are obvious. There is no difference in the appearance of the sexes but it is easy to confuse the young of red-leg and grey partridges.

Apart from the grey forecrown, the overriding colour of the upper parts and chest are dull olive-brown. The throat is white, descending into a wide bib of white and black streaks before giving way to the buff of the upper chest. The colour feature of the red-leg is the lavender-grey flanks, barred vertically with thin white and thick black and chestnut lines, eight or nine in number.

The juvenile has neither the flank bars nor the head pattern but can be distinguished from the grey by its more striped head, a near-white throat with spots beneath and fewer pale streaks and dark mottling on the upper parts and flanks. The legs, in promise of the future, are rose.

The adults begin moulting after breeding is complete, starting with the body and inner primaries between late June and late August; the tail begins slightly later. The moult of the body and tail is completed in October, but the wing can be complete any time between late August and mid-November.

As with the grey, the range of calls is much wider than is commonly appreciated. The usual rally call is a staccato 'chuk . . . Chuk . . . chuk . . . Chukuk . . . chuker'. The contact call is a soft, contented, chuck and the advertisement call of the male has been described as sounding like the chuffing of a locomotive, with more of a 'chak' than a 'chuk'. There are calls for food, hostility, territory, pairing, a nest-call, ground alarm, hawk alarm, suspicion, protest, sexual-pursuit and copulation-intent.

The red-leg has a length of 32–34 cm and a wing-span of 47–50 cm, the male being larger than the female. The weight of the adult male normally ranges from 500 g up to about 550 g and the adult female from 500 g down to about 450 g except before laying when the average is above 500 g.

The distribution of the red-leg is much narrower than the grey partridge, its main stronghold being Spain. It exists widely over much of France, although not the north, and in northern Italy, but, in recent years, has retreated south in West Germany and Switzerland. Introductions have been made, without success, to various Continental countries but have succeeded in the Azores, Madeira, the Canary Islands and, of course, Britain. Recent reports suggest the Channel Island population has now died out. Small

pockets of red-legs, through rearing, can be found in Belgium, Luxembourg, Netherlands and Denmark, but it is doubtful if these would survive but for shooting.

The habitat preference of the red-leg is for dry and sandy areas, with light soils and some permanently open areas interspersed with low, open, vegetation in which it enjoys both visibility and the freedom to run from danger. These preferences stated, however, it is adaptable and will inhabit almost any ground between the extremes of forest and swamps. Surprisingly, in suitable country it can be found as high as 2,000 m. It is well content with typical English countryside.

As with the grey partridge, red-legs are monogamous and form long-term pair bonds. They are also gregarious, a fact well appreciated by keepers whose nightmare is to see a flock of several hundred crossing over the guns at once, after which the next few drives are blank. There is no point in describing the social pattern and behaviour of the red-leg where it is similar to the grey and I will only identify areas of difference.

Roosting is one point of variation, for the red-leg sometimes roosts in trees and often frequents at least the outer fringe of woodlands, sometimes appearing in a drive among the pheasants.

A few months before I wrote this chapter, Dr R. E. Green, under the supervision of Dr G. R. Potts, Director of Research at the Game Conservancy, completed his final report to the National Environmental Research Council of *The Population Ecology of the Red-Leg Partridge*. It is a work of considerable length and detail and considerably advances our knowledge of the red-leg in various areas. Space, however, makes it impossible to do more than abstract the main conclusions.

On pre-breeding dispersal the main finding was the degree to which first year females dispersed from the wintering area when the winter groups broke up. Some birds moved as far as 16 km but older females and males dispersed very little. The void left by the first year females was quickly filled by incomers who paired with the first year males. These couples nested in or close to the wintering area of the yearling male; but the fewer the hedges, and therefore the less the cover, the more the couples were obliged to nest further away. Additionally, the more abundant the hedge cover, the less the males chased and fought one another. The females rarely behaved in such an unseemly fashion.

Most of the research was concerned with breeding biology and I will detail that which was already known before considering the new discoveries of Dr Green.

The red-leg is, of course, a ground nester, laying between ten and sixteen eggs, but averaging twelve to thirteen. The eggs are oval, smooth and glossy, and yellow-cream or pale buff, spotted with red-brown or grey. The average weight is 21 g and they measure some 40 × 31 mm. Incubation takes twenty-

7. Red-legs are relatively easily bred.

8. At this age partridge chicks are very vulnerable to wet and cold.

three to twenty-four days. It was known that the female sometimes laid two clutches, after which she would incubate one clutch and the male the other. It was estimated that this practice, known as double-clutching, was followed by some 20% to 40% of pairs. Dr Green found that while this forecast might be reasonably accurate for yearling females it was far too low for adult females (24 months or more) where some 60% to 80% attempt to lay two clutches. The pair remain together until both clutches are laid, so that incubating of both clutches, and therefore hatching, occurs about the same time. After hatching both parents care for their broods independently of the other. The fact that the first clutch lay unincubated while the second clutch was laid had little or no effect on the percentage to hatch successfully.

Another factor studied in detail was a comparison between the susceptibility of red-legged and grey partridges to nest predation. It was concluded that red-legs are more susceptible to nest predation during both laying and incubation, a critical sentence reading: 'The combination of higher rates of nest predation per day and the longer period of exposure of nests to predators during laying due to double nesting in the red-legged partridge would be expected to make the species more sensitive to predation pressure than the grey partridge.' Doubtless very true, but it does occur to me that birds who have the ability to hatch two broods where others only hatch one can stand a little extra predation pressure.

Once hatched the young are largely self-feeding, although they are brooded by the parent in a specially made scrape. It was already known that red-leg chicks are less dependent on insects than grey partridge chicks, but Dr Green extended our knowledge in this area. Both species of chicks eat a similar range of food. We have already covered the insects in the grey partridge chapter and suffice to report that the plant foods included grass seeds, particularly *Pod annua*, cereal grains, dicot leaves, especially carrots and kale, and dicot seeds, especially *Stellaria media*. As we have already seen the grey chick eats mainly insects in the early stages, turning eventually to grass seeds and then cereal grain. By twenty-five days old Dr Green found the diet of grey chicks resembled that of adults.

Red-legs, on the other hand, ate 'much' plant food from the beginning with only a slight increase with age. They also differed from greys by preferring different forms of plant food at an early age, dicot leaves being important and cereal grain forming a prominent item from an earlier age than the grey. As a result, young red-leg chicks can survive well on a diet of leaves or grass seeds and are therefore largely unaffected, in contrast to grey chicks, by the destruction of a large proportion of the insect population by sprays. Red-legs may, however, be affected by the loss of grass weeds due to herbicide spraying.

Red-leg chicks seem much more susceptible to poor weather conditions than grey. However, greys are by no means independent of the weather for, as we saw in the previous chapter, cold, dull, weather in May affects the insect supply when the grey chicks hatch.

Other observations from the report included chick activity. Broods are fairly inactive for about two hours after first light, irrespective of temperature. The period of greatest activity is from mid-morning till late afternoon, and activity, at any time, is reduced by cold, rainfall and dew. At any given temperature red-legs are more active than greys. The greys, however, grow increasingly active up to ten days of age, whereas the reds remain constant. Once adult, the diet is similar to the grey partridge, except for the addition of sugar beet roots, field beans and larger seeds of trees.

In managing the red-legged partridge for sport the main principles are exactly as for the grey partridge. However, as I explained earlier, the choice of red-legs rather than greys is dictated by their willingness to remain in the release area. This does not, however, mean they can be turned out willy-nilly and be relied upon to be present and correct in the first half of October. The right management policies have to be followed and I can but urge you to acquire the Game Conservancy's booklet, in that famous series of green booklets, and follow its instructions assiduously.

4

The Pheasant

All the inhabitants of England, and to a lesser extent Wales, Scotland and Ireland, have good reason to be grateful to the pheasant. For a small minority, the sportsmen, it is the most important single species we have, and without it the whole pattern of the sport of shooting would change. For the great majority, the pheasant has played a vital part in the appearance of the countryside. Because of it, the economic pressures to rip out every obstruction and convert the country into a much smaller number of much larger fields has been resisted. Not only have existing woods been saved but new ones have been planted. Farm managers anxious to remove hedges or take out rough corners, have been told where the owner's priorities lie. Foresters keen to plant single species of fast growing softwood have been instructed to select a mix calculated to please pheasants rather than accountants. It is no exaggeration to say that the pheasant has had a substantial influence on the appearance of modern day England.

Although I write casually enough of the pheasant it is hard to define exactly what bird I mean. As with most game birds, the pheasant is of the order *Galliformes* and the family *Phasianidae*. The Latin name is *Phasianus colchicus* and it was the custom in sporting and natural history books at the end of the last century and the first half of this to dwell at length on the other forms of the pheasant. However, interbreeding among the races has now continued for so long that the exercise is pointless and (apart from green, Reeve's, Golden and Lady Amherst's pheasants) the practice in this country is to regard a pheasant simply as a pheasant. It is likely that the original introduction into this country was *Phasianus colchicus* and this form lacked any white neck-ring. This feature appeared with *Phasianus colchicus torquatus* and has now developed to the point where a pheasant without any form of neck-ring is very much the exception.

Up to 1933 most sporting and natural history books state, with varying degrees of authority, that the pheasant was introduced to Britain by the Romans, a belief based on an early discovery of pheasant bones in a Romano-British midden at Silchester near Reading. However, in that year Dr P. R.

9. Cock pheasant along a Hebridean estuary.

Lowe announced that the bones in question were merely those of an ordinary domestic fowl and added: 'No authentic fossil Pheasant bone unquestionably contemporaneous with the Roman occupation has been described. I have so far been unable to discover any material in museums which would point to the existence of the Pheasant in the British Isles contemporaneous with the Romans.'

Legend says the common pheasant was first brought to Europe by Jason and the Argonauts, about 1300 BC, when they returned from Colchis to Greece in the Argo after their search for the golden fleece. Geographically this is correct, for *Phasianus colchicus* came originally from Colchis in Georgia (from whence, doubtless, it derived its name), and Armenia on the southeastern borders of the Black Sea. Confirmation that Colchis was the original home of what we might describe as the common pheasant came in AD 77 by Pliny the Elder (AD 23–79) in his *Historia Naturalis*. About this time the Roman epicure M. Gavius Apicius gave recipes for pheasant and rabbit rissoles, so we may assume the pheasant had, by then, reached Italy. In AD 350 another Roman, Rutilius Taurus Aemilianus Palladius, gave instructions on rearing pheasants which would suffice to this day (although we might jib at sprinkling wine on their barley-meal).

Surprisingly, Vesey-Fitzgerald, in his *British Game* of 1946, makes no mention of Dr Lowe's announcement in 1933, but does state, without further detail, that pheasants appear in a document from Waltham Abbey of 1059. In fact the manuscript in question is dated 1177 and is now in the British Museum. It contains details of the rations of the members of the canon's household at the monastery between Michaelmas 1058 and Ash Wednesday 1059 and equates one pheasant with a brace of partridges, a dozen blackbirds or two magpies.

The pheasant was therefore with us well before the Norman Conquest, although possibly still as a captive domestic bird. Quite when they became naturalised we will probably never learn, but in 1100 a licence was granted to the abbot of Malmesbury to kill hares and pheasants which, presumably, were in a wild state. From this time on there are regular references to the pheasant in contemporary literature, usually as an item of food rather than sport. Nicholas Upton, writing before 1446, describes how pheasants were reared and fattened for the table.

By the late fifteenth century a couplet on the Battle of Otterburn suggests the pheasant had reached at least as far north as Northumberland; and Fynes Moryson confirmed it was plentiful in Ireland between 1599 and 1603. There is also a sixteenth century poem by Gruffydd Hiraethog saying that pheasants 'fill everywhere' in the Llanddwye area of Merionethshire. In 1578 Bishop Lesley wrote that in Scotland, 'the fasiane' was common with other nations but 'scarce with us'. However, by 1594 a Scots Act forbade the killing of various creatures, including 'phesanis', in or near the royal policies.

The Chinese ring-necked pheasant, *Phasianus colchicus torquatus*, which was to stamp its distinguishing feature so widely on our present day mongrel, is first mentioned in 1768 by Thomas Pennant. In 1783 Tatham wrote that the ring-necked pheasant was not now uncommon in our aviaries and a few years later said, 'several noblemen and gentlemen have turned out many pairs into their neighbouring woods for the purpose of breeding'. They were to succeed better than they probably expected.

Although some argument rumbles on, it is generally believed that our melanistic mutant pheasant originates from the Japanese pheasant, *Phasianus versicolor*. John Gould, in his *Birds of Asia* 1857, stated that a pair were purchased by the Earl of Derby about 1840, but that during the journey from Amsterdam the female died. This was mated with a common pheasant producing 'The Green Pheasants, now becoming so numerous in the British Islands'. More Japanese pheasants were imported during the remainder of the nineteenth century and early in the twentieth.

The shooting season for the pheasant begins on October 1 and finishes on February 1. At the start of the season many birds are not fully grown and none of the young of the year have the strength of flight they will enjoy a month or so later. Hence sportsmen who conduct themselves properly either do not shoot pheasants at all at this time or select only the more testing shots.

As the pheasant is so widely spread, it is a quarry for the majority of sportsmen in this country, the distinction being not whether they shoot pheasants but how. The rough shooter takes what pheasants come his way; and these may vary from one or two a year to a substantial bag if his ground borders a keepered shoot. The great majority of pheasants are shot at formal driven shoots on ground which is keepered, and a percentage of the bag, greater or lesser depending on the ability of the ground to sustain wild pheasants, will be reared. Driven pheasant shooting on a large scale developed during the middle of the nineteenth century and rose to a peak in the last decade or so of that century and the beginning of the twentieth. The great social changes arising after the First World War led to heavily increased taxation and the break-up of many of the large estates. Towards the end of the nineteenth century Richard Jeffries observed a trend for the wealthier members of commerce to join together to take shooting, and this early beginning of the shooting syndicate has grown to the point where the majority of pheasant shooting is done by syndicates rather than private shoot owners. Put very simply, the essence of a syndicate is that the members share equally all the costs, pleasures and obligations of a formal driven shoot.

Economically and socially, pheasant shooting plays an important part in the countryside. If it finished, nearly every keeper south of the Border would be jobless, as would many of the staff of gun and cartridge manufacturers. There would also be a severe impact on many peripheral activities, including outdoor clothing manufacturers and those concerned with specialised vehicles, rearing equipment, footwear, leather goods, country hotels and a wide range of other goods and services. Not least affected would be the thousands of men, and the occasional women, who turn out every Saturday for a day's beating, or 'brushing' as the East Anglians will have it.

For those who have to pay to produce an adult pheasant flying over the guns, the difference between what it costs to put it there and what it is worth when it hits the ground a few seconds later is extremely depressing. However, cost apart, the sport produces some millions of very tasty birds for the table every season.

Due to its regular appearance on Christmas cards the pheasant is one of the very few birds the average town-dweller could describe with any accuracy. On such cards, and indeed any other scene, the male is always given pride of place, and the unfortunate drab female has a background role. Whatever the mix of races the male always has a battle-green head, with similarly coloured tufts behind each eye, and a red face with a broad wattle. Basically, the body and tail plumage are purple-chestnut, with the body feathers iridescent and containing black scallops and chevrons. The centre of the belly and the vent are almost black. The magnificent tail, which immediately distinguishes it from the hen in poor light, is widely barred with shallow V's. The wings are paler than the body, and basically yellow-buff.

The female is yellow-buff with a hatched pattern of feather markings and a chestnut wash to the neck. The tail bars are double, black and chestnut. When young both sexes resemble the female, but the cocks begin to show a darkening of the rear of the head and a chestnut tip to the mantle and chest from six to seven weeks onwards.

The adults moult after breeding, the cock beginning in June and moulting heavily in July and early August, taking about three months in all. The hen starts later, after the young hatch. The young have acquired most of their juvenile plumage by ten days and start to lose this and acquire their post-juvenile plumage as early as three weeks old. Subject to food and weather, the young are in their first adult plumage when four and a half months old.

The bill of the adult male is pale horn-yellow or green-yellow; that of the female horn-brown. The male's foot is horn-grey, tinged brown; the female's grey-brown. Both are small-headed, long-necked and deep-bodied, with short, broad wings with rounded tips. Including the tail, a cock pheasant measures about 89 cm and a hen 53 cm. Respectively, the tails are about 47 cm and 20 cm. The cock has a wing span of about 90 cm and the hen 70 cm. Weights vary considerably but a reasonable average for January would be 1,150 g for a cock and 850 g for a hen.

Before man began a long series of introductions, some successful and many not, the home of the pheasant was the southern Palaearctic and the north-eastern Orient. Here it ranges from south-eastern Russia and northern Asia Minor as far north as the Aral Sea, Mongolia and Manchuria, east to Korea,

Japan and Taiwan, and south to Burma and south-western China. It is now found in many parts of the world, including North America, New Zealand and Hawaii. The pheasant is also common throughout much of central and western Europe, including the south of Norway and Sweden. In Britain and Ireland it is present in all areas except much of the north-west of Scotland, and some of the islands.

The pheasant can be found in a wide variety of habitats, including foothills and dry uplands. However, by choice it is not found on the hills and is rarely found above 700 m in the west Palaearctic. Essentially the pheasant is a bird of the fringes; that is to say, its preference is for the edge of a wood, or other thick cover, where it can feed and run in the open yet remain close to shelter. Nor is it happy with any wood, but looks for the twin features of protection from the weather, particularly wind, and nesting cover. In the latter case it is noticeable that most nests are found within a few yards of the edge of the wood or an internal ride. The typical 'tree factory', growing regimented lines of softwoods, producing a thick overhead canopy resulting in no ground cover, is quite useless for pheasants. The old fashioned hardwood plantations with coppice underwood and some conifers for roosting were ideal; and it is to the credit of shooting that much of the woodlands planted in recent years owe their hardwood content to the owners' love of the sport. Where new planting is planned, and it is desired to attract pheasants, a mix of hard and softwoods is ideal but if economic considerations make it essential to grow only softwoods, then avoid spruces, firs and cypresses. These produce a completely bare floor, whereas pine and larches allow a reasonable amount of undergrowth. However, no matter how attractive the tree species, the time comes when the lower branches die and fall off and the wood becomes draughty. The solution is a perimeter hedge, preferably of quickthorn. Pheasants are also happy in wetland areas and I know one part of the Itchen valley in Hampshire where the birds reared in the summer by the farmer, and released and nurtured in his coverts, take to the reed beds adjoining the river immediately the weather turns cold.

The proximity of a food supply is, of course, of paramount importance, and cereal farming provides a range of food throughout most of the year. An ideal combination is relatively low-lying, draught-free woods with ample cover along at least the fringes, adjoining cultivated fields. A network of hedges to give cover as the birds move about would be a bonus.

Given these reasonable conditions, the pheasant is sedentary and severe weather causes increased deaths rather than initiating movement. When compelled to take to the air, the pheasant is a strong flier and will rise almost vertically, even through a canopy of branches. It cannot, however, sustain this power for long and descends as soon as it has reached a place of refuge. A pheasant has been recorded crossing 6½ km of water, but this is regarded as an exceptional feat.

We have a considerable amount of data on movement from birds ringed before release on shoots. Although many keepers, being naturally pessimistic, believe their birds are great wanderers, the truth is that movements over 1.5 km are exceptional. Hens are more inclined to wander than cocks and most dispersal from the breeding or release point occurs before November.

By nature pheasants are gregarious and flock in winter, often with the sexes segregated. The males tend to restrict their groups to less than ten but the females are more companionable and will have up to thirty in a flock. Not surprisingly, the hens are not very status conscious, but rank is important among the cocks.

Though a monogamous pair-bond is not rare, the normal pattern is for a cock to gather a harem of hens, each of which has a monogamous bond with that cock only. The size of the harem is often small—as indeed it must be where the numbers of the sexes are relatively even—but up to eighteen hens have been reported. Both sexes are sexually mature at one year, when all hens will breed. However, some first year cocks will not overcome the competition from older cocks for territory and mates. The hen selects the nest site, incubates the eggs and looks after the young, although the cock may occasionally join the brood. Some reports exist of the cock both brooding and tending the young, all of which seem to have occurred where the numbers of cocks and hens in the population have been fairly even and occasional monogamous pair-bonds have resulted.

Some cocks may begin to establish their territories as early as the autumn, but the majority commence in late winter with limited displaying towards the hens and aggression to other cocks. At the moment we are not sure why cock pheasants establish territories. It can hardly be to protect a food reserve, as their territorial behaviour only begins after the period of greatest winter food shortage. Nor can it be to ensure good nesting cover for their hens, as they frequently nest outside their cock's territory. There may be a good reason as yet undiscovered or it may simply be that all male animals, including humans, need to set up personal territory and then defend it against intruders.

It is common for a subordinate cock to attach himself to a dominant cock during the initial territory-forming process and his presence is accepted. Once the territory is fully established, the dominant cock drives off his satellite, but the latter will not usually vacate the area and remains on the fringe. Here he is a constant nuisance, molesting the hens and often killing chicks. For this reason the practice of thinning out the cocks in the later part of the season is very sound. In an American experiment, one cock successfully mated fifty hens so the possibility of over-shooting the cocks is far less than the risk of leaving an excess. It has been estimated that between 15% and 28% of cocks, in each year, behave as satellites. Presumably, although I cannot trace any information on the point, the percentage of satellites increases or decreases according to the ratio of cocks to hens; it is hard to imagine a cock behaving as a satellite when there is an excess of hens.

One authority says the size of the dominant cock's territory depends upon the food supply, population density and habitat structure; which is logical enough except that most territories contain between forty and eighty times the food requirement of a single pheasant. Perhaps, in the manner of males, the cocks have an exaggerated idea of their attractiveness to the opposite sex. The maximum area taken is rarely more than 5 ha and must include open spaces for courtship and feeding. Exceptionally, a territory can be as small as 0.5 ha but 2 ha is usually the minimum. In a reasonable habitat in England an average territory is about 3.5 ha and on this the hens form a loose-knit harem with occasional recruits and desertions throughout the season. Within, and around, the territory the nest-sites of the hens are well dispersed and a re-nesting hen will frequently move well away from her previous site. As individual hens disappear to begin incubating, the harem reduces and when the last hen goes the cock abandons his territory.

Young pheasants normally roost on the ground for the first two to three months, and, where tree roosts are scarce, adult pheasants will also ground roost, seeking out dense, safe cover. However, their preference is to roost in trees, thereby making themselves safe from foxes and highly vulnerable to human poachers. They have a preference for small copses on the outer fringe of larger woods, probably because they take the nearest roost to their feeding source. Pheasants are often inclined to communal roosting, particularly the hens outside the breeding season. The old cocks are more solitary, although in bad weather they tend to roost together.

Birds going to roost walk under their selected tree, then fly up at a steep angle, settling on the outer end of a branch and then working in towards the trunk. If roosting in tall trees, they often flutter up in a series of several steps. The call of the cock pheasant, on its way up to roost, is a very familiar winter sound of the countryside.

Roosting pheasants are normally awake for several hours after perching. When sleep comes they adopt a forward leaning posture with the tail hanging free and in the morning they will be active for up to an hour before descending. If disturbed at night the cocks emit their crowing call and the hens and juveniles hiss.

Although the young cocks are aggressive towards one another in their first autumn, there is little real antagonism among the males until the breeding season, when the establishment of territories begins. At the outset, a cock will merely patrol its intended territory without defending it, but in March and early April the casual patrols settle to fixed routes and it begins to use the crowing call. This is the most familiar of the pheasant calls, and similar to that of the domestic cockerel. Additionally, wing-drumming begins, in which the cock mounts a prominent site, draws himself up, makes a few preliminary wing-flaps, calls and performs a vigorous wing-drum, sometimes cocking his tail and sometimes pressing it against the ground as a brace. One rather fine specimen has been performing this routine on the dwarf wall outside my study window for several weeks now, and it is surprising how much noise can be achieved by simply beating the wings against the body. At the height of the breeding season, males with a harem will wing-drum at intervals of not more than fifteen minutes, but non-territorial males will often not call at all.

Wing-drumming is often used in boundary disputes between opposing cocks, who will also follow a variety of threat routines. These include walking in line with heads held high, wattles swollen and the plumage on the back of their necks erect, meanwhile uttering the threat-call. An alternative is facing one another with a head-ducking action and plucking at grass and, as aggression develops, the grass is torn and thrown forward, the legs are jerked straight and the bowed head is tossed up sharply. This situation will often progress into a fight in which the birds peck at one another's wattles or leap at the opponent using beak, claws and spurs. Deaths are rare, as the weaker bird usually runs away at an early stage pursued by the victor, running with his head held low.

In the intimidatory lateral display a cock will stand sideways to his opponent and trail the nearer wing, meanwhile holding his head high. This display appears to strike fear into the opponent who invariably retires. However, the probability is that the matter of domination had already been settled before the display began. Some aggression occurs among females forming a harem in April, but actual physical contact is rare.

When alarmed, both male and female make an early retreat into thick cover and both prefer to run rather than fly. I was once hidden in a hedge-hide, decoying pigeons, in Hampshire, and with an extensive view over a valley. Two rough shooters appeared, a mile away, working a narrow tree belt down the centre line of the valley and from which hedges ran off at right angles up the valley sides. When they were still more than half a mile away there was a rush of pheasants up my hedge, running vigorously away from danger. Many shoots fail to realise how rapidly pheasants learn to recognise danger sounds and to vacate the area. Bringing January pheasants over the guns demands a quiet approach and adequate stops.

In addition to the crowing call the pheasant has a variety of other calls. The alarm call is commonly known as the 'cucket' note, but is better described as 'gogOK, gogOK, gogOK'. It is used when uneasy or excited and particularly when hearing a distant noise or feeling a tremor, when the call is often taken up by other cocks over a wide area. There are numerous tales of cocks in England responding to shelling in France during the First World War and to air raids on London in the Second. The threat call is a hoarse growling note, used in low intensity antagonistic encounters, which can develop into a louder, richer note as the conflict increases. Other calls include a protest-call,

PHEASANT

Phasianus colchicus

Colourful, strident, aggressive: a common and welcome sight in the English countryside.

BLACKCOCK

Lyrurus tetrix

For the majority the sight of a blackcock is a rare
event, although the lyre-shaped tail provides instant
recognition.

guard-call, distrust-call, the most descriptive conversation-croon, titbitting call, and hiss. The female lacks many of the antagonistic calls of the male and replaces these with a contact-call with the cock, a pre-copulatory call, protest-call, distress-calls and brood-caution and brood-gathering calls.

The pheasant is omnivorous, eating grain, seeds, berries and other fruits, roots, green shoots, small arthropods, molluscs and, occasionally, small vertebrates. Most of the food is taken either on the surface or up to a depth of 8 cm underneath. To reach the latter it either digs with its beak or scratches and will readily clear a way through snow. Grain stands high among the pheasant's preferences, with wheat favoured before barley, oats and maize. However, feeding pellets are preferred to wheat and where a mix of the two is fed in the release pen the pellets are always taken first. Acorns are very popular and a good year for acorns is a bad one for keepers, trying desperately to stop their charges spreading out widely over the surrounding countryside. There is little a pheasant will not take, including beetles, bugs, flies, grasshoppers, spiders, millipedes, earthworms and slugs. Frogs, lizards, voles, shrews and small snakes are also in danger. Given this list one is hardly surprised to learn that laying females and young under two months also take pebbles of less than 5 mm in diameter. They appear to be able to detect the composition, selecting those with the higher percentage of calcium. These pebbles have a mechanical function but are also the source of micro-elements.

Breeding commences with the cock performing the lateral display to the hen and strutting round her in semicircles with head low and tail spread. The hen usually runs off and there follows a series of displays and runs which may cover as much as 150 m. In all courting activities the wattles and tufts of the cock are swollen and erect. Normally the hen eventually squats and the cock mounts, but it is quite common for the cock to use force.

Laying takes place from late March to early June, and the nest site is normally on the ground and in thick vegetation. A shallow depression is selected rather than formed and little or no lining provided. The eggs are oval, smooth and glossy, coloured olive brown, but occasionally pure olive, brown or grey. There is no speckling or mottling. An average size is 45 × 36 mm and they weigh about 33 g. The clutch varies between eight to fifteen eggs and anything over eighteen is probably the work of two hens. The mean of observations in England showed an average clutch size of 11.8 eggs. Each hen has only one brood, although up to two re-layings may be attempted if previous clutches are lost. Eggs are laid every one or two days and are often deposited in the nests of other species as well as pheasants.

Needless to say incubation is by the hen alone (the cock being far too busy with his other commitments) and it takes twenty-three to twenty-eight days. She begins incubating on laying the last egg and all hatch about the same time. Once hatched, the young are largely self-feeding. For the first ten days their food is principally invertebrates, and they concentrate on foraging in

low grass and dead vegetation for spiders and insects. Only after this period do they turn their attention to green plants. An investigation in Czechoslovakia found insects made up 80% of the diet in the first week, and a similar enquiry in Denmark showed the same pattern.

For the first three weeks, the brood remain in the general area of the nest site, often following the tracks used by the cock on his spring territorial patrols. The pheasant has the reputation of being a bad mother, which is somewhat unfair, as her sole offence is that of not being able to count. Provided she is followed by several chicks, she is content and will often leave the odd chick to die, lost in long, wet, undergrowth. By ten to twelve days the young can fly short distances although they remain dependent on their mother for up to seventy-five days. When contented, or settling for the night, the young have a particularly pleasant call of 'ter-wit, ter-wit' which changes to a louder 'teweep' when suspicious or alarmed. The flocking-call, which, in view of their mother's disposition to lose individuals is much needed, is a repeated 'tee-erp'. It is also used to signal hunger, cold or distress generally. The same call, but louder and more pronounced, is the fright-call and sends the rest of the brood to cover.

In the late 1970s the Game Conservancy recorded the progress of 402 pheasant nests from 21 estates in twelve English counties. Many of the results merely confirmed existing knowledge, but some other interesting data emerged. 35% of the nests were in woodland and only 16% in hedgerows, which contrasted with a survey of partridge nests, where the respective percentages were 13% and 73% (this preference for hedgerows by partridges is yet another reason why partridges are under pressure). 61% of all the nests hatched, and of those which failed predation accounted for 57% and desertion for 36%. Of those, predatory foxes were responsible for 30% and in nearly every case the hen was killed.

One particularly interesting result was that the earlier hatching broods survived better than later ones, and this trend was significant to the degree of being more important than the weather on the day of hatching and on the subsequent ten days.

Applying this to management theory, there may be a case for shoots feeding wild pheasants well in the late winter and early spring to encourage early laying.

There has been little intensive investigation into the survival rates of wild pheasant, although much is known about managed populations. However, the latter figures are of relatively little use, as they principally reflect shooting pressure. A Danish enquiry showed a mean annual mortality, in their first year, for cocks of 78.1%, and hens 62.3%. In subsequent years this dropped to 58.4%, presumably as any bird surviving its first year had gained considerable experience in survival. I personally ringed several thousand reared pheasants for two successive years and found the recovery rate by shooting in

10. Hen pheasant.

11. Newly hatched pheasant chicks.

their second year to be under 5%. However this percentage is not very significant for, shooting apart, the area of the release ground was relatively small and some undoubtedly strayed. The oldest ringed bird I can trace in literature was 7 years 7 months. My personal best was 5 years, 6 months and this was recovered less than 200 m from the original release point.

It is extremely difficult to investigate the natural history of the wild pheasant in Britain, for they are keepered and husbanded to such a degree that there can be few truly wild birds. Even birds described as wild may be the survivors of a rearing programme of a year or two previously, and a wild-hatched brood may have one or both parents who were reared. Certainly the survival rate is improved by the standard practice on shoots of regular and ample feeding. One result of this concentration on improving populations is that we know less about the details of the private life of the pheasant than we do about most of the other important game species. The money and time available has tended to go into perfecting the science of rearing and releasing, rather than looking at behaviour in the wild. However, the Game Conservancy has recently announced (January 1983) that they are launching a new research project, concentrating on wild pheasants. The work will concentrate on factors affecting breeding populations in the wild, together with the contribution that released birds make to the total harvest and to subsequent breeding populations. Subsequently radio-telemetry will be used to study breeding season, brood movements, chick survival and diet in the wild.

Predators are, of course, a threat to pheasants, although the degree to which they take pheasants is often exaggerated. Some useful data is available from the work of Dr David Macdonald of the University of Oxford who studied the fox–pheasant relationship for some nine years. The most important conclusion is that foxes may be getting about 10% of their food in the form of pheasants during August, and, taking a very broad average, this would mean about two pheasants per fox. Dr Macdonald concluded that the impact of foxes was only responsible for reducing the bag by about 5% each year. However, the shoot upon which he carried out part of his investigation was intensively keepered and this must have had the effect of reducing the fox population upon the adjoining, unkeepered land. Earlier observations on the Continent showed that where rabies decimated a fox population, the bags of pheasants, partridge and hares all increased by 50% to 100%.

Earlier Game Conservancy data also suggest fox predation is more serious than concluded by Dr Macdonald. In 1958, and on a well-keepered estate, foxes took 12% of all pheasant nests. Even more emphatic was a survey around a wood at Rockbourne in 1978. Of 38 nests foxes took 6 (16%) in only four days despite vigorous attempts at control.

In the first half of the 1970s the Game Conservancy investigated the effects of avian predation, resulting in the conclusion that birds of prey killed about 1% of released—as distinct from wild—pheasants. (It is reasonable to assume that wild birds, with the benefit of a mother, would suffer less.) In southern and eastern England more than 90% of the kills were made by tawny owls, but in the west this fell to 25%. Here buzzards killed 39% and sparrowhawks 36%.

In fact the figures may exaggerate avian predation, as those shoots suffering losses tended to report them and those with none did not. There is, in any event, nothing that can be done about such losses as birds of prey are now all protected.

Stoats sometimes, but rarely, kill sitting hens. Their greater threat is as a predator of the eggs and one survey showed them taking the eggs of 10% of all known nests. However, the real villains in egg destruction are the corvids who, in the survey in question, accounted for no less than 37%. The proximity of housing also leads to some losses to domestic cats and dogs. Surprisingly, I could find no figures for the depredations of rats, although these unquestionably occur.

The list of diseases to which pheasants will succumb is of a frightening length. Probably the greatest threat is coccidiosis, which results from the invasion of the bird's digestive tract by single-celled protozoans of the genus *Eimeria*. (Protozoa are primitive, free-living, single cells living on other animal or plant material. Malaria is an example of a protozoal disease which attacks man by destroying the red blood cells.) The oocysts, that is eggs of *Eimeria*, are picked up in the food and when the digestive juices dissolve the oocysts wall, eight minute sparozoites are released and enter the epitholial cells lining the gut. These divide up into fifty to a hundred merozoites which infect other epitholial cells and further multiplications take place. Eventually male and female cells are produced which unite to form oocysts identical to those originally ingested by the bird. The scale of multiplication is quite staggering: one oocyst can produce half a million eggs in its life cycle and one infected bird can produce 69 million oocysts. Given these figures it will be readily appreciated that the spread of infection can be rapid.

Coccidiosis usually affects poults, with the peak period of susceptibility at three to four weeks. The birds droop, lose their appetite and look ruffled. Some froth around the beak may be observed but the most obvious sign is a white scour around the vent.

Several efficient drugs are now available to treat coccidiosis and losses among reared birds should be relatively few provided the signs of illness are detected at an early stage.

The second greatest threat to reared pheasants is syngamiasis or, to give it the common name, gapes. This is caused by the roundworm *Syngamus trachea* which, in its adult stage, lives in the trachea of the bird. Each female worm is about 2–5 cm long and has, permanently attached, an adult male of about a quarter this length. Between them they produce fertilised eggs which are coughed up by the pheasants, swallowed and expelled with the droppings.

12. *A well-marked cock pheasant.*

Some of these eggs may be picked up by another pheasant along with food materials, but if not, all is not lost for the egg. With luck it will be digested by an earthworm, or other invertebrate when the larvae will encyst in the muscles of its host, remaining dormant for several years if necessary, until host and worm together are eaten by an unfortunate poult.

The sign of gapes in chicks is coughing accompanied by a sideways flick of the head, both actions being intended to dislodge the irritants. With young poults the death rate can be serious, but prompt diagnosis and action will minimise fatalities. Various remedies exist but, as with coccidiosis, the critical need is to spot the trouble at an early stage. Coccidiosis can often be controlled by adding a low level of coccidiostat to the food of reared birds but no preventive treatment for gapes is possible; action can only be taken when the symptoms are observed.

The science of managing pheasants has been very extensively studied and the conclusions tried and evaluated over many years. For shoot owners it is not so much a question of what measures can be taken, but which of the various well-proven techniques are most applicable to the particular circumstances of their own ground. One essential question to be answered at an early stage is the degree to which their finite resources of labour and money should be concentrated on assisting the wild population to breed and rear the best possible numbers; to let the wild birds manage as best they can and devote all efforts to rearing; or a combination of both, and if so in what proportions. The subject is much too large and complex to attempt here and, in any event, would be out of context in a book of natural history.

It is a pleasure to record that, contrary to the position with so many other species, there is no reason to fear for the future of the pheasant as long as the sport of shooting survives. However, in the unhappy event of extreme political views producing legislation to ban shooting, the days of the pheasant would be numbered; for it is far too tasty a meal to be left in peace and the rate at which it disappeared into poachers' pots would greatly exceed the capacity of a truly wild stock to breed.

5

The Ptarmigan

The ptarmigan stands high on my list of favourite birds. One compelling reason is the admiration one must feel for a bird which not only survives but breeds in harsher conditions of surroundings and weather than any other creature in this country. Another stems from gratitude for a kindness shown. As a keen amateur wild life photographer I am accustomed to disappointment. One beautiful April morning I set out to climb Ben Buie on the Isle of Mull in response to little more than a rumour that there were ptarmigan on the summit. It was a 2,000 foot-plus haul with a rucksack of camera equipment and I was resigned to the probability that this would be yet another wild goose, or more correctly wild ptarmigan, chase. Eventually, and somewhat wearily, reaching the summit I found, within a few yards of the Ordnance Survey trig. point, three ptarmigan seemingly lined up for photography. One was in full winter plumage, one had completed the change to breeding plumage and the other was mid-way. They stood quietly and patiently while I photographed them from various angles and waited while I changed from black and white to colour film. Such consideration has never been shown me, before or since, by any other bird or animal and in return I have never shot a ptarmigan, nor ever will.

The friendly, or, more accurately, frequently tame, ptarmigan (*Lagopus mutus*), is of the order *Galliformes* and the family *Tetraonidae*. As such it is closely related to the members of the grouse family which include the capercaillie.

The ptarmigan shares the same shooting season as the red grouse, that is August 12 to December 20 but as quarries their importance is at opposite extremes. The grouse is famous, even glamorous, and pursued by many. The ptarmigan is much less well known and sought by very few. In part this is due to sharing its habitat with the red deer, and the disturbance of ptarmigan shooting would not be tolerated on a deer forest. However, even without the deer, few rough shooters would have the fitness and tenacity to climb to the home of the ptarmigan and then walk-up exceptionally rough ground. The final drawback is that, when eventually discovered, the ptarmigan is frequently semi-tame and nothing puts off a good sportsman more than a trusting quarry.

Occasionally, but only very occasionally, ptarmigan are driven. The artist-sportsman, John Guille Millais reported in his *Game Birds and Shooting-Sketches* (1894) that 27 brace of ptarmigan were killed in a single drive at Gaick Forest in 1886. He also reported a novel technique, used by the old Highland poachers, for capturing ptarmigan with just a beer bottle and corn. The bottle would be thrust, neck down, into the snow at dusk and corn scattered around and into the hole. During the night the snow would freeze, thereby rendering the walls of the hole hard. Next day the ptarmigan would eat the surface corn then, in thrusting ever deeper to gather the ears at the base of the hole, trap itself head down. It is a method I would view with reservation, except that Millais wrote that his mother had often watched the poachers in Glenfinlas.

There are eight races of ptarmigan in the Western Palaearctic but they vary only slightly. On average the ptarmigan is some 10% smaller than the red grouse, with narrower wings and a slighter build. The male is 5% larger than the female and the male and female can be distinguished by plumage differences except in winter. The juveniles resemble the female.

There are three distinct seasonal variations of plumage. Taking the adult male first, the breeding plumage offers extreme contrasts. Both surfaces of the wings and the underbody are pure white, while all remaining parts are dark grey-brown and black. This superficially drab upper coat is vermiculated and barred with white and covers not only the body but head and neck. The tail-feathers are black. By autumn all the dark feathering, with the exception of the tail which remains black the year round, has moulted and been replaced by paler grey. This point is the completion of the post-breeding moult and the final plumage phase is triggered off by falling temperatures. The winter moult is considered to have begun when all newly growing feathers are white and, when complete, the ptarmigan is entirely white except for the black tail-feathers and lores. It hardly needs stating that the reason for the colour change is to provide camouflage, for at the heights at which ptarmigan live snow lies throughout the winter.

The pre-breeding moult does not begin until May and merges into the post-breeding moult from July to early September. With the female the pre-breeding moult is quicker and is completed in May. In summer she can be distinguished from the male by her rather browner upper coat with ochre or tawny markings, and in the autumn is darker.

The young of the year have three stages of plumage, downy, juvenile and immature autumn, the later similar to the non-breeding female.

Both sexes have a kidney shaped bare area over each eye and a fringed comb on the crown. In the display season these areas are coloured vermilion to scarlet in the male and orange-red to vermilion in the female. At other

13. Ptarmigan in full winter plumage.

14. Ptarmigan midway between winter and summer plumage—photo-graphed in early April.

times they are reduced in size and are pale yellow-red. The bill is black and the claws blue-black.

In attempting to describe the voice I will take refuge in *Birds of the Western Palaearctic* which states the 'calls almost defy description', but then recovers its scientific authority and says the calls are 'variations of a predominantly low-frequency pulse burst of cyclic clicks'. This I do not doubt, but in trying to convey to the reader the strange and eerie noises I have heard in various remote high places I prefer an alternative description—pulling a stick across the slats of a picket fence at varying speeds.

The ptarmigan measures some 34–36 cm in length, of which the tail represents about 8 cm, and has a wing-span of 54–60 cm. Combining the sexes, the average weight is about 450 g, which is almost exactly one pound Imperial.

In broad terms the ptarmigan may be said to live on the top of the world, although as even this tough character declines the North Pole the distribution map looks rather like a necklace around the north of the globe. Apart from this extensive area, small pockets exist in the Alps, the Pyrenees, some high mountains in central Asia, and Hondo, Japan. In Britain the Lake District population died out in the last century and it is now extinct in England. In the same period the ptarmigan also disappeared from south-west Scotland, Arran and Rhum and in the 1930s from the Outer Hebrides. In 1946 Vesey-Fitzgerald wrote that there were, 'still a few in Jura, Islay and Mull, and rather more in Skye'. Now, I would reverse the positions on Mull and Skye. Apart from a couple which went past me at great speed on the main ridge of the Cuillins I have never seen ptarmigan on Skye, but on Mull, at least up to five years ago, there was a healthy population in the Glen Moore area. The exclusions apart, ptarmigan are found on most of the mountains of mainland Scotland from Ben Lomond northwards. Why they have died out in some areas in the last century puzzles me. Nearly all losses of wild creatures derive from the activities of man and the preferred habitat of the ptarmigan is one of the few areas to be left virtually untouched.

The belief that the ptarmigan chooses to live only at high levels is only accurate so far as this country is concerned. What the ptarmigan seeks is not height but low temperature conditions, and the further north one travels the lower the ptarmigan will be found until, at the northernmost limits of its range, the bird is found at sea level. The criterion is access to its plant food, and to achieve this it will move seasonally, although as little as possible. Its range descends, but only just, to the higher fringe of the tree-line, where stunted trees and scrub lead a precarious existence. The preferred surroundings are open, exposed and rocky, with alternating areas of moss carpets, lichen and dwarf heath plants, stones and mountain rubble. In this, to us, entirely hostile world the ptarmigan can find food, shelter, look-out points and, in due time, sheltered nesting sites. Wet ground is avoided, although there is a preference for nearby water.

In Scotland the majority of the population lives in the 600–1,000 m range, although they can be found as low as 200 m.

The ptarmigan is rarely seen alone, being a gregarious bird by nature. When not in pairs in the breeding season, it is normally in either a family covey or larger pack. The usual pattern is for winter packs to form after the coveys break up in September and October; and packing intensifies in bad weather and deep snow. Towards the end of February and in March, the packs break up as individuals settle territories. Monogamous pair-bonds are usual, although, as the males frequently outnumber the females, those unsuccessful in finding a mate will often form summer flocks of males. Pairing commences early, sometimes in the preceding autumn, and firm pairing is evident from January. In many overseas populations, the males desert the females during incubation, but in Scotland the males usually remain loyal until a little after the chicks have hatched. This leaves the full burden of the young on the female until the covey splits up some eleven to twelve weeks later when the young are fully grown.

The night roost is often on bare ground, but where it is exposed some shelter is taken behind stones. Snow appears to be favoured for roosting, with the ptarmigan forming hollows for protection. Large groups of adults often roost together, although rarely closer to one another than 50 cm, but family groups roost with the young almost touching until nearly fully grown.

In flight the ptarmigan is lighter than the grouse. It is also nimbler on the ground and more reluctant to resort to flight. Once the grouse feels it is observed it usually takes wing, whereas the ptarmigan will run with agility and scale surprisingly steep rock faces. When ptarmigan flush they appear faster fliers than grouse, but this may be partly because, being lighter, they accelerate faster, and partly because in escape they prefer downhill flight. Whether their maximum speed on the level exceeds that of grouse, I rather doubt but, not surprisingly, there are only opinions on this question rather than hard evidence.

The diet of the ptarmigan differs from the red grouse as a result of its preference for higher ground, but where they overlap they compete for the same food items. (The question occurs as to whether the lighter ptarmigan does not actually prefer higher ground, but has been driven there by the grouse. However, I think this unlikely for I know several areas where the grouse population is very sparse but the ptarmigan stick rigidly to the heights.) In general terms the ptarmigan inhabit the tundra and grouse the scrub and the former must therefore live on the limited plant life which exists in such harsh conditions. This is usually heather (in the more sheltered areas), bilberry and crowberry. These plants provide 90% of the dry weight of intake in the winter and 60% in summer. The berries of the bilberry and crowberry are taken in summer and in winter it is an enthusiastic digger, with its feet, to reach snow covered plants. It will feed in trees on buds, twigs and seed, where these are available, and in Iceland the winter diet is mainly willow shoots, catkins and buds from the downy birch and the dwarf birch. A list of food items taken around the world shows ptarmigan can live on a wide range of plant material, and what is eaten in any area is mainly a matter of availability rather than preference. It is known that the chicks eat plant material in the first few days but it is suspected that the diet in the first week is mainly insects. Vesey-Fitzgerald reports watching a pair drinking from a shallow depression but I could find no other reports. Logic suggests ptarmigan do drink, for their plant diet is relatively dry.

Not surprisingly, ptarmigan nest on the ground, usually partly sheltered but otherwise in the open. The nest is a simple scrape or hollow, lined with plant material and sometimes a few breast feathers from the female. Unusually, the male is involved in nest building, and both he and the female make several scrapes before one is finally selected.

When first laid, the eggs are oval and glossy, coloured rich cinnamon-red ground with deep brown markings. As incubation proceeds this fades to yellow-buff with black markings. They measure approximately 41×30 mm and weigh some 20–24 g. Scottish records put the average number of eggs to a clutch as 6.6, although in the periods of population decline this falls to four to six.

Normally there is only one brood and eggs are laid at intervals of one or two days and covered with loose grass between the female's visits. Incubation is by the female only and takes twenty-one to twenty-three days. The young leave the nest as soon as they have dried and are largely self-feeding. Millais thought the chicks could fly within a few hours of hatching and Vesey-Fitzgerald said they could 'cover a good many yards long before they are ten days old'. However, Adam Watson, whose authority I would not doubt, states they are capable of precocious flight at ten to fifteen days and exceptionally, or in a strong wind, at seven to ten days. The young become independent at ten to twelve weeks.

We are again indebted to Adam Watson for the information that in an observed 24 clutches there were 147 eggs of which 90.5% hatched. Most of the young who perish do so before they are twenty days old and the main causes are bad weather and lack of food. Over an eighteen-year period of observation the average of full grown broods varied between 1.2 and 6.2.

Ptarmigan populations show considerable annual fluctuations and there is some evidence to show these are cyclic at intervals of approximately ten years. The British population is thought to lie in the range of 1,000–10,000 pairs and is believed to have remained fairly constant during this century. Sweden appears to have the highest national population with approximately 75,000 pairs.

Ptarmigan populations are basically resident but some movement takes place with seasonal and weather changes. In late summer, after breeding is complete, they often move uphill following the retreating snowline. Conversely, when the weather hardens, they move downhill once more. In deep snow the Scottish ptarmigan descend to the heather zone, where they merge with the grouse. In Greenland, Iceland and other northern areas where weather conditions are severer, ptarmigan migrate over large distances to winter further south.

Compared with other wild creatures, ptarmigan are relatively little troubled by predators, for the simple reason that few predators, or indeed any other creatures of any size, live in their ecological niche. In Scotland, some are undoubtedly taken by golden eagles, but the eagle population is low and can also normally find richer pickings at a lower level. The same reasoning will apply to the fox and all other predators who will naturally seek their food where the supply is best.

The greatest pressure on the ptarmigan comes from the hostility of its environment but, conversely, this threat will also be its saving, for there is no financial gain for man to be found on the remote hill-tops and the birds are likely to be left in peace.

The Woodland Grouse

The next two chapters deal with the black grouse and the capercaillie, members of the grouse family who frequent woodland habitats. All the woodland grouse have suffered severe population declines, both in numbers and range, during the last century or so, and have disappeared from many areas in which they were once common. The position is serious, and throughout Europe much is being done to investigate the reasons and reverse the trend. We should be proud of the fact that a major force in this work is the World Pheasant Association, an organisation born in this country in 1975 mainly as a result of the initiative of Dr Tim Lovel, Major Iain Grahame, Mr Keith Howman and their wives.

In 1982 the World Pheasant Association instituted a research project on the woodland grouse to be carried out by N. Picozzi, to concentrate mainly on the habitat requirements of hens and their broods. In his first report, issued in November 1982, he dealt with the techniques used for trapping and monitoring wild birds using radio telemetry; the movement and breeding performance of marked birds; the food and habitat requirements of adults and young; and the main food plants of cock and hen black grouse in the study area throughout the year. Obviously this is an important and much needed investigation which will almost certainly yield important results.

However it is questionable whether the organisations and individuals concerned with the welfare of woodland grouse should wait for further information before taking some action. There is often conflict between scientists and laymen, with the latter calling for 'something to be done', and the former pointing out that it is firstly necessary to determine the right actions. Writing as a layman, I would suggest there is now a very substantial volume of material recording the natural history of woodland grouse and whilst we need to extend our knowledge to the maximum, it is equally important to set in train practical measures to halt the decline as quickly as possible. We may still have large gaps in our knowledge but, I would humbly suggest, the fundamental causes are already obvious. The old forests, carved by wind and fire into a mix of various species of trees, mainly pine and of varying age ranges, the whole interspersed with open glades offering ground cover and plant foods, have been largely cleared and replaced by uniform ranks of identical trees, usually Sitka spruce which is not favoured by woodland grouse because it forms an unbroken canopy which effectively prevents ground cover. At the same time, human disturbance has increased very considerably. While a programme of recreating the old favourable habitats might lack scientific exactitude, it would almost certainly work most effectively.

This simple solution unfortunately suffers from an equally simple, but dominating, drawback—money. Landowners and foresters have to manage their estates and business activities in the most profitable ways and even if they are sympathetic towards woodland grouse, the financial pressures of our times may make it difficult to take any action. Nor can we seek the answer in sporting rents, for the income is most unlikely to compensate for the losses the necessary alterations from normal woodland management practices would create.

There is no single answer and I suggest the major effort should now go into seeking different paths leading to the one objective of habitat improvement. Some forestry organisations might be persuaded to incorporate suitable mixed areas in future plantings as a goodwill publicity exercise. Large landowners might see it as their personal long term bequest to the countryside (with a suitable plaque erected by the World Pheasant Association?). Existing reserves could be managed with a greater priority given to the needs of woodland grouse.

There may be other and better ideas, but the quicker we take positive action, the more likely we are to preserve these fascinating birds into the future.

6

The Black Grouse

As I write, dawn has just broken and if I look northwards through my study window the sun is picking out the tower on Leith Hill, part of the North Downs ranging east/west across rural Surrey. It is indicative of the state of the black grouse that little more than a century ago, in the 1870s, they were living on Leith Hill and in various other parts of Surrey. Indeed, a pair were seen at Hindhead in 1906. Now I would have to journey north for nearly 300 miles to see wild black grouse.

Of the order *Galliformes* and the grouse family *Tetraonidae*, the black grouse has the Latin name *Tetrao tetrix*. Like the other members of its family it has inhabited these island for a long time and remains have been found as far back as the early Upper Pleistocene, that is to say, some 150,000 years ago.

The shooting season is from August 20 to December 10. There are few areas where the population is sufficient for black grouse to be the prime object of a day's shooting and it more normally figures as one of the species in a mixed bag. This is not, however, to diminish its importance in the sporting scene, for it provides a colourful feature and is regarded as a rather special quarry for all but those living in its home territory.

Both the male black grouse and the female are larger than the red grouse, but smaller than even the female capercaillie. As a result of its magnificent lyre-shaped tail the male black grouse is 30% larger than the female, but its wing span is less than 20% greater.

The distinction in appearance between male and female is further marked with the former having a head, neck, upper parts and tail of glossy blue-black and a black underbody. The wings are brown-black with a white bar at the base, a white patch at the shoulder, and white under the wing-coverts. The undertail and thighs are white and these white areas of the body and wings stand out in contrast to the remainder of the bird when in flight. The white areas however are not the main distinguishing feature for, when viewed from below, the fork of the magnificent tail provides instant identification. In late summer the male assumes a duller, partial eclipse plumage, when the head and neck become mottled with brown and black.

The female is a warm brown above, but assumes a greyer, paler shade below the chest. Overall she is freckled and with strong black barring. The wings have the colour of the underbody but with a pale white wing bar. The tail is coloured as the underparts and has a discernible fork. Apart from size, it is easy to confuse the female black grouse with the female capercaillie.

Standing in a grouse butt, and particularly against a strong light, it is also easy to confuse black grouse with red if they come separately. However, together the size difference is distinct and also the slow, more deliberate wing beat of the black grouse. Black grouse also normally fly higher than red grouse—sometimes very much higher—and will also glide for prolonged distances in outstretched wings.

The bill of the male is dark blue-grey to black and the female's brown-black. As with the other males in the grouse family there is a bright red comb over the eye which is largest in spring. The feet are dark grey-brown and the claws brown-black. According to sex the length varies from 40 cm to 55 cm, and the wing span from 65 cm to 80 cm. The male weighs approximately 1,250 g and the female 950 g.

The extent of the decline of the black grouse in Britain can best be appreciated by considering where it could once be found. As late as the last decade of the nineteenth century Millais could write that black grouse were in 'Westmoreland, Cumberland and Northumberland—though they are found here and there in almost every county in both England and Scotland, having been shot in every county from Caithness to Cornwall.' Now, black grouse have disappeared from most of the English counties. Small populations exist in parts of the West Country, Wales, Derbyshire and the North-West. Scotland is the stronghold of the black grouse and, happily, the range has extended slightly over the last twenty years or so.

Elsewhere it is found in suitable habitat throughout much of Continental Europe and Northern Siberia but in most areas it is a story of retreat and decline. Sometimes the evidence upon which estimations of variations of wild life populations is based is rather scanty, but with the black grouse we have some detailed reports. In Denmark a count in Jutland in 1942 showed a spring population of 2,400. By 1966 this was down to about 1,100 and by 1973 had dropped again to approximately 400. 1978 saw a fall to about 100 black grouse and there is now a grave risk of total extinction in the area.

In Poland numbers fell from 40,000 in 1976, to 33,000 in 1977 and 29,000 in 1978. The Netherlands also report a decline, which in one study area saw the cocks fall from about 3,000 in 1950 to less than 200 in 1980. A Norwegian report begins: 'Since 1967–8 populations of woodland grouse decreased markedly in Norway.'

There is no need to labour the point: black grouse numbers are falling in most areas and the only good news is that many responsible people and organisations are very concerned.

The preferred habitat of the black grouse is the mixed area between open moors or grassland and continuous dense forest. Trees are essential, but they must be in small scattered groups and preferably not tall. Most favoured are areas offering a combination of suitable trees for roosting, open bare land for display and a good supply of the right food plants. A study in Scandinavia produced some detailed results. Black grouse show a strong preference for woodland with a high proportion of birch. On the ground the ideal shrub coverage seemed to be between 61% to 80% and areas with less than 40% shrub cover were avoided. There was a strong preference for areas with bilberries and areas without were thinly populated.

By nature black grouse are gregarious with the males, in particular, forming the equivalent of men's clubs. As with other species given to flocking, the trend increases as the temperature lowers and in USSR flocks of 200 to 500 occur. In Scotland immature males and females tend to flock separately to the older males. These latter groups are mainly composed of adult males from the same lekking arena. (I write of 'lekking arena', with the black grouse but later of 'display area', with the capercaillie as the latter is not so strictly defined.) However, these flock compositions are not rigid and various mixes of age and sex are possible, although it is usual to find that one sex constitutes some 70% to 85% of a flock. Radio tracking of individual males in Scotland showed home ranges of 303 to 639 ha although much smaller areas were used regularly.

As one would expect from males who club together, they are a promiscuous bunch, meeting the females for copulation, then leaving them to get on with the entire business of breeding on their own. The scene of these brief love affairs is the traditional lekking arena at which the males congregate to display at morning and evening in spring and in mornings only in autumn. Occasional use occurs at other times in the year but it is feeble compared to the spring. In some arenas abroad, activity at various levels occurs through most of the year. The lek is usually situated in the centre of an open area: a glade or clearing, meadow, forest edge or bog. The centre of a peat bog is particularly favoured. Arenas are often found within sight of one another and a case is recorded of a gap of only 200 m. The males using the arena are usually those whose territories surround it, although 'intruders' may appear for brief spells. However, regular members of the club are not equal but appear to divide into two categories of 'central' and 'marginal', the former performing the great majority of the copulations.

Reports from various observers, over long periods and in various countries, show there is a complex territorial and ranking system. For example, it is thought that every 'marginal' male, in spite of his lowly position with the ladies has a segment of the group's home range upon which he ranks highest. And he, in turn, has an even lower ranking male who, when he is a safe distance away, assumes top rank in that particular segment only.

Male establishment of a territory, and subsequent dominance behaviour, is frequently triggered off by courtship and a male 'intruder' to the arena will, if he is successful in courting a female, fight to resist eviction by the resident males and frequently establish a new territory.

Depending on the country and the weather, males may attend the lek every day or neglect it for months but activity in the arena becomes intense once the first females arrive in mid April. The beginning of the display immediately changes abruptly to first light, and activity rises daily to a peak fortnight in early May after which it declines slowly until, by the end of June and with the females occupied with nests and young, it has died to almost zero.

The males do not assemble at the lek but gather some distance away with excitement mounting as more birds join the flock and time passes. At early twilight they fly or walk to the arena, showing such impatience that if one breaks into a run or flight others will immediately follow suit. On arrival, the males hold their heads high and ruffle the feathers around throat and nape as a threat posture, followed by what observers have termed the 'crowing-hiss' and 'rookooing'. Briefly, in the 'crowing-hiss' the body is raised, the neck, nape and throat feathers are tightly compressed and a harsh, angry sneeze is emitted, described as 'whush-EE'. Each male may perform this two to three times per minute. Crowing-hissing is frequently preceded by flutter-jumps or simple wing beating.

However, most arena activity is devoted to the 'rookooing' display in which the male adopts a forward posture and cocks and fans its tail to ruffle the rump feathers into a hump. The neck is swollen and horizontally outstretched while the call is made. This is a musical, resonant, dove-like bubbling, lasting 2 to 3 seconds and can be heard over a considerable distance. As the name suggests the call resembles 'rrooo-OO-rroo-rroo'. The sound of a number of singing male black grouse has been described as 'a cacophony with powerful reverberating character'.

There are many detailed accounts of lekking and territorial performances, some of which merge into a common pattern and others which appear to be individual but there is neither space nor need to detail them. Merely, I record that the behaviour of the black grouse is fascinating, not least because of the frequency with which one recognises similar human responses and attitudes.

After the females have viewed the proceedings from a distance for a few mornings, often perching in trees, they then visit the arena proper and commence some preliminary flirting. This takes the form of a self-explanatory invitatory-crouch display. Condensing a lengthy and complicated ritual into a few words, the male circles the female with short rapid steps, often for up to 10 minutes. A male will often circle more than one female and the more ambitious will contain as many as five. The male then mounts for 2 to 4 seconds, although one bewildered male faced with an experimental stuffed female remained in position for 30 seconds. Whilst copulating the male holds the nape of the female in his bill and flaps his wings violently.

It is thought that each hen only mates on one or two days each season and that 25% of copulations occur within the ten day height of the season. One study found that 70% of the hens copulated within 15 minutes of arriving at the arena.

Reverting to rather quieter behaviour, black grouse generally roost on the ground at night and, surprisingly, only rarely in trees. However, Scottish black grouse show a preference for trees on rainy winter nights. When there is deep snow on the open moor they favour the forest floor, but move out to the open ground when the weather improves. It is rare for them to roost alone, preferring groups of three to ten, although these are scattered rather than close-knit.

In Continental areas where exceptionally severe winter conditions are encountered, black grouse actually dig a burrow in the snow for shelter. Using both feet and bill they tunnel forward a distance of two to three times their own length and, by hiding the excavated snow rearwards, close the entrance hole behind them. The faeces dropped during the night are used as a platform to insulate the feet. To emerge, it pushes its head clear, peers round, then often bursts straight into the air like a rocket from a silo. These excavated roosting sites are traditional and birds usually leave and return by flying, presumably to prevent predators following their tracks. In the worst conditions black grouse may remain underground for several days. (As a comparison, during the very severe winter of 1961–2 I found hares forming and living in snow burrows on a freshwater marsh on the Isle of Sheppey.)

Black grouse are normally residents, rarely moving outside their home ranges, although on the Continent severe weather will force movement, sometimes over long distances. One ringed female travelled over 1,000 km and a male some 500 km which included a 20 km sea crossing.

The adult black grouse is essentially a plant eater, feeding on the ground whenever possible, but being driven into the trees and shrubs in winter. As food choices are limited in winter, it is not surprising that crop examinations vary according to what is available in the locality. Birch catkin is a great favourite, Scots pine is taken freely and juniper less so. Other winter foods include the stems of bilberries, heather and deciduous tree buds. Summer choices include bilberry, bog whortleberry, cowberry, crowberry, heather and sedges.

An interesting paper in the report of the 1978 Woodland Grouse Symposium reasoned that the black grouse selects its winter food for its potential metabolic energy. Much of the supplementary diet is relatively poor in crude protein but rich in total sugars—for example the larch is preferred to the Arolla pine because its total sugar content is higher. Protein is not important to the black grouse in winter whereas energy is vital to maintain body temperature and to allow it to acquire and warm food.

The female black grouse selects a nest site among thick ground cover, although on rare occasions it will utilise an old tree nest of another species. The nest is a simple scrape, lined with grass or mosses and laying can begin from late March onwards. The eggs are oval and glossy, coloured pale olive or buff, and lightly spotted red-brown or yellow-brown. They measure approximately 51×37 mm and weigh about 36 g. Eggs are laid at intervals of 36 to 48 hours and the clutch size varies between four and fifteen eggs. Incubation takes some twenty-five to twenty-seven days and is carried out solely by the female who takes three feeding periods during the day.

Once hatched, the young are cared for by the female, who broods them at night for any period between ten and twenty days depending upon which authority you choose to believe. The female may lead her brood over relatively long distances in the first few days—records show up to 400 m in the first two days and 900 m by four days—in search of a suitable area in which to spend the next few weeks. Interestingly, one Norwegian study observed a brood which hatched in poor weather conditions. For the first five days it was wet and raining and the brood moved no further than 200 m. The weather then improved and from the tenth to the seventeenth day the brood moved no less than 5.6 km.

Observations suggest precocious flight begins at any time between seven to fourteen days and the young are independent at about three weeks. Below the weight of 100 g the chicks take mainly animal material: insects, with a strong leaning to ants and spiders.

Although the foregoing data demonstrates that we have a good volume of factual information on the natural history of the grouse we are less well informed on its population structure and more particularly all the reasons for its decline over most of its range. Shooting is certainly not the reason, for even where it has been prohibited by law, numbers have still fallen. Obviously habitat destruction is an important factor, but we cannot say precisely how important each aspect of the habitat is. A good indication of this appears in the progress report for the World Pheasant Association by N. Picozzi. In one area he found nine nests in mature heather and well concealed. Of these, three deserted and one was killed by a predator. Four nests hatched but the young of three had all died within fourteen days. The fourth reared 4 young and the fate of the ninth nest is unreported. Of the 8 nests whose fate is known, only 4 young were reared.

Subsequently Picozzi searched for previously unobserved females with dogs. He found 8 with a total of 3 young and suspected 2 more hens without young. If this nesting failure rate is common, then the decline in black grouse is understandable. However it may be significant that the most successful hen did not nest in the same glen as its sisters but an adjoining one where, apparently, the nesting season was a good one for black grouse. The glen in question has more cover which may mean more insect food for the very young chicks.

A French study tended to disprove the common theory that cold, wet weather is responsible for poor chick survival. The authors drew a comparison between the Northern Alps with its cool, humid climate in which the peak of the annual rainfall occurs in June, July and August, and the Southern Alps with their warm, dry summers. The best breeding results could be expected in the south but in practice there was little difference with the balance, if any, in favour of the north.

Nest predation will obviously account for some losses but a Norwegian study suggests the black grouse should suffer less than the capercaillie. This showed that black grouse almost invariably select denser nesting cover than the capercaillie and the effectiveness of this measure is demonstrated in the statistics. Of 41 capercaillie nests 13 were robbed by predators but only 1 of 24 black grouse nests.

F. J. J. Niewold, writing on the decline of black grouse in the Netherlands, said there were two factors seriously affecting reproduction: firstly, the failure of a 'substantial number' of hens to incubate a clutch and, secondly, the high mortality of chicks at an early stage. His conclusions were based on extensive observations and distilled down to the belief that the decline was due to the changes which had occurred in the last decade or two to the cultivated land surrounding the heath and peat areas favoured by the black grouse. As a result of wider and deeper drainage ditches, the chicks were confined to unfavourable habitats with low survival chances. Other factors, leading to a disappearance or scarcity of cover and also food for chicks, were increased mechanisation, changing crops, larger fields and increased agricultural production.

One interesting theory is that tetraonid populations may be related to those of small rodent populations. The reasoning runs that when there is an ample supply of easily caught rodents the grouse family is left alone by the corvids, stoats, foxes and weasels, and during this time they can build up their numbers. However, in due course the rodent population crashes and the predators turn their attention to harder prey. The hypothesis is attractive but it cannot explain the general and prolonged decline of the black grouse.

In management for sport one naturally thinks of rearing and preliminary reports of an experiment in Southern Germany are encouraging. In 1978 black grouse were released in an area from which they had previously disappeared in the early 1970s. At the same time, a major programme of fox control was carried out in the area. Observations suggest that a reasonable percentage of the birds have survived to date, although there is no indication of breeding so far.

Encouraging though this is, the practice of rearing and releasing in areas where the wild stock has either died out or is much depleted does not make much sense other than to improve the short term shooting. If conditions were such that the natural wild stock had died out there is little prospect of reared birds creating a viable population. The correct approach is to improve the habitat so that it will hold and maintain a natural population; and to do this we must know what conditions black grouse need and how they can be reproduced most economically. The future of the black grouse is very much in the hands of the World Pheasant Association and kindred organisations overseas.

7

The Capercaillie

If the space allocated in this book to the capercaillie was in the same proportion as the number shot in relation to the other quarries then it would, at best, receive a couple of paragraphs. However, such a large and colourful character deserves far better treatment and it is my pleasure to give the caper generous attention.

Essentially the capercaillie is a very large grouse, belonging to the same order, *Galliformes*, the same family, *Tetraonidae*, and with a Latin name that somehow fits, *Tetrao urogallus*.

Common names include cock of the wood, mountain cock and wood-grouse but the most popular is old man of the wood. One suggestion for the derivation of capercaillie is that it derives from Gaelic, being a combination of *capull*, which means great horse, and *coille*, meaning a wood. The name gives scope for a variety of spellings and these include caperkellie, capercaley, caperkally, capercalze and capercaili.

The threat of man to wild life is well illustrated by the capercaillie in Britain. Now it clings on precariously over a restricted range, but its history in Britain goes back a long time. Remains have been found in the Forest Bed of Norfolk, laid down in the Cromerian interglacial, along with the mammoth, sabre-toothed tiger and cave lions. Later, in the early Upper Pleistocene, there are more capercaillie remains, in a remarkable period when cave bears and grouse, forest rhinos and partridge, cave wolf and ptarmigan, and many other species, some of which are very familiar and others which we only know from reconstructions, all inhabited Britain.

Taking a giant stride in time we know the capercaillie was present in England at the end of the twelfth century, from the writings of Gerald of Wales, who also mentioned white-fronted geese, the hobby and the merlin. The capercaillie was also quite common in Ireland, but died out in the last years of the eighteenth century.

Quite when the capercaillie became extinct in Britain is a matter of some doubt. In *Letters from a Gentleman in the North of Scotland*, in 1754, Edward Burt said the Cobber-kely, was 'very seldom to be met with'. John Latham

79

wrote of it in the past tense in 1783 and *The Old Statistical Account of Scotland* (1798) spoke of the last caper-coille having been seen about forty years ago. *The Handbook of British Birds* gives the authoritative opinion that the capercaillie became extinct in Scotland and Ireland about 1760 and had disappeared from England about a century previously.

There is, however, an inscription on the back of a painting in Balmoral Castle, 'Two coileach-coille, capercailzie, shot on the occasion of a marriage rejoicing in 1785'.

Whenever the precise death of the last survivor, the more important fact is that the loss of this magnificent bird was caused by massive forest-clearing and, in the later stages, over-shooting of the much depleted population. However re-afforestation programmes began in the eighteenth century and by 1828 Fleming in *British Animals* could write of the capercaillie that 'recent attempts have been made to recruit our forests from Norway, where the species is still common'. The first, somewhat ill-conceived, venture was a pair taken to Norfolk in 1823. This failed, as did several efforts by the Earl of Fife on his Mar Lodge estate at Braemar between 1827 and 1831. Other unsuccessful attempts were made at various times and in various places, some recorded and some, judging by the occasional reports of solitary capercaillie turning up in odd places, not.

The credit for the first successful introduction goes to a team rather than an individual. In 1836 Sir Thomas Fowell Buxton requested Mr Llewellyn Lloyd to obtain capercaillie for his friend Lord Breadalbane at Taymouth Castle, Perthshire. Lloyd offered rewards to the peasantry of Sweden and in due course 48 capers reached the Castle. Sixteen more followed in 1838 and by the following year the head-keeper estimated there were between 60 and 70 living wild on the estate. By 1862, and with no further introductions, Lord Breadalbane estimated numbers had risen to about 1,000.

There is a long history of the efforts, some unsuccessful and some not, of other introductions, spurred on, no doubt, by the achievements at Taymouth Castle. However, the details are unimportant to this book. What matters is that by 1914 breeding populations existed as far north as Golspie in Sutherland, westwards to Cowal, Argyllshire, south-west to Stirling and eastwards to Buchan, Aberdeenshire.

Relatively little expansion has been noted since then, partly due to large timber felling operations necessitated by the two World Wars. In particular, little if any movement westwards took place and this failure was blamed on very high rainfall coupled with the practice of replanting almost exclusively with Sitka spruce, a species less favoured by the capercaillie than native Scots pine. However, in a paper presented to the Second International Symposium on Grouse, in 1981, Mr I. Brodie said that in the five years 1975–80 a 'significant westward expansion had taken place' resulting in some birds reaching the west coast of Argyll, during 1980, at the head of Loch Craiguish.

Mr Brodie argued that the belief that capercaillie disliked areas of high rainful might well be mistaken. They might, he suggested be inhibited by this factor but not positively limited. Instead he suggested the main barrier to westward movement had been the very high percentage of Sitka spruce plantings, amounting to 80% in some areas. However, in the mid 1960s these forests suffered major damage from exceptionally heavy winds (I recall the major storm lifting a partly built bungalow off its foundation in Skye) which broke up the regimented age classes of trees and created irregular compositions. A decade later the devastated areas had regenerated and the remainder was well matured, resulting in much more mixed and natural areas of forests. The capercaillie were attracted to these new and suitable habitats, and the crossing to the west was a natural consequence. This encouraging westward movement apart, the capercaillie is well established in the valleys of the Tay, Dee and Spey, throughout their tributaries and in Morayshire and Banffshire.

The shooting season for capercaillie is from October 1 to January 31. Although the prospect of bagging a capercaillie will doubtless be attractive to many shooting men, I doubt if this alone sends many sportsmen to Scotland. The caper is more probably the icing on a cake which may include grouse, pheasants of above average quality, geese or a mix of all three—or, perhaps best of all, autumn salmon and the chance of a caper. Whatever the magnetism offered by the capercaillie, its importance as a quarry must be limited by the low population. Nor do the relatively few sportsmen who pursue it have prolific sport. Among the many statistics of a report on the management of woodland grouse I found some figures on caper shooting. Some 30 shoots had been observed and 1,531 capercaillie were seen. Of these 169 were bagged. If we assume ten guns at each shoot, this gives 300 man/days for 169 capercaillie, which means a gun would average about one caper for every two days' shooting. This said, however, the capercaillie undoubtedly plays a part in bringing income to isolated parts of Scotland where it is most welcome.

The capercaillie is one of our most easily recognisable birds, if only by virtue of its sheer size. The sexes are very dissimilar, and not just in colour but size, as the male is up to 40% larger than the female. In flight the broad wings and tail, together with the large bill, are very noticeable.

At a distance the male appears to be dark slate-grey. In fact the flanks, belly, tail and lower-head are almost black, the chest is green-black and the upper mantle and wing-coverts are dark warm brown. The female is basically brown—rufous on the back, chestnut on the chest and paler elsewhere. There is heavy black barring above and black and white barring below. As with other grouse there is bare skin over the eye which is bright red in the male but paler in the female. The bill of the male is pale yellow and that of the female dark-brown to grey-brown. The toes of both sexes are grey-brown and the claws black-brown. The male begins his moult in May, once the display period is over, but the female varies between late May and early July, depending on the hatch of her young.

The flight action of the capercaillie resembles the other members of the grouse family except that the wing beats are slower but very powerful. For their size they walk and run with surprising ease, the female being faster than the male.

In length capercaillie vary between 60–87 cm, of which the tail can occupy 19–28 cm. The wing-span varies between 87–125 cm (34–49 inches). Scottish capercaillies weigh less than their Continental counterparts with adult males averaging 3,920 g against 4,240 g in Norway and 4,715 g in Central Germany.

A little earlier I wrote of the dislike of the capercaillie for extensive areas of unbroken Sitka spruce of even age. When considering its likes rather than dislikes, the best description comes from Pennie (1950): 'the preferred habitat of the capercaillie is the old open pine woods on the hillsides with an undergrowth of heather and blaeberries'. In natural forests centuries of gales, fires and other forces have created a mix of pine trees of varying ages and densities, including free standing trees with large crowns for roosting and winter feeding. On the ground the 'sky windows' caused by the many gaps in the tree canopy allow extensive vegetation for summer feeding. Conversely, plantation blocks lack virtually all these features.

It is significant that capercaillie prefer the oldest trees in a forest, commonly called 'grannies'. These have ceased to grow and the sharp canopy has adopted a rounded or irregular profile which is more convenient for the capercaillies. Other preferences are fern or other ground cover for hiding, gizzard grit and water. Finally the area needs to offer a good variety of plants fruiting at different seasons, for the capercaillie is reluctant to make seasonal movements and seeks a year-round food supply.

According to the season, the capercaillie can be gregarious or solitary. After the dispersal of broods in the autumn flocking occurs, although adult males tend to remain solitary. Firm pair-bonding is absent, with either promiscuous mating or only temporary polygamous pair-bonds. Lacking pair-bonding, the female alone cares for the young.

Male capercaillies meet at traditional display sites which have been frequented by generations; some sites in Sweden are known to have been in regular use for over a century. Male activity on the display area can begin as early as the New Year and continue sporadically until late autumn. However, the peak of the active ground display is restricted to three or four weeks, during which time the females visit the site. The use of the display area has a major influence on the behaviour of the male capercaillie, for one estimate suggests he spends up to a third of the year close to the site. One interesting theory advanced by Ingemar Hjorth at the 1981 Grouse Symposium was based on the 'piece of cake hypothesis'. Put simply, the belief is that the male capercaillie have their individual territories around a central display area and each territory is wedge shaped with the sharp end of the 'piece of cake' forming a segment of the display area. To this the individual males come for their communal displays and the nearer they come to the sharp end the more aggressively they defend their territories.

At the height of the season the males will commence singing from their tree-perches some one to two hours before sunrise. They then drop down to the display area to continue the song-display on the ground, performing in the process a 'slow-march' with the head tilted upright and the neck stretched. Meanwhile the primaries are scraped noisily across the ground and the bird emits a clicking noise with the interval between clicks shortening until merging into a quiet roll. This is interrupted by a cork-pop note and the occasional deep grunt and, to add yet more variety, the bird may run, crouch, flap its wings noisily and even make short flights.

The prime purpose of this behaviour is to intimidate other males rather than attract females and fighting is common. Rival males advance on each other with lowered heads and emitting the self-explanatory 'belch-call'. When fighting the males stab and peck at one another, occasionally rearing up close together and thrashing at the opponent with their wings. The loser will flee the area, and it is thought that while few deaths occur during fighting, subsequent deaths from injuries are not uncommon.

In the more pleasant matter of mating, the females appear at the display area in groups and begin by watching the performance from the trees, emitting occasional cackle-calls. Over a period of several days they move closer to the action and eventually fly down and are immediately courted by the males. Usually the female will be wary and uncooperative for several days but eventually crouches while the male circles, grasps her nape feathers in his bill, and mounts.

The one or two dominant males in the display area will usually fertilize the majority of the females and will sometimes mount several females in rapid succession.

The foregoing is a very abbreviated description of the long, and frequently varied, activities around the display area but there is not space to cover all aspects. A major difficulty in assembling a concise yet accurate report is that scientists and natural historians are still in the process of observing, recording and reaching conclusions. As a result there is a wealth of detail of individual observations but, as yet, no simple synopsis of what happens and why.

Many snippets of information and opinion can be gleaned from the papers of the two symposiums on grouse, organised by the World Pheasant Association. From these we are told that the song of the cock has a territorial motive and is not concerned with courtship; that 'bowing' is directed only at rivals and never the hens; that the centre of the display area is always occupied by the dominant male; that the visits to the area by females to mate are mainly confined to April (in West Germany—the same dating does not necessarily rule in Scotland); and, in direct contravention to conclusions in this country, that the males seldom fought and when they did injuries were very rare and then usually not severe.

Through the spring, summer and autumn (unless there is snow cover) the capercaillie feeds on the ground, but in the winter it turns to the crowns of trees for nourishment. In the summer and the interseasons some of the major food items are cow-wheat, crowberries, cloudberry, sedges, marsh andromeda, horsetails, the leaves, stem and berries of bilberry, bog whortleberry and the leaves of woodrush and aspen. In winter the preference is for Scots pine, with the consumption being more than 80% needles. The balance is shoots, with small cones making up less than ½%. Where Scots pines are absent any variety of conifers are used but, significantly, where there is a choice the Sitka spruce, much favoured by foresters, is rarely taken.

A detailed study of the capercaillie's food was carried out in eastern Finnish Lapland in the period September to December by examining the crop content of 312 birds. Pine needles were taken in September, before any snowfall, destroying the theory that they are only taken when there is no alternative. However, in the early autumn, between 70% and 80% of the crop contents came from only a few varieties of ground level plants. As the snow arrived, so the proportion of pine in the diet increased until, in December, it varied between 81–100%. Not surprisingly, as the pine content went up the nutritive value of the food went down, but it was concluded that the capercaillie could survive severe winter conditions with a diet containing only 7.0–7.3% crude protein.

In contrast to the dramas of the display area, the hen selects a nesting site at ground level, in thick cover and often at the foot of a tree. In Scotland and central Europe laying takes place in the second half of April and early May but in harsher climates is deferred. The nest is shallow and lined simply with pine needles and grass. The eggs are yellow-white with the occasional brown streak and oval, smooth and glossy. They weigh about 50 g and measure some 57 × 42 mm. The clutch normally contains seven to eleven eggs, with eight being the most common number and incubation taking twenty-four to twenty-six days. The hen only incubates, normally leaving the nest twice a day for anything between twenty to seventy minutes.

Once hatched the young are cared for exclusively by the female, who broods them in the early stages. As with so many other species the chicks have a preference for animal food when young. In one experiment 53% of the intake of chicks up to the age of twenty days was animal material, while a Finnish study put the percentage as high as 71%. However, in one of the Grouse Symposium discussions, Dr Adam Watson pointed out that the nutrient value of newly growing heather shoots was high and that grouse chicks could survive and grow well on a diet containing as little as 5% dry weight of insects.

The young make their first attempts at flight when only two to three weeks old and are fully grown at two to three months. They become independent soon after but the males do not normally breed until they are three years old. The females, unfettered by having to compete with others of their sex, breed earlier.

Reports of population trends over the last twenty to thirty years make mainly depressing reading. Declines are reported from France, Spain, East and West Germany, Sweden, Finland, Poland, Austria and Italy. Finland appears to have the largest population with an estimated 214,000 pairs. An illuminating paper on the Norwegian situation, by Per Wegge, appeared in the 1978 Woodland Grouse Symposium report. The 1960 Norwegian population was put at roughly 3–400,000 capercaillie and, based on shooting returns, it was felt numbers had fallen by 60–80% in just a decade. One factor revealed by the studies was an increase in nest losses from 25.2% before the decline to 41.1% in the years 1968, 1976 and 1977. The mean size of broods reared was also low, varying between 1.4 and 3.8 and the percentage of females without chicks increased. The net result was an annual juvenile autumn recruitment of 34.3%, although unfortunately no comparable figures exist for the earlier years.

The author suggested several reasons for the decline, one being natural fluctuations which appear to result in very large populations about every ten years. Unfortunately the peaks have become progressively smaller. Next, and in line with Scottish experience, he blamed extensive timber felling operations for destroying good habitat. Acid air pollution also came in for a suspicious glance, not least because the heaviest declines have occurred in those areas suffering the greatest pollution. Another, most interesting, line of thought was the large quantities of rubbish created by modern society. The resulting rubbish dumps, he reasoned, sustained a much higher predator population than could have survived under natural conditions. Finally he blamed modern recreation, which led to considerably more human disturbance, over the whole year, in isolated areas which had previously enjoyed solitude for most of the time.

Some useful information on population dynamics emerged from ageing capercaillie shot on a Scottish estate over a period of several years. The proportion of young varied from 42% to 53% and it was concluded that, in the long term, the annual mortality rate of all age classes must average 49%. However, this does not mean 49% die each year irrespective of age, for obviously the young and inexperienced are more vulnerable than the older birds. A suggested mean mortality rate is 59% for young cocks and 39% for the older cocks.

Managing capercaillie to increase the population, whether as an end in itself or for sport, presents a problem in that we know what to do but it is economically difficult. In a nutshell, and as with so many other species, if we improve the habitat, the capercaillie will do the rest. Where suitable forests exist felling should not be in large blocks but smaller areas and the mature 'granny' trees should be preserved. Ideally the open areas should be left to provide ground feeding. New planting should be not just different varieties of pines, but planted at intervals of several years to give a forest of different age groupings. Regrettably, all this is contrary to the management policies necessary to maximise forestry profits and the capercaillie are likely to come second to economic pressures.

If the earlier suggestion that approximately 49% of the autumn population is young is correct, then if 16% of the population is shot the breeding population by the spring should be at the previous year's level. As, you will recall, a drive through an area to standing guns bags about 15% of the population, it follows that one day's shooting is as much as an area can stand without being over-shot.

Capercaillie have been successfully reared in France, but one of the first lessons learnt in this country, when heavy game rearing began in the nineteenth century, was the ineffectiveness of releasing reared game into an inhospitable environment. We will do far more good for capercaillie by improving habitat than rearing and releasing youngsters into unbroken forests of Sitka spruce.

To simplify a complex subject, it is probably no exaggeration to say that the future of the capercaillie in Scotland depends upon the willingness and ability of forestry managers to plan their affairs with its interests in mind.

PART II

VARIOUS

CAPERCAILLIE

Tetrao urogallus

This, the largest of the British gamebirds, owes its
existence in this country to re-introduction by man.

WOODCOCK

Scolopax rusticola

A will o' the wisp among birds, the private life of the
woodcock has been a mystery until recent scientific
discoveries.

8

The Woodcock

The secretive life-style of this most attractive of birds has made it the subject of many strange beliefs, some false and some true. Their great diversity of plumage and weight deceived many nineteenth-century countrymen into thinking there were several different varieties, but this error is more easy to accept than the true fact of it being the only bird with a backward facing brain.

Until recently there were large areas of its life history, ecology and behaviour of which we were almost entirely ignorant; and even now there are considerable gaps. A major breakthrough began in 1976 when the Game Conservancy initiated an intensive study by Dr Graham Hirons, under the supervision of their Director of Research, Dr G. R. Potts. An important aspect of this study was the extensive use of miniature radio transmitters weighing 7–8 g, which were attached to woodcock netted for the purpose, and then released. For the first time an accurate non-stop record could be made of behaviour patterns.

The European woodcock is of the order *Charadriiformes*; the family, *Scolopacidae*; the sub-family, *scolopacinae*; the genera, *Scolopax*; and the species, *S. rusticola*; from which emerges its name *Scolopax rusticola L.* Among others it is related to snipe, sandpipers and curlews.

It is thought the origins of Scolopacid birds began in South Asia. Bone fragments indicate a woodcock in North America about a million years ago, but the oldest evidence for the British Isles is in the late Ice Age.

The status of the woodcock as a quarry in this country is in no way related to the annual bag which, as with all facts about the bird, is not easy to determine. The National Game Census of the Game Conservancy makes an uneasy forecast of a minimum annual kill of 4,000–6,000, which modest figure would leave the woodcock a minor player on the sporting stage were it not for its very special qualities. High pheasants, rocketing teal and exploding partridge coveys are all very well; but the sudden, silent, appearance of a woodcock, flitting ghost-like through the trees, offering the merest chance of a shot and then gone among the bare winter branches, rouses a unique excitement. Except in Ireland, and a few favoured spots in the West Country, the presence of woodcock in any numbers is never sufficiently certain to warrant special shoots, but when ground is blessed with an unexpected 'fall' of cock it will be a talking point for the rest of the season.

Estimates exist for some European countries, but only one reports really large bags. West Germany averages 20,000–30,000, Switzerland 1,900, Holland 2,000–5,000, Denmark 10,000–35,000, Norway 10,000, Finland 300–500 and Spain 30,000–40,000. Russia was the exception, shooting about 1,000,000 annually with some 400,000 being shot in the spring. However, in 1967 spring shooting was prohibited, so the annual bag is now probably around 600,000.

So much about the woodcock contains question marks that it is no surprise to learn it is a webless wader and its behaviour as a migrant varies between staying firmly in one area to travelling several thousand miles. The three prominent features are the stoutish build, exceptionally long bill, and beautiful, large, liquid eyes. Indeed, it is the eye which most often gives its presence away on the rare occasions it is spotted on the ground. This feature apart, the mottled plumage of red-browns, black and greys provides perhaps the best camouflage of any bird. It is the enormous eye sockets and the need to support the bill which have led to the changes in the skull which, in turn, have required the brain to face backward.

In very general terms, a woodcock measures about 350 mm from bill tip to tail tip, of which the bill itself takes up some 68–79 mm. The wings are relatively short and rounded, varying between 184–208 mm. The tarsus of the legs varies between 34–38 mm and the colour ranges from blue-grey to pinkish-yellow. The tail, of twelve feathers, has a darker colouring, giving the effect of a black band, and is some 71–82 mm long. The weight varies from bird to bird and with the seasons but an average is about 325 g.

The ability of nature to develop creatures to their special way of life is well illustrated in the woodcock. Here is a bird which lives in the shrubby wood margins, flies mainly in the twilight and feeds in rather than on the ground. It is furnished with superb camouflage, large eyes, which give not only good vision in poor light but allow full rear viewing whilst probing, and a long, strong, bill coupled with short, thick, legs. The bill has the remarkable ability to detect and capture living creatures, mainly earthworms, underground and to this end the last 30 mm of each mandible has many nerve endings. Additionally the last 35 mm of the upper mandible is bowed, although this can be either towards or away from the lower. The purpose, I imagine, must be to improve the hold on the quarry.

The uncertainties continue with the matter of moulting. The fledging period is unknown, although it is believed young can fly at 19–20 days. In general terms, adults moult completely between July and September, but also moult partially between February and May, when the details are less clear. Doubt also exists over the details of the juvenile autumn moult and there is also a suspicion that, among adults, the male begins the summer moult before the female.

This, and many other questions as to possible differences between the sexes, is greatly complicated by the fact that there are no obvious external differences between them. Over the years various possible indicators have been examined, including the shape and coloration of the light patch below the bill, the silvery markings on the back, the black streak between eye and bill, and differences in primary feathering and size. None of these are significant except the latter, where more females are found in the heavier range than males. Additionally, the bills of females are usually larger whereas their tails are normally shorter. However, woodcock vary in size, weight and colouring far more than most birds and there are too many large males and small females for size to be conclusive.

It is not easy to detail the world distribution of the woodcock in a few words, as it varies with the seasons, and the weather. It is, however, very widespread and a simple definition is that woodcock may be found anywhere between the July isotherms of 53°F in the north and 75°F in the south. This range includes such far flung areas as the Canaries, China, Sweden, Burma, Italy, much of Russia and Tibet. Very occasionally, but only after prolonged easterly winds, one will be reported in North America.

In Britain our permanent residents are supplemented each winter by migrants from the Continent; but as they are rarely observed in the winter except when flushed, and move readily and secretly from area to area with weather changes, it is impossible to form an accurate assessment of densities. Even records on breeding birds are suspect for they are often based not on nests discovered but the presumption that a roding woodcock indicates a breeding pair. In the event not everyone can identify true roding flight and even the real thing does not invariably mean a nest.

All we can say with accuracy is that in winter woodcock may be found in every county in the British Isles, although they are much more plentiful in some than others. The Game Conservancy report that the maximum numbers are almost invariably shot in Norfolk and Cornwall.

The habitat requirements of the woodcock are well understood, but the reasons for its preferences are not quite so clear. Evergreens are favoured, particularly holly, laurel and rhododendrons, although whether to provide overhead cover from predators or because their shiny leaves prevent heat-loss through radiation is not known. Certainly quiet is essential and woodcock are rarely found among high densities of pheasants or rabbits. Although they spend much time in wet areas, woodcock want dry, warm, places to roost and a combination of shelter and sun is very popular. De Visme Shaw, in the *Fur, Feather and Fin* series, wrote that a captive woodcock, 'is never so happy as when allowed to bask in the warmth of a fire'.

An ideal woodcock wood would provide wide rides, to give flight paths, a broken canopy to allow entry and egress from above, an irregular rather than straight perimeter, much of the ground level open and unimpeded with the remainder giving dense low cover of bramble, bracken and mixed bushes and the whole well dotted with evergreens and numerous boggy patches.

In fact, the habitat preferences of woodcock may owe more than we realise to the habitat preferences of earthworms. It may be that woodcock select their areas not so much because they like the combination of soil, damp, light and vegetation, but because the worms do, for evidence shows that woodcock populations are related to earthworm density.

Although the *Fur, Feather and Fin* series was an outstanding collection of natural history books for its time, the ignorance of the ways of the woodcock are shown by the near twenty pages devoted to migration which are mainly pure speculation. One conclusion reached is that migrating woodcock travel at 150 miles per hour, a speed which I very much doubt they could attain at all in level flight, never mind sustain for several hours.

However, fact can now largely replace speculation for great progress has been made in migration studies since De Visme Shaw mused in 1904. Contrary to popular belief it is now thought that woodcock migrate as individuals and not in groups or flocks. The fact that 'waves' reach an area together is simply because they all, as individuals, took advantage of favourable weather conditions. Of the resident British population of woodcock something like three-quarters are sedentary, moving only short distances or not at all. Those that migrate do so to escape the hard weather and therefore mainly leave Scotland and Northern England, the majority for Ireland and the remainder for Southern England, France, Spain and Portugal. Logic suggests that if many woodcock head for Ireland the resident birds are unlikely to move far and this is confirmed by ringing results showing that 94% of Irish woodcock are sedentary.

While European immigrants begin to arrive in this country as early as the end of August, the migration proper takes place from Mid-October onwards and the return journey in February and March. In many years the majority arrive in two very large waves, rather than a succession of smaller ones, weather conditions—a combination of frost or threatened frost on the feeding grounds and good flighting conditions—probably being the trigger. The winter visitors to Britain come from a wide area, including the Baltic States, west Russia, north Germany, southern Sweden and Norway. They strike the east coast (which explains why Norfolk is a leading county for woodcock shooting) then move south and south-west, travelling overland, or down the Western Isles and the west coasts of Scotland and England. Most of those on the west head for Ireland, arriving mainly in the north by mid-October. One of the more accurate observations of the nineteenth century was made by R. M. Barrington, who studied migration as observed by the Irish light-stations, and concluded that the great bulk of woodcock first reached Ireland in the north and then moved southward, mainly down the west coast.

It is normally the third week in October before woodcock reach the south coast of England, although some may then continue southwards and rejoin the Continent, having merely used Britain as a form of aerial motorway. There is some evidence to suggest that birds which migrate at night are more subject to being drifted off course by winds than daytime travellers. Certainly the increased navigational problems make this logical and we may owe some of each autumn's arrivals to easterly and south-easterly winds over the North Sea.

Any observant countryman or sportsman will be aware that woodcock fly at dawn and dusk and for years it has been believed they fed at night and roosted during the day. However, the facts of natural history rarely follow a clear and sharply defined pattern and Dr Hirons' study, assisted by the radio transmitters, proved this a case in point. In March and early April, that is early in the breeding season, the birds behaved as expected, flying out to fields at dusk where they were active all night. The average distance flown was about 1,000 m and most of the woodcock returned to the same pasture field every night. They returned to the woods at dawn and roosted in heavy cover until dusk.

However, as the breeding season progressed the pattern reversed and the birds began feeding during the day and roosting at night. The feeding grounds also changed, to arable fields or woodland clearings, but there is no reason to think the new feeding areas caused the change from nocturnal feeding. With the approach of winter the birds reverted to their normal pattern and this was maintained until the next breeding season.

Of all the question marks attached to this mysterious bird none have created greater interest than its habit of roding, the term given to a repetitive display by the male woodcock in which it flies above the woodland canopy, calling repeatedly. It has long been appreciated that roding is part of the woodcock's mating process, but hitherto it had been believed roding males maintained exclusive territories. Although some aggression is displayed between roding males, the truth is that there are no exclusive territories and males will often roost close to one another.

As the breeding season progresses the length of the roding period increases, peaking in May and June. During the roding period most males spent approximately one-third of the time actually roding, and this time was roughly twice as long at dusk as at dawn.

Some male woodcock were considerably more successful with females; these birds were among the first to commence roding and the last to stop. They also showed the ability to pick the areas most attractive to females and achieved at least four females each season. The less successful males, who devoted less time to the chase and often worked poor areas, sometimes failed

15. Photographs of woodcock in flight are rare.

to mate in the entire breeding season. On finding a receptive female the male stops roding and stays with her constantly for several days until she begins egg-laying, when he would resume roding. A few will continue to return daily until incubation begins.

Whether or not a woodcock carries her chicks in flight was an argument which rumbled on for very many years. I write 'was' because, in my view, at least, there are so many recorded sightings that the practice is proved beyond all reasonable doubt. I accept that in contentious matters some people's imagination runs away into wishful viewing, as distinct from wishful thinking, but chick-carrying has been reported by many very responsible and knowledgeable people and can be accepted as a fact.

Writing in 1904, De Visme Shaw stated categorically, 'In open weather the food of the woodcock consists almost entirely of worms, other diet probably not constituting more than 2 or 3 per cent of the total food consumed.' This would mean that the stomach content of *every* woodcock would contain not far short of 100% earthworms, yet in an examination of 64 stomachs by Dr Hirons 12% contained *no earthworms at all*. This is not to say that earthworms are not the major food source of the woodcock—they are—but many other creatures are regularly sought and eaten.

A really thorough investigation of the food of the woodcock, covering not only a full year but also varieties of weather, has not yet been undertaken. However, there is considerable evidence from various watchers over a wide spread of countries and at different seasons. Clearly woodcock regularly eat a wide range of insects and larvae, various small freshwater molluscs and plants. Some scientists believe plant seeds are only taken in an emergency whereas others consider it a regular practice. One report suggests woodcock regularly take rowan berries, bilberries, elderberries, maggots from carrion, and beetles and larvae from dung.

However, interesting as these more exotic foods may be, the earthworm, or rather the 34 different species of earthworm in Britain, are unquestionably the woodcock's staple diet. Studies in North America show a clear relationship between the supply of earthworms and the occurrence of woodcock and, significantly, sites which were dry in summer and had neither worms nor woodcock became attractive to cock in the spring when the damp conditions brought worms near the surface.

Although the general belief that woodcock feed at night is largely correct, there are, as described earlier, both exceptions and doubts. For a start, it is by no means certain that cock spend the daylight hours in the woodlands just roosting. As they favour thick cover it is practically impossible to observe what they are doing in it. One investigation, in 1976, looked at the guts of 76 cock shot between 18.00 and 19.00 hours and only 4 were empty. However, Dr Hirons concluded that in mild weather woodcock feed almost entirely at night, but there is ample evidence that in hard weather they also feed by day, including a crop of sightings in the severe winter of 1962–3.

Turning to the subject of breeding, we need to look in more detail at roding. Although it cannot be stated conclusively that females never rode, the overwhelming majority of roding birds are male. (We know this because shooting roding woodcock is common practice in some European countries.) During roding the cock use two different calls, a shrill two-syllabled call which carries well and, between these, a low croaking sound, repeated several times and with little carrying power. Most roding activity takes place at dusk, but dawn roding is common and there are various reports of daytime roding. It is, of course, restricted to the breeding season and the extremes of recorded sightings are late February to late July.

We now know from Dr Hirons' work that male woodcock are successively polygamous, but do not defend either an exclusive or specific area. Essentially roding is searching over an extensive area for a mate, rather than any form of territorial marking.

Female woodcock, unlike the majority of males, breed in their first summer. The nest is simple: a hollow, lined with dead leaves or, less frequently, some other local vegetation. Until the use of radio-telemetry little was known of events at this stage but Dr Hirons reports that the female chooses an area in which to nest, then moves to the edge of an opening and calls to a roding male. The two birds then return to the nesting area. A female may be involved with more than one male in a breeding season.

Egg-laying can take place between early March and early August, but the peak period is believed to be mid-March to mid-April. However, this conclusion may be biased by the greater difficulty of finding the later nests due to growth of ground cover. An average of 100 British eggs gave a size of 44.2 × 33.5 mm. The colouring is variations of a buff background blotched with reddish-brown. The average clutch size is four with some healthy dispute on the intervals between laying, varying between twenty-four hours and four days. Incubation takes about three weeks with reports varying between twenty and twenty-four days. In this period Hirons has again cleared a fog of uncertainty and we now know that the female alone incubates and cares for the chicks. From sunset to sunrise she never leaves the eggs, and when she does walks and never flies. Those females observed (that is to say, tracked by radio) fed not more than 80 m from the nest and did so not less than five times during the day nor more than nine. The average time of absence was a little over 20 minutes.

There appears to be a relationship between rainfall and the duration of the breeding season. One indication is that roding stops earlier in a dry summer, but more telling is the absence of June broods. In summers of average rainfall it is common to see approximately 50% of the broods in June. Following the pattern through shows that earthworms are, for obvious reasons, less available to woodcock in a dry summer, although whether this is coincidental or a prime cause of the earlier end to breeding activity is unclear.

There is a strong view that the woodcock is double-brooded, but no firm evidence exists either way. The movements of the bird are so secretive that even where a nest is used twice in a season it could simply be another female following on. One of the strongest arguments is that the single-brooded American woodcock concentrates its breeding span into only five to six weeks. Doubtless the truth will emerge before long.

Chick weights at hatching are in the order of 17–20 g and for the first two to three days they live by absorbing the remaining egg yolk. After this they search for their own food, for the female does not feed them, although it is thought she may scrape surface litter aside, possibly to expose surface insects or alternatively to facilitate shallow probing.

From this stage on little is known of the development of the chicks, which is hardly surprising considering that their time is passed in deep cover and it would be difficult to find the brood, let alone observe it. Fledging is well advanced by two to three weeks and a Swedish report on ringed chicks said they weighed about 130 g at four weeks. Lönnberg (1921) confirmed this approximate growth, and said that at one month they could fly as well as adults. This I find hard to accept. There is no useful evidence of brood mortality between hatching and flight.

Whatever brood mortality may be, the life expectation of a young woodcock when it first faces the world on its own is not great. Enough ringing has been done to produce reasonably reliable results and this is confirmed by the extent to which the studies agree. Approximately 55% of British reared woodcock which have survived from hatching to August die before the following July. Among adult birds the figure is naturally lower; about 37%. Both classes of Continental woodcock have higher mortality rates, which is no doubt due to their extensive migratory journeys.

In the middle 1940s Alexander produced an interesting table of the longevity of 507 woodcock ringed as young in Britain. 314 died in the first year and 93 in the second. By the end of the sixth year only 8 were alive and of these 3 died in their eleventh year, one in the twelfth and the last in its thirteenth year. Interestingly, a similar study carried out a few years earlier also saw the last survivor die in its thirteenth year.

Given that the above figures are reasonably accurate then, if the population is to be maintained, every 100 adults must produce sufficient chicks each year to ensure that by August 1 84 are still alive.

Little is known about the effects of predation. Hawks, owls, foxes and even stoats are listed as predators but no-one has attempted a forecast of the level of predation other than Hirons, who reported 47% of the nests on his study area lost. However this is nests lost, as distinct from hens killed, where the figure was 13%. The annual overall predation on the radio-tagged birds was 42%, and if this was increased to allow for birds shot it would take the annual loss well over the estimated 37%. In practice the number of birds radio-tagged was too small to be really significant.

The vast majority of dead woodcock handled by humans have been shot and therefore no systematic study of woodcock diseases has been carried out. One would expect earthworms in fields to build up organo-chlorine residues and to pass these to woodcock but, again, no serious investigation has been done.

Most shooting readers will be aware of the classic anti-townee joke about the wealthy business man who took up shooting and, on missing a small, fast-flying, brown bird, enquired as to its identity from his keeper. 'That, Sir, is a woodcock.' 'Really,' said his new employer, 'well, rear a couple of thousand for next season.'

Perhaps one day it will be possible to rear woodcock in numbers: personally, I hope not, but in the meantime increasing a local woodcock population is a matter of creating the right habitat. Even this presents problems, for to be sure one is doing the right things it is necessary to keep a careful record of population variations and this is difficult with a bird which is rarely seen and whose numbers rise and fall periodically as migratory cock travel through. However, some basic essentials are known and the proof of their effectiveness, although not entirely conclusive, is demonstrated by increased bags of woodcock on estates where they have been implemented.

Alexander summed up the essentials as: 'Special treatment of the coverts, keeping down the numbers of pheasants and rabbits, allowing no shooting after the New Year, and keeping the coverts quiet during the breeding season.'

Immediately one sees a problem for the formal pheasant shoots, for they will be well content to keep down the rabbits but must have a high pheasant population in the woods from August to January. Additionally, stopping shooting from the beginning of January would curtail the season too much and the only requirement presenting no problem is the need for quiet coverts in the breeding season. We must, I think, accept that the high pressure shoot will always have a lower resident population of woodcock than would be otherwise possible. The best that can be done is to reserve a suitable covert for woodcock and avoid feeding it for pheasants, although the latter will doubtless populate it to some degree as disturbance mounts elsewhere.

Where pheasants do not rule much can be done to improve woods which are already attractive to woodcock, but if cock are never or rarely seen it is almost certainly a waste of time and money to try.

The availability of food is a strong magnet for all wild life and, as mentioned earlier, there is strong evidence that woodcock populations vary with earthworm density. This in turn varies under different species of trees, with sycamore and ash being two of the most highly favoured. Therefore planting these trees in sufficient numbers should be effective, although results would take years to achieve.

More rapid measures should be aimed at making woods warm and sheltered, although the frequent recommendation for a dry floor should be treated with care. For a bird which probes to feed, damp areas are vital. Another factor to bear in mind is the cock's habit of walking not inconsiderable distances when feeding. Continuous, thick, ground cover should be avoided and some of the best 'woodcock estates' make (or made, when finances allowed the employment of specialist woodcock keepers) tunnels through the rhododendrons, which are often features of good woodcock ground. Maintaining woods in the right condition requires not just attention to that which exists but forward planning to take out old areas, from time to time, and replant for the future.

From a practical viewpoint it is unlikely that many shoots will be able to do a great deal to encourage woodcock. Shooting rents are so high that the maximum sport has to be extracted from the ground and this comes from pheasants not woodcock. However, the appearance of the occasional woodcock, whether bagged or not, adds so much pleasure to the day that any measures taken are well worth while. And, sport apart, they are such beautiful and appealing birds that any country lover will wish to help them.

The non-shooting reader, on registering the last sentiment, may well feel a constructive gesture would be to stop killing them. Granted, and yet again we reach the anomaly of sportsmen who love their quarries. In fact the evidence is that shooting is not harmful to woodcock numbers. Certainly there has been no significant change in the numbers shot in this country in the last twenty years and this chapter can be neatly closed by quoting once more from Dr Hirons, 'At present shooting in Britain is not considered to be an important factor limiting the number of woodcock since predation is probably density-dependent and survival or production rates can compensate for shooting losses.' Or, in simple terms, if we shot fewer woodcock the increased population would attract more predation and the numbers would not improve.

9

The Common Snipe

When I think of the snipe my thoughts fly north to the Hebrides where, at the end of a full day on the hills or by a river, I stand at deepest dusk and gaze at the great inverted bowl of the night sky. In this enormous void of limitless space a myriad of stars twinkle, ending only where a black band marks the horizon. If one remains still for long the murmur of the night sounds gradually separate into individual components—the slow coming and going of gentle waves thrusting through the waving arms of the kelp: the distant throb of a homeward bound fishing boat: rustlings of small things in the grass: cattle stirring in the field; but almost always the drumming of snipe. These strange islands are the perfect setting for what, in the darkness, is an eerie and fascinating sound.

The common snipe, *Gallinago gallinago*, is of the order *Scolopacidae* and the family *Gallinagininae*. More commonly, and because the sound of its drumming resembled the bleating of a lamb or goat, it was often known as 'heather-bleater', or in France, 'flying nanny-goat'. However, the stranger character of the bird, and one from which the name snipe derives, is the very lengthy bill. Most of the European languages follow suit, with the French becassine, from bec; the Portuguese Narseja from nariz; and the German Schnepfe from schneppen. In Anglo-Saxon, both the bird and a nose were snite and while nose gradually became snout so the bird changed its t for a p. Lydgate, a Suffolk poet, writing shortly after Chaucer used a very early spelling:

> All one to three a falcon and a kyghte,
> As good an owl as a popingaye,
> A dungbill duck as dainty as a snyghte

Shakespeare, nearly 200 years later used snipe but his contemporary Sir John Harrington, in *Epigrams* had the interim 'snytes'.

The importance of the snipe as a quarry has diminished as this century has progressed. In part this is through the considerable growth in driven pheasant shooting (which has tended to overshadow most branches of the sport) but the greater factor by far is the steady reduction in the wet areas so essential for the snipe. The greatly increased areas of reservoirs and gravel pits have provided to some extent substitute habitats for the ducks deprived of their water meadows and inland marshes; but these are not viable alternatives for the snipe, who need damp, muddy ground. There is a West country hotel whose advertisements invite guests to come specifically to shoot driven snipe and doubtless many of the wildfowlers who journey to Ireland have them in mind as a principal quarry, but for the great majority of shooting men the snipe is simply the occasional, albeit difficult and exciting, opportunity on a rough shooting day. Economically they play no part although in the old days, before the extensive wetland of England disappeared, they were commonly sold. The household book of the Earl of Northumberland records that in 1512 snipe were bought at threepence a dozen. Nowadays the season begins on the 12th August and ends on the 31st January.

Among the considerable variety of waders, the snipe is of medium size and the immediate and obvious characteristics are the long bill, the striped head and back and the dark brown plumage. However, as ground sightings are comparatively difficult, the snipe is usually only sighted as it takes off, at which moment its erratic flight provides means of identification.

A detailed description of the colouring of the snipe runs into a lengthy and bewildering schedule of brown-blacks, black-browns, dark and olive-browns and buff-whites, arranged in stripes, bars, streaks, mottles and patches. For our purpose it is sufficient to say that it is an essentially brown bird with a heavily streaked and patterned plumage in which the brown-black crown of the head stands out, as also do the boldly barred flanks. The bell is pure white. In flight there is a broad white trailing edge to the secondaries and inner primaries of the wings.

In relation to the body the wing is broad, long and pointed. The tail is fan shaped and the number of feathers cannot, as the old naturalists believed, be used to distinguish between common, great and jack snipe. Although 14 is usual, there can be as few as 12 or as many as 18. The upper mandible of the bill is slightly longer than the lower and ends in a terminal bulb. The bill is dark brown at the tip, shading to red-brown at the base. The leg and foot range from yellow-green to blue-grey and the claws are black-brown.

The adults moult after breeding, usually commencing in July, but some individuals delay while raising a second brood. In some cases moulting is only completed in the winter quarters. The sexes are similar at all stages of plumage.

An adult snipe measures 25–27 cm in length (bill 6–7 cm) and has a wing span of 44–47 cm. It is some 25% larger than the jack snipe (recently made a protected bird under the Wildlife and Countryside Act 1981) and this size variation is sufficient to make recognition in flight a fairly simple matter. It is not quite so easy to distinguish it from the great snipe, for although it is less bulky the wing span of the largest common snipes are marginally greater than the smallest great snipe. Moreover the bill of the common snipe is usually slightly longer than that of the great snipe.

The weight can vary over a relatively wide range and results over several European countries gave an average, in winter, of 107 g and in summer of 101 g. However, the mean of wintering birds in India was only 96 g.

The snipe can be found virtually throughout Britain and Ireland, though it is patchy in some areas in the west country and south-west Wales. In 1976 the breeding population in Britain and Ireland was estimated at some 80,000 – 110,000 pairs. On the wider scale, the bird is distributed throughout the northern half of the Western Palaearctic in summer with a southern movement in winter. While Sweden has an estimated breeding population of 150,000 pairs and Finland 90,000, Spain has probably under 200, Italy about 100 and Belgium even fewer.

The essence of good snipe habitat is that drainage has been impeded to create soft and accessible feeding grounds. Ideally this damp ground needs to be fairly open but dotted with tussocks or clumps of vegetation; it should be rich in food organisms and reasonably near shallow water, either fresh or brackish. These conditions are, of course, best provided in water meadows, liberally dotted with soil enriching cowpats, and now so often destroyed by drainage improvements. One of the best snipe bogs I know lies at the foot of a gentle heather clad hill in the Hebrides. On the slope above there are three crofters' cottages and for several centuries the untreated sewage has been discharged down the hill.

While frequently found alone, the snipe is not truly gregarious, although any large concentrations will usually have gathered for a good food source rather than social reasons. Snipe are monogamous, and from such a neat, dapper little bird one would expect high standards. Sadly, observers report that both sexes are given to frequent promiscuity. The males arrive in the breeding grounds a week or two before the females who, on arrival, mate with various males until they gradually spend more time in a particular territory and eventually settle down with the resident male. Whilst the hen is occupied with incubation, the male is not to be trusted with any female entering his territory and, on hatching, the brood is divided between the parents who immediately lose contact and the pair-bond breaks up. Not what could be termed a strong marriage!

Territorial aggression is restricted only towards other snipe displaying by either calling or drumming, which means feeding areas are available to all, whether or not they lie in an individual's territory. Observations suggest a female may return to the same breeding site for several years.

Twilight is the time of greatest activity, although there are suggestions that in winter the snipe feeds throughout the night. At dusk most, perhaps all, of the birds in an area fly for up to half an hour; on moonlit nights this activity

16. *The photograph vividly illustrates the size of the bill in proportion to the head.*

17. *A snipe springing.*

lasts considerably longer. Drumming-flights form a large part of this, and it is only in recent years that we have had a clear understanding of how this remarkable sound is produced. At the turn of the century drumming was the subject of much speculation. Having noted that the noise only occurred during flight descent, naturalists eliminated the voice as the likely source and concluded it was either vibrations set up by wing, tail or both together; by wing action; by wing action throwing air on the tail, causing it to vibrate; or by actual contact of the tips of the wings with the outer feathers of the tail.

We now know the sound emanates from the two outermost feathers of the tail which stand clear during the drumming-flight and are vibrated by the bird's passage through the air and the wing movement. Usually the snipe flies in a wide curve, rising slightly before commencing a switchback flight in which the ascent phases increase to about 30° until reaching a height of about 50 m. It then banks to one side and dives at 40 – 50° with the tail formed and the two front feathers standing visibly clear. The wings continue to beat during the dive and the performance concludes with a brief glide, after which it regains height and commences again. Normally drumming lasts 1.5 to 2 seconds, but records of up to 4 seconds exist. Drumming is principally carried out by the male during pair formation, to define and defend its territory, and around the incubating female; although reports suggest that as incubation advances this last tendency fades. Drumming appears to be more important as a heterosexual behaviour than for territory marking, but it takes place in various circumstances, including migration.

There are a variety of descriptions by observers of specialist forms of flight carried out in the process of mating. Their names—wing-arch flight, rolling-flights and flutter-leaps—are self-descriptive. Copulation is preceded by both birds circling round one another, on the ground, cocking and fanning their tails, dropping wings and calling. Flutter-leaps, which are simply wing-assisted jumps, occur frequently and the level of activity intensifies until the female lies flat on the ground with outspread wings and the male mounts.

When threatened by predators, the snipe squats close to the ground with neck drawn in and feathers sleeked to reduce size. However, once it decides flight is the best resort, it flushes in the low, rapid, zig-zag pattern which makes it such a difficult shot. Sportsmen of the last century were convinced the snipe used its bill as a lever to assist its take off—a form of vaulting pole. The belief arose through regular reports from observant men who had seen the snipe in the air with its bill still in the ground. Eventually, however, the truth dawned that these birds had been surprised in the act of feeding and were simply flushing and withdrawing their bill from the ground in one and the same movement. The zig-zag flight pattern is only used for escape and in migration and other normal flights of any distance a straight path is followed.

In Britain many of our snipe are resident throughout the year, but their numbers are reinforced by migrants from the north and east who are forced south in winter. Others continue southwards and large numbers winter in Africa, south of the Sahara. The whole pattern of migration is very complex and while much has been discovered by ringing, there is a great deal more to learn. We do know that much of the Continental movement is west and south-west rather than a simple southern movement.

The autumn passage in the far north and east starts in July and the peak numbers in Denmark and the Netherlands occur in September–October. However, the earliest migrants leave the Continent before then and in Chad, south of the Sahara, snipe are observed from the first few days of September. By November all are in the wintering areas, although severe weather will move them on once more. The return movement begins in March, and the birds are back on their breeding grounds by April to May.

In addition to the noise of drumming the snipe usually emits an alarm call, when flushed, which I find defies description, but others have reported as 'scaup' or near variations. Other variations exist for different circumstances but the snipe is one of the less vocal birds.

The bulk of the snipe's food is invertebrates, mainly larval and adult dipteran flies and beetles. However, many other invertebrates are taken, as is plant material of various forms. Proportions vary, with earthworms some-times predominating and sometimes insects, but availability is more likely to be responsible than preference.

Most of the food is taken under the ground by probing and conditions must therefore be soft and wet. Water margins and the shallows are favoured and the snipe probes in a semi-circle around itself before moving on to a new stance. Four to twelve probes in one spurt are normal and a snipe has been timed to average eight probes per minute. Food is located by touch and eaten without the bill being withdrawn unless it is an earthworm or similar large prize. I can trace no information on the food of the young, but logic suggests it will be the same as the adults.

Grass is the normal choice of a nest site, followed by rushes and only about 10% of snipe select alternative vegetation. The nest is a simple scrape, lined with fine grass and laying begins about late May. The eggs are oval, smooth and slightly glossy, ranging from pale green to dark buff with small dark or red-brown blotches. They weigh about 17 g and measure approximately 39 × 29 mm. The great majority of clutches have four eggs, and most observers believe there is only one brood. Incubation is by the female only and takes eighteen to twenty days. Observations suggest both parents are normally present at the hatching, when the male takes the two older chicks and the female the two younger. At this moment the parents split permanently, with the female tending to remain near the nest site with her two young.

In the early stages the adults process the food in their mandibles and then feed the young, mouth to mouth. From the beginning the young can hide effectively and run to cover on the alarm call of the adult. After about six weeks the relationship with the parents breaks down and the young snipe form groups prior to the autumn migration.

Annual fluctuations through migration, coupled with local movements due to weather conditions, make accurate population estimates difficult but Britain certainly has one of the highest populations in Europe. Annual mortality appears to be in the order of 50%, with various studies varying from a low of 46.9% in Finland to a high of 69% in West Germany (perhaps because shooting pressures are higher in West Germany than in Finland). The oldest known ringed bird is reported by the British Trust for Ornithology as 12 years 4 months.

Given the absence of economic pressures it would not be difficult to manage snipe for sport. As the removal of wet areas by drainage has destroyed good snipe habitat, so the creation of new wet areas would replace it. Unfortunately the value of snipe shooting is far less than the value of the farmland created by the drainage and I fear the snipe population is likely to fall lower. Nor are the substantial new water areas created in recent years a solution, for many are simply deep holes in the ground filled with water rather than the shallow wet areas needed. However, the problems are only localised, for there are still sufficient wet areas, particularly in areas of marginal farming land, to maintain a reasonable snipe population and it is in no danger at the present time.

10

The Golden Plover

This most attractive little bird rarely receives the attention its beauty and sporting qualities warrant. The Lonsdale Libraries' *Game Birds, Beasts and Fishes* (1935) granted it just one page in 255 and Vesey-Fitzgerald in *British Game*, (1946), was even more parsimonious with two paragraphs. In fairness, it is not one of the glamorous quarries, whose financial importance warrants extensive scientific research, but it is both numerous and widespread and most sportsmen will encounter it periodically.

The golden plover, *Pluvialis apricaria*, is of the order *Charadriiformes* and the family *Charadriinae.* Surprisingly for a bird with its haunting call it appears to have no vernacular names other than goldie.

There are two races recognised: one, the 'northern' *P.a. altifrons*, found principally in Iceland and also from northern Scandinavia to central USSR, and the 'southern' *P.a. apricaria*, inhabiting the range from Ireland to southern Finland. The majority of the British breeding birds are of the southern race, although some 'northerners' breed in the higher areas of Scotland.

Its shooting season begins on September 1 and ends on January 31. As a quarry it is very much a minor, occasional and rarely planned participant: most welcome when it appears but usually unpredictable.

A description of the colouring of the golden plover is much complicated by the seasonal variations. In the breeding season the upper parts are black with a yellow spangling of spots around the margin of black feathers. The wing-coverts are dark grey, tipped with yellow, except for the major coverts which have a white edging. A white band crosses the forehead and continues down each side of the neck and along the top of the flanks. The under-parts are black, except under the tail-coverts which are white. The beak and legs are also black.

As the summer passes, the yellow fades until the autumn moult when the colouring lightens. The breast and sides of the face become white, as do the inner primaries and the tips of the major coverts. The fore-neck becomes tinged with yellow, spotted with dusky mottlings.

Juveniles resemble the adult winter plumage, but are distinctly more golden above. In down they are pale gold mottled with black. Adult lengths range between 26–29 cm, with wing-spans of 67–76 cm. Weights vary between 175–275 g, depending on season and sex.

The normal home of the golden plover is in the more northerly latitudes, ranging from arctic and tundra to the unenclosed upland moors of this country. Wherever height, temperature and wind combine to prohibit tree growth there one may find the goldie and always in sparse vegetation which allows it to run freely. In Britain it is unusual to find it above 600 m and it has a strong preference for gently sloping ground with small raised areas to serve as look-out points.

In winter our resident birds combine with the large numbers of visitors and feed, often in large flocks, on permanent pastures, stubbles and open farmland generally. Although they are encountered below the high water mark, the coastal birds prefer the open ground above it and the adjoining farmland.

The golden plover is only partially migratory in Britain, and it is thought many simply drop down to the lowlands adjoining their nesting area. However, hard weather causes the entire British wintering population to move south and west. All the birds breeding outside Britain and Ireland are migratory, and this country, Ireland, France, Iberia and Maghreb are the most important wintering areas. It is estimated that the winter population for Britain and Ireland is approximately 400,000, which is some 40–50% of the total wintering population of western Europe and North Africa. By October the average estuaries count is almost 186,000, but this drops to about 130,000 by winter, when it is estimated that about double this number are inland.

The southern movement from the northern breeding grounds begins in July-August and the main southward movement through Europe occurs in October–December. However, the Icelandic birds arrive on their Irish wintering grounds in October–November. These Irish birds begin their return journey in March, re-occupying their breeding grounds in mid-April to early May.

The resident golden plover who remain nest on most of the moors and mountains of Britain, with the highest densities in the eastern Grampians, the Pennines and the eastern Southern Uplands. Height is not an important factor, although maximum densities occur mostly between 300–600 m and few nest much over 1,000 m. The preference is for flat or gently sloping ground and few nests are found on an angle exceeding 10°. Considerably more nest in Scotland than England, with D. A. Ratcliffe (*Bird Study*, V. 23, no. 2, June 1976) estimating the breeding pairs in Southwest England at only 10, Northern England at 7,550, Southern Uplands 3,850, the Highlands 15,515 and the Hebrides 2,000. Ireland, in spite of the large numbers to be found there in winter, had only an estimated 900 breeding pairs. Broadly speaking, the farther north, and to some extent west, the lower the level at which breeding occurs.

The golden plover normally selects short cover for a nest site, usually less than 15 cm, presumably to allow it to spot danger at a distance, for its preference is to slip away from the nest rather than sit tight. It has no strong bias for the vegetation among which it nests, favouring, if anything, mixed and broken ground, but this must be unenclosed. Fields, to the golden plover, are just for feeding.

The nest is very basic, simply a scrape lined with local vegetation. The eggs are of a yellowish stone colour, spotted and blotched with brownish black, approximately 51 × 34 mm and weighing about 35 g. Whether or not the male assists in incubation is a matter of contention among ornithologists. In most years egg laying begins by the end of March and peaks between the last half of April and the middle of May. The loss of a clutch, either through predation or weather, will be followed by as many as three further attempts. The norm is four eggs and where a nest is found with less the cause is usually predation or the hen not having completed laying. Incubation varies between twenty-seven and thirty-four days, with an unusually long chipping period of two to three days. The young fly in about five weeks and from early July flocks of adults and young begin to move back to the lowlands.

The flight of the golden plover is straight and swift, with steady, rapid wing beats. Flocks often assume V or W formations and would be less vulnerable to shooting if they did not pack so densely in flight. Nor are their survival chances improved by a trick of diving on hearing a gunshot rather than veering away.

For those of us who love the high, open places there are few more beautiful sounds than the call of the golden plover. More often than not the sound is heard before the bird is sighted and, usually heard miles from civilisation, this clear, pure note has a haunting eeriness. Various attempts at phonetic descriptions of the musical double whistle have been made, but none awaken a response in me. Perhaps Dixon, in 1893, came nearest with 'klee-wee'. The alarm is a single note, a plaintive sound more of sorrow than concern, and there are other calls restricted to the breeding season. All are uttered both when flying and stationary.

As with all waders, the golden plover devotes much of its time to feeding, living mainly off invertebrates. Inland, worms, slugs, snails, all insects and their larvae are taken, and on the shore, molluscs, crustaceans and shore worms. Some vegetable matter is eaten and also grit. Nearly all is taken from the surface or from a depth not exceeding 2 cm. I could trace no information on the diet of the young but it is assumed to be similar to the adults.

It has been calculated that adult mortality in Scotland is 22%, which is very much lower than an Icelandic report of approximately 46.5% and a Netherlands ringing enquiry in which 53% died in the first year after ringing. The oldest ringed bird was 12 years 2 months.

Predation does not have any significant effect on the adults, being restricted to the relatively scarce hen harriers and peregrines. Foxes will also take nesting birds and, possibly, the occasional roosting plover. However egg losses are certainly heavy, particularly to hooded and carrion crows, although both species of black-backed gulls, black-headed gulls, rooks and ravens are also culprits.

It is believed that the golden plover reached its maximum breeding population in the middle of the nineteenth century and has declined since in many areas. There is no single and obvious reason, although large scale afforestation of moorlands has destroyed many breeding areas. Ratcliffe has advanced various suggestions and eliminated others. For example, he doubts whether pesticides have any effect but suggests the long-term exploitation of many moorland areas has reduced their carrying capacity for invertebrates—the essential food of the golden plover. Other factors considered are increased shooting pressure from the middle of the nineteenth century, moor burning, military training on moorland, vehicles on moors, and increased public access; but none of these can be shown to have exerted major pressure except on a localised basis. He observes that there are many areas where population reductions have occurred, where there are no obvious changes in the appearance of the habitat or in human pressures.

One interesting theory connects the decline in the numbers of golden plover to climatic changes. For the first 45 years of this century temperatures in northern Europe increased, but from 1950 onwards the mean temperatures of spring and summer have fallen. Nethersole-Thompson has suggested the fall in the British population of the snow bunting and the dotterel and their subsequent recovery was due to this and it is reasonable to suppose that the golden plover, similarly a bird of cold places, was equally affected. The theory is slightly dented by the failure of the plover to recover its numbers in recent years, but there are grounds for believing it may be less swift to respond to climatic change than other species.

While the golden plover may have declined, there is no reason to fear for its future. Its feeding grounds seem secure, for it is difficult to imagine a system of agriculture which dispenses with grasslands. Equally, the preferred breeding habitat is relatively safe, for while some may be lost to forestry the majority has no obvious future beyond sheep and grouse. Nor is shooting a factor of significance.

Hopefully, that delightful call will please us for many years to come.

11

The Brown Hare

I grant both species of hares rather more space than their importance as quarries justifies for two reasons. Firstly, much has been discovered about them in recent years, and secondly, because they are such attractive animals.

In the order *Lagomorpha* the hares, *Lepus*, are the dominant genus with some twenty species covering most of the world. Apart from small areas in the Pennines and North Wales, the only hares encountered south of the Scottish border are the brown or common hare, *Lepus capensis L.* Local names abound. Sally and Sarah are common in East Anglia and in *The Leaping Hare* there appears a late thirteenth century poem listing no less than seventy-seven variations, including Old Big-bum and dew-hopper.

There is evidence that several species of hares existed more than a million years ago and the two species of European hares probably date from around the middle of the Pleistocene and certainly from the late Pleistocene; that is to say, some 100,000 years ago. In this country the remains of hares have been found in a Devon cave along with those of mammoth and woolly rhinoceros.

While many Continental sportsmen rank the hare highly, in Britain its status is much lower. Most formal driven shoots ban ground game for safety reasons and few rough shooters would set forth with hares as their principal quarry. For most shooting men the hare is another of the species which make for variety, while some decline to shoot them at all. It is almost certain that the majority of hares shot in Britain each year are bagged at the annual hare shoots which have control rather than sport as their main objective. This view would not be shared by many of the participants, who often have few opportunities to shoot and look on their annual invitation as a high point in their social and sporting calendar. Safety standards are often low and many a wise landowner leaves the organisation to his keeper and finds good reason to be absent.

This criticism made, however, hares can provide excellent sport. Leaping from a form in the rushes and zig-zagging away through the heather clumps, it is by no means an easy shot. But if you cannot kill it within twenty-five yards, hold your fire. A going away hare, with head tucked down and the powerful rear thighs acting as shields, presents few vital areas and is easily wounded.

There is no close season for either the brown or mountain hare but some protection is offered by the ban on selling them from March to July inclusive. Additionally, on moorlands and unenclosed non-arable lands, hares may be shot only by the occupier and persons authorised by him between December 11 (July 1 in Scotland) and March 31.

The economic value of the hare as a quarry is limited. Although it may provide an additional attraction to Continental sportsmen, it does not bring sportsmen to an area nor generate work for local people. Even on the large hare shoots the beating is mainly done by the invited guns. The market for the carcasses is variable, as many are exported and the demand fluctuates with the supply of Continental hares. A further drawback lies in the great variations in supply. For most of the year there is a relative trickle until the end of the pheasant shooting season sees the start of the hare shoots. Throughout February the market is flooded until the ban cuts off supplies abruptly in March.

The relatively inexperienced observer will sometimes have difficulty distinguishing between a rabbit and hare in the field but the more knowledgeable will not, even though he or she might be hard pressed to explain why. Various small pointers—where the animal is seen, the surrounding growth, how it reacts—all add together and produce a positive answer which, when a clearer view is obtained, is usually right. The long, black-tipped ears are, of course, the first and principal clue and, when it moves, the long legs and loping gait. In the hand the nasal passage is noticeably wider. The coat is another clear distinction, for although rabbits' coats vary widely the norm is considerably greyer than the hare's, which is a warm brown. The underside is white, the insides of limbs and feet yellowish and the tail is white with a black stripe on top.

The moult into the thicker, reddish, winter coat begins in late summer or early autumn, beginning at the feet and legs and progressing upwards. Mid-February sees the start of the spring moult which occurs in reverse, starting along the back and proceeding down the limbs to finish on the head.

In snow or mud the trail is easily distinguishable from the rabbit by its size. The rear feet impressions are side by side and greatly elongated. They show five toes, whereas the front feet are placed asymmetrically, show four toes and leave only small, round impressions. The droppings are not easy to distinguish from rabbits, being only slightly larger, paler and more fibrous.

A survey in Aberdeenshire gave an average weight for adult male hares as 3.54 kg and adult females as 3.71 kg. In a Norfolk survey on size, in which both male and female were averaged, the mean length of head and body was 544 mm with a range from 520 to 595 mm. Tails, with hairs, averaged 106 mm and ears 99 mm.

18. The black tips to the ears of the brown hare are prominent.

19. Hares at dawn in Cambridgeshire.

Few mammals have as large a range as the hare; they occur throughout the whole of Europe, below the coniferous forest zone, and, in similar acceptable conditions, across Asia as far as Central China. It is also found, through introduction, in North America, Chile, Australia and New Zealand.

In Britain there is virtually no part of the lowlands where it cannot be found, although some areas, for no apparent reason, do not hold hares while neighbouring areas, showing no obvious differences, do. The hare is not native to the Hebrides, but has been introduced to many of the Islands and is firmly established in some. Skye is a good example, for although *The Handbook of British Mammals* merely says 'It has been recorded since 1960' on Skye, hares can be seen there in substantial numbers.

In general terms the principal habitat of the brown hare is agricultural land. This is less obvious in areas of overall farming activity for there is no alternative to illustrate the fact, but in the Hebrides it is noticeable that brown hares are rarely found far from the crofts. A survey in the Peak District found the range of the brown hare lying between 120 and 150 m, while mountain hares were mostly between 300 and 550 m.

Stephen Tapper and Nicola Parsons, in their paper *The Changing Status of the Brown Hare in Britain*, published by The Game Conservancy, offered the interesting suggestion that hare populations vary with the proportions of tilled land. Far fewer hares are shot in the western British counties than in the Midlands, East Anglia and Scotland and they conclude a major factor is the higher survival rate of leverets in the better cover provided by cereal fields.

Cover alone may not be the only factor, for Pielowski (1976) has shown that leveret deaths due to agricultural practices are high in forage and grass fields (lucerne—44%, meadow—18%, clover—17%) and low in cereals (spring barley—4%, winter wheat—1.7%).

Even this may not complete the story for, in 1980, Strandgaard and Asferg suggested that soil type and climate may also play a part, partly through a higher incidence of pseudotuberculosis in the wetter, western regions. This disease is common in hares and often fatal.

The brown hare population has been falling gradually over the lasty twenty years, not just in Britain but over Western Europe generally. The Game Conservancy estimates the average decline at about 3% per annum and in 1980 began 'The Hare Project', a research programme aimed at discovering the reasons for the decline and proposing any practical measures to reverse it.

The first annual report of 'The Hare Project', published December 1980, contained hitherto unknown, or at the least, unpublished, information on the effect of livestock on the use of pastures by hares. Put briefly, it was found that hares rarely fed in the same paddocks as livestock and serious feeding would not begin until about four days after stock had been removed. Data based on some 1,500 observations showed that where the stocking density of livestock was low, a few hares would use the pastures. Their behaviour showed they were actually disturbed by the presence of livestock (unlike rabbits, who are unaffected). Hares would cease feeding or resting when livestock approached within 30 m or less and would flee when they felt threatened. This behaviour may help to explain the relatively large area over which individual hares will range.

Work carried out in Europe suggests that hares make considerably greater use of tree stands than had hitherto been suspected, and the general conclusion drawn from the research is that the average density of hares in tree stands was about three times higher than in open fields.

In small stands (up to about 1.5 ha) the average density was several times higher than in larger stands, although this general conclusion could be upturned by the ground cover. Stands with dense ground cover, offering good shelter from the weather, always carried a higher density of hares than more open woods or shelter belts. Obviously the main advantage to the hare was shelter in the winter months, particularly in conditions of hard frosts and little snow when form digging in the open fields was difficult. However there is doubt as to whether tree stands are actually beneficial to hares, as the advantage of shelter is offset by the increased risk of predation by foxes.

Our knowledge of the behaviour of hares has been greatly assisted by radio tracking, a technique used in the preparation of 'The Hare Project' reports, referred to earlier. Essentially, hares are captured and fitted with a collar containing a lightweight radio transmitter emitting a signal having a range of almost 1 km. By 1981 a collar had been evolved which weighed only 34 g (that is about 1% of the hare's total weight) and would transmit for about seven months. The position of the radio-collared hare can then be established by taking two intersecting bearings, in any weather and at any time of day or night.

Such positive information eliminates much that has previously been guesswork. For example, in *British Game* Vesey-Fitzgerald wrote that the hare is 'not gregarious—in fact it is distinctly unsocial'. In fact, night-time radio observations suggest quite the reverse and that their distribution during darkness is clumped. Dawn and dusk visual observations support this, showing that 50% of all hares are accompanied by one or more other hares.

Prior to radio-tracking we were aware only of the general pattern of the hare's behaviour; namely, to spend the day hidden in grass, crops or forms, becoming active at dusk and feeding at night. Now we can be more specific. One striking observation was a slow but positive decrease in the use hares made of cereal crops as the year wore on. In January and February between 60–90% of the hares were in cereal crops but by July only 10% were in cereals and the emphasis had swung to grass leys and permanent pastures.

Individual hares have their own areas although these may range quite widely and the use will vary throughout the year. One tracked female used two spring barley fields and a winter wheat field during May and June, but by July was concentrating on a rye grass ley. After harvest this hare moved into woods in daylight, only emerging on to adjoining fields at night. Another demonstrated the hare's objection to the presence of livestock in its use of pig fields. It spent the daytime in unstocked pastures but at night, when the pigs were asleep, moved into their field.

As, with the progression of the year, hares feed less on the developing cereals, so they turn their attention increasingly to grass leys and permanent pastures. Until recently there had been few systematic observations but an analysis of droppings, reported in the 1981 report of 'The Hare Project' gave a clear and interesting picture. Monocots (other than cereals) and herbs were eaten throughout the year, the former remaining fairly steady at 5% of the total intake, while the herb content rose from about 5% to 7½% during high summer, dropping back to 5% in late autumn. In winter the remaining 90% of food intake was divided approximately 60% to cereals and 30% to grasses. The proportions then began to change in favour of grass with the arrival of spring, until in mid-summer grasses provided 60% and cereals the balance not made up by other monocots and herbs.

Some interesting Continental research has been carried out on the effect of hares on the yields of cultivated plants. Tests involved both fencing hares out of some areas and fencing them in others. In the latter it was found the daily weight of dry matter consumed, per hare, was 144 g. During the winter, when vegetational growth had ceased, consumption by both hares and roe deer amounted to up to 11% but the final crop yields showed no significant reduction.

Although grasses and cereals form the major proportion of a hare's diet, both local opportunities and weather conditions will cause variations. Tree bark is torn and eaten, although the habit is much more frequent in snow cover. In turnip-growing areas these are regularly eaten and in 1977 Raymond Hewson, of the Department of Agriculture and Fisheries for Scotland, wrote a brief paper on food selection in turnip and cereal crops. Part of the investigation concerned the extent to which the hare's choice was affected by the treatment of cereal crops with nitrogen but no clear preference emerged. Other considerations, for example variations in the degree of damage according to the time of harvesting and preferences for different varieties of turnips, were investigated. Slight variations were observed but nothing emerged so clearly as the degree to which the hares invariably fed most heavily on the turnips or cereals forming the outside rows of the observed blocks. Measurements on three plots of barley showed the grazing of the two outer rows accounted for 76%, 85% and 90% respectively. The authors' main conclusion for the practice of fringe grazing is that it improves the ability of hares to see approaching predators.

Like rabbits, hares also practise refection, that is to say that they re-ingest soft droppings produced during the day-time.

Although the spectacular courtship antics of hares in spring, including leaping, chasing, enurination and 'boxing' are well-known and are in part responsible for the superstition and mythology attached to the animal, there is no systematic account. Observations in north-east Scotland showed that pregnant hares could be found in every month of the year, rising from 11% in January to over 90% in April and May, declining to 11% in November and 4% in December. It is reasonable to assume that the winter percentages would be rather higher in the milder climate of southern England. There is some confirmation of this assumption in the work of Flux (1967) who showed that after cold springs, females start breeding later, produce fewer litters and have less young per litter than in years with warm springs. We also owe to Flux, working in New Zealand, the knowledge that the breeding seasons in New Zealand, Australia, Canada, Scotland and USSR all start soon after the shortest day, irrespective of the environmental conditions.

Work done in both Scotland and Poland agrees that a female hare will produce 3 to 4 litters per year. In the Scottish investigation embryo counts varied from means of 2 in January to a peak of 3.2 in May. It does not follow that births would be at the same level for hares, as rabbits, will reabsorb embryos.

The Polish study was very thorough, involving large groups of hares over a period of eight years. This confirmed the Scottish study, showing that in the Central European areas studied the annual number of litters was again 3 to 4. Some of the statistics of the Polish study show the scale of the investigation. For seven years, from 1966 to 1973, between 600 and 2,400 hares were netted every autumn and winter for examination to determine the percentage of young (current year's) hares in the population. Additionally 491 litters of hares less than five days old were inspected.

One major conclusion was that the mean size of an average litter is 2.3 young. The study also confirmed an earlier conclusion that litters follow upon each other at two monthly intervals and a typical female hare will either produce four litters, in March, May, July and September, or three litters in April, June and August. This gives an annual average increase from each female of 7.4 young.

In fact, matters are not so arithmetically simple for the number born each year is not just the number of breeding females multiplied by 7.4. The annual 'crop' varies quite widely according to the level of implantation and re-absorption of embryos and, although not yet understood, it is felt some natural limitation of numbers takes place. Gestation lasts 42 days and the young, when born, are fully furred and weigh about 110 g. Adult weight is reached in about 240 days which dispels the popular country belief that large hares are old. Breeding can take place in the first year of life.

Much of the behaviour of both mother and young during the nursing period had been the subject of speculation but scientists from the Research

Institute for Nature Management in Holland were able to observe a litter for a full five week period; and, while it cannot be assumed that the behaviour was entirely representative, it is likely to be typical.

The litter of four leverets were still wet when found during the mowing of a field on 27 May, 1974. The immediate area was left unmown and a caravan, with spot lights for night viewing, was positioned.

It was the popular assertion of earlier writers that the female hare gave birth to her young in different places. Other, usually later, writers contended that the doe separated the young after birth by taking the scruff of their neck in her mouth. However Koeren, in 1956, wrote that nests of four leverets are found regularly and that the young disperse themselves under various conditions, including heavy rainfall. Rongstad and Tester (1971) attached small transmitters to six day-old hares and concluded that the dispersal was a willing act and not one created by stress conditions. They found the young dispersed each night after having previously assembled for nursing during the twilight period.

In the case of the Dutch litter the four young stayed huddled together during the first day. By the second day two only remained in physical contact and the other two had made their own forms nearby. After this day one of the adventurers disappeared, never to reappear. From the fourth to tenth day two stayed in the grass and one under hay only three metres away. On the ninth night one leveret moved away and was never seen again. The following night the two survivors travelled 80 metres to the edge of the field where there was good cover. There they spent every daytime until the end of the fifth week and the maximum distance they moved from their birth place was 120 metres. However, every evening they returned to the birth place for feeding.

Nursing stopped in the second half of the fifth week; the young moved into another field and in the sixth week one was seen 400 metres away from the birth place.

In the early days the young waited to be fed by the doe at the birth place, but by the fifth to eleventh evening they waited a few metres away and after that would wait even further away, in the direction from which the doe usually came. However, the doe was anxious to nurse closer to the birth place and would jump away from the young to gain her position.

For the entire 33 days on which the young were nursed they fed only once a day, in the evening. The young arrived between 15 to 60 minutes after sunset and always in advance of the doe. Nursing took place between 45 to 95 minutes after sunset, and although the observers could not be certain that when the young were under the doe's belly they were feeding without interruption, the intervals so spent varied from 2 to 4.5 minutes, and usually lasted 3 minutes. On the last 2 days before nursing ceased the time dropped to 1–1.5 minutes.

20. Leverets will freeze at the approach of danger rather than run.

21. Keen sight and powerful legs are the hare's main defences.

Not surprisingly the leverets remained motionless in their hiding places when anything or anyone passed during the day. However, with the approach of dusk, and feeding time, their behaviour changed and they would follow other hares, both adult and young, and on one occasion a black-tailed godwit.

The young hares were first seen to nibble grass on the thirteenth day and by the fifteenth and sixteenth were eating effectively. This confirmed previous observations of captive leverets who commenced eating green food on the twelfth day. Whether the youngsters would have continued suckling from their mother beyond the thirty-third day or not could not be established, for she ended the matter by not turning up at the rendezvous, after which the young were no longer seen at the nursing area.

While this particular litter was obviously observed with meticulous care, there must be some slight doubt that its behaviour was entirely representative as the grass around the birth place was mown and the area of open ground to be crossed before reaching fresh cover may have inhibited dispersal in the early stages. However, the behaviour pattern was very similar to the findings of two other scientists who observed other litters and provides yet another example of how wild creatures develop survival patterns best suited to their individual needs. In the case of hares, the act of dispersal must limit predation as they can then only be taken individually. It is only when they draw together to feed that the entire litter is vulnerable; and this risk is reduced to a minimum by feeding only once in twenty-four hours and keeping the duration of the feed short. Additionally the feeding takes place after sunset when the main avian threat, that is all the birds of prey—crows, magpies, blackback and herring gulls and short-eared owls—are no longer active.

A few pages previously I mentioned the commencement of 'The Hare Project' and the initial report. By the summer of 1982 results pointed to three main factors: a succession of poor breeding years brought about by bad weather: increased predation from a spreading and increased fox population: and a severe reduction in available grazing due to loss of agricultural grassland and early ploughing of stubbles. In respect of the last factor, the evidence suggests it is changes in farming practices that are significant, rather than the amount of land farmed. Between the turn of the century and 1938 the amount of cultivated land in Britain fell from 18.4 to 11.9 million acres, but during the war years rose to 17.5 million. There was no corresponding increase in the hare population.

To assess the impact of weather, the Conservancy compared the annual bags of hares, both at regional and estate level, with temperature and rainfall. The conclusions were that winter weather has only minimal effect on the population and the late summer and autumn weather only marginally more. It is the early spring temperature which is of overriding importance with, obviously enough, cold springs producing lower than average hare bags.

February, March and April are the critical months, whereas cold, wet summers make no difference.

A more intensive investigation on the effects of weather on hare population was carried out by the Polish Hunting Association between 1966 and 1974. Earlier work had concluded that the reduction of the hare population by the direct influence of weather was only about 2% but that indirect influence could be substantial, for example by favouring the development of disease or parasites, or affecting reproduction processes.

Some of the results merely confirmed the obvious—for example, the longer the occurrence of snow cover the thicker it is, which results in a lower mean air temperature and a greater death rate of hares. Others did not. Commonsense would not have suggested that the death rate for adult hares in the breeding season (March–November) would decrease when the rainfall in spring increased, and also increase in dry summers and autumns. Nor would one expect more adult hares to die with an increase in air temperature, particularly in spring and during cloudy summers. Increased survival of young in sunny Mays is understandable, but why should the same trend occur in wetter autumns? There is obviously much more to discover about the relationship between weather and the hare population.

Relatively little work has been done on population structures in this country. Consulting Polish studies, we learn the hare, spared disease and predators, has a physiological life of 12 to 13 years, but in the harsh conditions of the wild only 6% were found over 5½ years old and no males over 4 years. Still in Poland, a 1965 study found 34% of the autumn population under one year old. (Up to about 8 months there is a notch at epiphysis of tibia or ulna.) This compares well with the figures of Lloyd (1968) who found 23–30% of 91 females killed in Cambridgeshire in January–February 1965 were under one year. (Some of the Polish hares would have died between the autumn count and January–February.)

Yet another Polish study put the mortality rate of adult hares from spring to autumn as high as 20% while winter losses were thought to be only a few percent. (Several studies concluded that in all but the very severest winters the winter weather had a negligible effect on survival.) A far more dangerous period was from birth to autumn, as the innocent youngsters first faced the natural hazards. Four scientists, working independently and in different years, predicted mortality rates varying between 39% and 90%. A longer study, over nine years on one shoot, produced an average of 77%.

Perhaps the most striking conclusion was that the average life expectation of a hare is 0.7 years and 90% of the population are less than four years old.

Sampling bags of shot hares shows a normal sex ratio of one to one. Polish estimates of density varied between one hare to 2.4 and 5.5 ha. An English survey in 1956 suggested one to 4 ha and in 1968 of one to every 2–3 ha. This result runs against the general decline, but the later figure was gathered by

Lloyd who, as we saw from the earlier paragraph, was active in Cambridge-shire. I know from personal experience that in the sixties hares were very numerous in that county and I suspect the result was obtained from there.

Many country dwellers felt the hare population increased when myxomatosis decimated the rabbits. I cannot trace positive evidence of this and there is no obvious logical reason for such a cause and effect. Indeed, there is a case for suggesting that fewer rabbits would mean heavier fox pressure on hares. A counter-argument suggested the hare population benefited from the absence of buck rabbits who had always killed young leverets, by kicking with their hind legs, whenever they came across them. However, lack of reports of such behaviour prior to myxomatosis rather suggests this was a theory dreamed up to explain a supposed increase.

Moving from buck rabbits to rather more threatening predators produces a relatively short list so far as adult hares are concerned. Leverets are, of course, vulnerable to a wider range, depending on their age. Once, on the Isle of Skye, I witnessed a dramatic incident involving a leveret about half the size of an adult rabbit. I had parked my car close to the shore of a sea loch and, with windows open, was watching sea birds when I heard a high pitched screaming. I turned and saw a buzzard fly from behind a small hillock, keeping a constant height of about six feet and dangling the leveret from its talons. The leveret was not struggling but was the source of the screaming. Suddenly I realised an adult hare, presumably the mother, was running beneath the buzzard and leaping frequently in an effort to reach its young. This pathetic scene moved quite slowly, but very clearly, across the road and the pasture adjoining until reaching a low but sheer outcrop of rock. Here the buzzard, apparently with great difficulty, rose over while the hare was forced to detour and lost ground. They all disappeared over the short horizon and I waited until, some ten minutes later, the adult hare loped back slowly and alone.

A buzzard could not, of course, take an adult hare—indeed there is evidence to suggest a buzzard will not (as distinct from cannot) attempt to take a rabbit—but a golden eagle would have no difficulty. In practice, in the areas I know well where eagles are in permanent residence, the two territories hardly cross. The brown hare lives in the cultivated lands around the crofts and the eagle patrols the wild hills. However, the eagles will take many mountain hares.

Needless to say, the Poles have considered predation in depth and found the hare a component of the diet of foxes, martens, domestic cats, badgers and buzzards. However, of these predators the fox was by far the most serious, with hares forming 37% of its diet in winter and almost 15% in summer and autumn. Presumably because it is easier for a fox to catch voles than hares, an explosion in the vole population takes the pressure off the hares, with voles providing over 90% of the fox's diet. (In the case of barn owls and buzzards the figure is 100%). In assessing the impact of the fox on hare populations it must be remembered that foxes will take both hare carrion and sick hares. Removing from the exercise the hare remains from hares already dead or shortly to die from other causes might produce a very different picture.

Further work done by the Polish Hunting Station showed that in 200 shot foxes 46% of the volume of the stomach contents were hare remains. It was calculated that foxes take nearly 3% of the adult hare summer population, nearly 2% of the winter population and slightly over 10% of the annual natural increase of hares. The figure of 46% of stomach content being hare remains is substantially higher than found in a similar study in this country by the Game Conservancy. Here a level of 24% was recorded, but this is probably explained by the higher hare densities in Poland. (The English foxes also contained 27% passerine birds and no less than 28% earthworm.) In factual terms the Polish studies concluded that in the course of a year one fox would eat, on average, nearly three live (as distinct from carrion) adult hares and 17.3 live young hares.

Many observers believe that certain sprays used in this country are fatal to hares, but little appears to have been done in this area. Again Polish work provides, at least, an opinion. Studies throughout a year showed that the chlorinated hydrocarbon level remained nearly unchanged and had no influence on hare reproduction. However, an organophosphorus insecticide, while not causing death, reduced the hares' activity and generally lowered their capacity for survival.

Rather surprisingly, the threat from agricultural activities is the much more direct one of hares dying as a result of being struck by machinery. Such deaths are restricted almost entirely to young hares but this in no way reduces the seriousness of the problem. The danger is greatest in green forage crops but still present in beet, potatoes, and spring cereals. It is suggested that no less than 15.4% of each year's natural increase is killed by machinery.

In Britain, rabbit fleas, sheep ticks and the sucking louse are common parasites on hares. The stomach worm, *Graphidium strigosum*, occurred in 63% of hares examined on the Berkshire Downs, but came a poor second to nematodes of the genus *Trichostrongylus* which achieved 100%. The tapeworm *Cittotaenia* came a poor third at 37%.

Although hares are subject to a wide variety of diseases, the greatest threat is coccidiosis. It is quite common to find dead hares with acute coccidiosis, particularly in autumn and the Game Conservancy study area showed that while in spring 95% of hares with coccidiosis had a low infestation, by the autumn the count at this level had dropped to 62%. Among those with coccidiosis some 28% had a level at which they were unlikely to survive, as against only 4% in spring.

In some areas of the Continent hares are managed to achieve a higher populaton for sporting purposes. However, in Britain shooting men do not regard the hare as a prime quarry, preferring to treat it as an incidental species adding variety to a mixed day. To some extent this reflects the good fortune of the British sportsman, who enjoys such a variety of quarries that he can afford to be selective. Were we ever to manage hares, the two priorities would be to reduce the fox population and to manage grassland activities to minimise killing young hares.

Current indications do not suggest the hare will become an endangered species. It is widespread over Britain and the evidence suggests that the decline in numbers has been restricted to the intensively farmed areas and is due entirely to changed agricultural practices. Even here the effect has been to reduce rather than eliminate the species and if the result is to do away with the need for the annual hare shoots this will be no disadvantage. I personally took part in a shoot near Newmarket, in the 1960s, when over a thousand hares were shot in the day and for many of the participants it was an unpleasant agricultural exercise in pest reduction rather than sport.

It is reasonable to expect our countryside will be graced by these attractive creatures for many years to come.

12

The Mountain Hare

Few wild creatures highlight the physical limitations of humans as vividly as the mountain hare as it flits, light as a shadow, up, down and across rough upland country over which we would be hard pressed to exceed a mile an hour and would make an untidy job of even that speed. Regrettably, space requires that we deal relatively briefly with this fascinating animal.

As with the brown hare, the mountain hare is of the order *Lagomorpha* and the genus *Lepus*. Their general name of *Lepus timidus* is varied with several subspecies including the Scottish named *Lepus timidus scoticus*, the Irish *Lepus hibernicus* and the American *Lepus americanus*.

You will, I trust, recall that in the last chapter I mentioned the brown hare had been traced back, in Europe, some 100,000 years or so. However, before it arrived on the scene there existed a subspecies, closely related to the mountain hare, named *Lepus timidus Anglicus*, which appears to have been widely distributed throughout Britain. This subspecies evolved into the two subspecies of the mountain, or blue, hare in Scotland and the Irish hare. By the time the brown hare arrived on mainland Britain, Ireland and the Islands had been cut off by the rising seas but it was subsequently introduced by man to most, but not all, areas. Where brown and mountain hares compete, the brown drives the mountain hare away, which explains how the unfortunate original species has now been forced into the harsh upland areas.

As with the brown, the mountain hare is not an important quarry species, partly because a successful shot is frequently followed by a long, hard carry. They are, perhaps, most at risk from bored grouse shooters, waiting in the butts and aware that transport is at hand for the bag. Certainly the economic importance of mountain hares for sport is very low.

All subspecies of *Lepus timidus* are smaller than the brown hare and of these the Scottish race is the smallest. One investigation gave the average length of the head and body of Scottish mountain hares as 502 mm and Irish hares 545 mm. The weights of Scottish hares varied with both sex and season, the adult males averaging 2.6 kg in spring and summer and 2.7 kg in autumn and winter, while the respective weights for adult females were 3.1 kg and 2.9 kg.

John Flux, in his most excellent study of the mountain hare, estimated the growth rate of leverets as 14 g per day. However, growth practically stops during the winter, even in late born young which may be only half adult weight. There is no significant seasonal change in the weight of the adult other than with pregnant females.

During the summer the mountain hare is distinguishable from the brown by its shorter ears, greyer coat and absence of black top to the tail. However, living on ground which will experience permanent snow cover for much of the winter, the needs of camouflage require a colour change and the mountain hare responds by moulting into a white coat. The degree of colour change varies from North Scandinavia, where the change is to almost complete whiteness, to Ireland where only a piebald effect is achieved. There are two autumn moults, a preliminary one that produces a coloured coat, after which the hair follicles contain no pigment-producing ferment. The subsequent white hairs of the winter coat are almost completely grown before the autumn coat is shed.

The colour change, in Scottish mountain hares, begins in early October every year and is therefore probably triggered by a constant factor, the most likely being shorter day length. A Scottish study showed that the complete change from brown to white was not achieved in the same time each year but for the first ten to twelve weeks was related to air temperature. However, from December until February the principal factor was the extent of snow-lie. Depending on temperature, the change back to brown began in mid-February and ended in late June, the complete change date being fairly constant and so, once again, probably being determined by day length.

In practice, the Scottish mountain hare is never pure white. An area of grey extends over the back, varying in size from animal to animal and also with conditions. Additionally the outer half of the ear, below the black tip, remains brown.

Lepus timidus is widely distributed throughout the northern Palaearctic with fifteen subspecies ranging from Ireland to Japan. In Scotland it is most commonly found on heather moorland between 300 and 900 m and is more common in the east than the north and west. It was introduced to many of the Scottish islands in the nineteenth century and still survives on most, although reports suggest it is now extinct on Islay and Eigg. Introductions to the Pennines in South Yorkshire and Derbyshire, about 1880, were successful, as were similar experiments in North Wales about 1885. However, the latter population is reported to have fallen substantially of late.

Mountain hares spend most of the day sitting in a form with their forefeet tucked under their chest and the toes of their large rear legs actually in front of their body. Although in this position the eyes are usually half closed, they appear not to sleep and, indeed, Flux never observed either wild or tame hares actually asleep.

At dusk hares leave their forms to feed, in fine weather often preceding feeding by jumping and chasing other hares in a playful manner. The distance from the daytime resting area to the night feeding grounds can be as much as 2.5 km and once there hares appear to remain until dawn. Unlike brown hares, mountain hares are indifferent to cattle and sheep and feed alongside them.

Mountain hares have a strange habit of digging burrows, usually some 1 to 2 m long, which they do not subsequently use. There is frequently a form close to the entrance, but only young leverets actually enter the burrow. However, there is no evidence to suggest the adults prepare the burrow for the benefit of the young and one theory is that burrows are prepared as an emergency escape from eagles.

In summer mountain hares move to high ground, but, less understandably, in winter they favour exposed hill faces. A possible explanation is that with the death of much of the summer ground cover they seek areas giving maximum visibility of possible danger.

Once disturbed from their forms, hares normally run uphill, a habit exploited by organised hare shooting parties. They sit tighter between May and October and tightest of all in hot weather, possibly because an animal so acclimatised to cold is even more averse than we would be to physical effort in high temperatures. Experiments over a whole year gave a mean flushing distance of 20.3 m, which, unfortunately for the hare, is quite close enough for the sportsman.

When travelling, hares often use sheep tracks but they also develop their own well-defined, and communal, runs in the same fashion as rabbits. The ranges of individual hares overlap and they appear to seek out one another's company during the night.

Although there is some dispute among the authorities as to percentages, the main food of mountain hares is heather. Hewson, in the *Handbook of British Mammals*, puts the winter figure as 90% and from April to October at about 50%, while Flux found the winter peak in January at 80%, dropping to as low as 20% in June. There may well be local variations according to heather quality but heather is certainly the staple diet, followed by cotton grass and then a fairly wide variety of other grasses depending on the season.

Population densities of hares on moors overlying base-rich rocks are significantly higher than where the underlying rock is poor, as a result, of course, of the better quality heather. However, irrespective of the overall quality, mountain hares are very selective, showing a strong preference for young heather of 4 to 8 cm tall and only moving to budding heather, 15 to 20 cm, when the former was overgrazed.

During periods of deep snow, or lighter snow with a frost covering, mountain hares turn to young trees as a food source and may cause substantial damage in plantations. Experiments carried out with captive hares showed no preference among the varieties of conifers used for moorland planting. However, they preferred rowan and willow to birch and the reported preference of Scandinavian hares for birch may be due to the lack of alternative species. Field observations suggest that, where a variety of trees are available, gorse and juniper are preferred to rowan and willow. I could trace no report of mountain hares observed drinking.

The beginning and duration of the breeding season is governed by the need to produce young when there is an adequate food supply. The males start to come into breeding condition as early as December but there is no immediate response from the females who are rarely found to be pregnant before February. Obviously the duration of the breeding season is shorter in the more northerly areas and the length of daylight appears to be the trigger for the females. Pregnant females are rarely found after August and the conclusion of the breeding season appears to stem from failing fecundity of the males in July.

Although in the breeding season mountain hares are often seen in pairs, these appear to be only temporary unions and there are various reports of groups of hares mating indiscriminately. At all times the females appear dominant and will attack males with their forefeet if their advances are unwelcome.

While four litters in a breeding season are possible, three are more likely. Flux found the average number of litters was 2.6, and the mean number of embryos 2.1. The average female produces six to seven young per annum. There is no certain evidence of the gestation period, but results with captive hares in Sweden suggest about fifty days.

Mountain hares can live for several breeding seasons and a life span of nine years or more is not uncommon. However, the population levels go through cycles of peaks and troughs and the age structure varies according to the population phase. When the numbers are high, and also in the immediate period of decline, a study on marked hares showed as many as 75% of adults and 84% of leverets dying within twelve months. However, when the population was low, and in the revival phase, survival levels increased to the point where 30% of leverets marked at that time were subsequently recovered between three and seven years later.

Population levels are highest in East Scotland, where up to 2.45 hares per ha have been recorded, and lowest on West Scottish moors and Irish bogs where a hare to 80 ha is quite normal.

As with brown hares, and ignoring man, the principal predator of the mountain hare is the fox. Wild and domestic cats take adult hares and it has been suggested that stoats kill occasionally. Hen harriers and buzzards take leverets up to, it is thought, twenty-six days. Golden eagles take mountain hares of all ages and my own observations in the Hebrides, one of the strongholds of the eagle, suggest that where eagles are present in any strength they prey quite substantially on mountain hares. This will apply particularly in rapid spring snow thaws when the colour change of the hares lags behind and they stand out clearly as white dots on the brown, winter-burned hillsides.

Ticks, rabbit fleas and the sucking louse are parasites commonly found on mountain hares, but nothing appears to be known about the frequency of infection. A very limited investigation (fourteen hares only) in Banffshire found the nematode worm *Graphidium strigosum* in 21% of stomachs and *Trichostrongylus* in 100%.

As man has the greatest influence, for good or bad, on the future of any species, the preferred habitat of the mountain hare should ensure its survival into the foreseeable future.

13

The Wood-Pigeon

A merely casual acquaintance with the wood-pigeon is misleading. Seen as large flocks of drab, grey birds, flapping slowly about their business of consuming vast quantities of our farmers' produce, they appear to offer neither beauty, interest, or other than average sport for the shooting man. The truth is very different.

Beside the wood-pigeon, four other species of wild pigeon exist in Britain; the stock dove (*Columba oenas*), often known locally as the blue rock; the rock-dove (*C. livia*); the turtle-dove (*Streptopelia turtur*); and the collared dove (*Streptopelia decaocto*). The latter arrived in Britain in 1952 and ten years later Dr R. K. Murton reported was 'steadily becoming established'. Now in many areas the numbers have grown to nuisance proportions.

Within the order *Columbiformes* and the sub-order *Columbae* there are a large group of pigeons and doves, although mild scientific dissent exists with Peters (1937) listing 306 species divided into 59 genera and Fisher and Peterson (1964) giving 285 in 48 genera. Five pigeon species have become extinct since 1680, including the passenger pigeon (*Ectopistes migratorius*), the last of which died in Cincinnati Zoo in 1914. The extermination of this once vast population of American birds was largely due to the irresponsibility of the shooting community. Perhaps the lesson learnt from the passenger pigeon was the stimulus for the Ducks Unlimited operation, in which American sportsmen reversed the alarming decline in their wild fowl population and redeemed their own reputation in the process.

The sub-order Columbae divides into two families, one, the Raphidae, including the extinct dodo. The other contains all the pigeons and doves and among them, in the sub-group *palumbus*, is the subject of our attention, the wood-pigeon *Columba palumbus* Linnaeus 1758.

Local names for the wood-pigeon include the quist, cushie doo, ring-dove, cushat and queest, the last three of which were listed in Blaine's *Rural Sports* in 1852.

The existence of true pigeons has been established for some twenty-five million years and Pleistocene remains (that is to say in the age range of from

130

six thousand to two million years) of the wood-pigeon have been found in most of the areas it now inhabits. However, this does not mean permanent habitation over this time span, for the Pleistocene saw four major glaciations affecting Europe. It requires a strong effort of imagination to visualise the full effect of these vast onslaughts of ice and snow and even more to consider the effects on modern society if, or perhaps I should write, when, the ice returns. In the context of the pigeon the deciduous woodlands were driven back as far as Spain and Italy and boreal species of birds, which include the pigeons, would have dropped back with the trees. It is 8,000 years since the end of the last glacial period and in the time-scale of evolution this is only yesterday. Pigeons would not have returned to Britain merely because the temperature rose but delayed until the changed climatic conditions led to the growth of suitable trees and vegetation. It took a further 4,000 years before the oaks returned and another 1,000 years for the beech; given acorns and beech nuts, the wood-pigeons must have been present, albeit in the modest numbers found nowadays in areas of good woods but unintensive agriculture.

Although the glaciations drove the pigeon from Britain and the rest of northern Europe, there is no reason to presume any interruption to its existence in the south. There is ample evidence to show that the ancient Egyptians not only regarded pigeons as a common bird, but kept them domestically. Regrettably, our own early literature treated pigeons mainly as a source of food and what little mention they received came mainly from a culinary angle. As man's ability to survive improved, and the pursuit of wild creatures became more a sport and less a necessity, so books on shooting became popular, a trickle in the eighteenth century becoming a minor flood in the nineteenth. These do not, however, tell us a great deal about the wood-pigeon of the time for, with the exception of a few such writers as Charles St John with his *Wild Sports of the Highlands* (1846) and *Natural History and Sport in Moray* (1863), the sporting writer with either real knowledge of, or deep interest in, the natural history of his quarries was a rarity. The renowned Colonel Peter Hawker was a prime example, for while he devoted entire chapters of his classic *Instructions to Young Sportsmen* (1816) to guns, shot, powder and techniques, his natural history was decidedly skimpy.

The status of the wood-pigeon among shooting men is somewhat unusual, for it is one of the few quarries actively pursued at all levels. Many sportsmen are excluded from shooting driven game by cost, and those forms of sport usually available to all, for example ferreting rabbits, are often disregarded by the more fortunate as unappealing. Not so the wood-pigeon, whose wariness, speed and ability to jink at the crucial moment make it a universally popular quarry. Granted, not everyone clamours for a seat in a pigeon hide on a wet, cold day, but a roll-call of the guns manning the woods at the first roost shoot in February would show a wide divergence of backgrounds.

Unfortunately the value of the wood-pigeon as a quarry does not go far beyond the test of marksmanship. Its pursuit generates no work for local people, nor is there a strong and steady market demand for the bodies. Continental house-wives, particularly the French, are regular buyers but the demand in Britain from this source fluctuates with variations in the wood-pigeon population of the Continent and other vagaries of the market. For a brief spell in the seventies demand was high, vast numbers were exported and the price rose to the point where those who allow money to enter into sport could make a profit. The British market is surprisingly poor, considering how tasty a pigeon pie or casserole of pigeon breasts can be. Rarely does the price rise to the point at which the cost of cartridges can be recovered and occasionally they are unsaleable. The fact that the greatest bags are made in hard weather, when the condition of the birds is poor, is another drawback to satisfactory marketing.

Unlike the game birds the wood-pigeon makes no significant improvement to the economy of an area by attracting visitors, at least not in any numbers nor for any length of time. One exception, within my personal experience, is in Wiltshire where an enterprising local flies parties of Danes over for visits of several days devoted entirely to decoying pigeons. The Danes enjoy shooting not otherwise available to them; the farmers enjoy crop protection at no cost; and the organiser does not do it through kindness.

Once in the hand, the full subtle beauty of the colouring of the wood-pigeon is revealed. The blue-grey of the upper parts shades to a darker grey on the upper wings and black on the upper tail, the whole changeable with variations in the light. The lower parts are mainly a paler grey, with the breast vinous, and most of the under tail black. This generally dull overall colouring is sharply contrasted in three areas: a broad white band across the under tail and wings and white patches either side of the neck. Above these neck patches are iridescent purple and green display plumage. The general health of all birds is indicated by their plumage and this is particularly true of the wood-pigeon, whose soft and delicate feathering normally has an exquisite sheen or bloom which I can only compare with the beauty of a mackerel the moment it is taken from the sea.

The bill commences as a soft white lump of fleshy membranes over the nostrils, hardens and changes briefly to pink, then to yellow throughout the greater length and finally brown at the tip. Dr Murton, beyond question the greatest authority on the wood-pigeon, described the eye as, 'particularly striking at close range, being straw-coloured with a small pear-shaped iris, and this gives the bird a very alert appearance'. However, a wood-pigeon looks alert at any distance, and certainly long before any detail of the eye is visible. It is not, I submit, the precise detail of the eye, but the constant neck stretching and head swivelling as it keeps a wary eye on its surroundings. A wood-pigeon looks alert because it is alert. The final discreet flash of colour comes from the dull red legs.

22. *At close quarters the previously dull grey bird reveals a myriad of subtle shades.*

It is a common belief among many farmers and shooting men that Britain is invaded each autumn by flocks of wood-pigeons from the Continent or Scandinavia, these birds being smaller and darker than our own and without the white neck markings. In fact, these are simply juveniles which have yet to obtain both adult size and feathering. The question of immigration is dealt with later, but there is no obvious difference between our wood-pigeons and those of the Continent and Scandinavia. Where a species of animal exists over a wide range, the northern populations are both larger and lighter in colour than the southern. However, the variations are usually very slight and can only be demonstrated by the average of many examples. It is quite impractical to take an individual wood-pigeon and say it is either a British or foreign bird by virtue of its weight, size or colour.

Adult birds may moult any time between February and November but moulting is heaviest in mid-summer. Juveniles normally moult at six weeks, acquiring a darker plumage than adults and without the green, blue and white neck markings which are used by the adult birds in sex display.

Blaine (1852) deals swiftly and positively with the statistics of the wood-pigeon. 'It weighs about 22 ounces; length 18 inches.' Either wood-pigeons have diminished in the last century or so or the author selected some fine specimens, for Murton gives the length as 16 inches (40 cm) and the average weight as a little over 17.5 ounces (500 grammes). Only twelve were examined for the details given in the *Handbook of British Birds* and, equally, I doubt Blaine's informant carried out a detailed study of many birds, certainly nothing approaching the five-thousand or more handled by Murton.

In fact, Murton makes the point that the knowledge of the average weight of the wood-pigeon is of little value as, like humans, they vary in size and weight, and also vary through the year, partly as a result of fat accumulation or loss. This is well understood by anyone who has shot pigeons after a spell of hard weather in late winter and compared the emaciated bundles of feather and bone with the plump, heavy birds of summer. A vivid example of the extremes is given in Murton's statistics with two female wood-pigeons, measured in February, one weighing 250 g and the other a little over 600 g. Neither was diseased. As a general guide Murton gave average weights in October, when weights were heaviest, of 559 g for males and 540 g for females; and in June, the month of lightest weights, of 477 g for males and 467 g for females.

A combination of wariness and a catholic taste in food has enabled the wood-pigeon to spread widely, breeding as far north as the 55°F July isotherm, which takes it well into the north of Sweden and Norway. Southwards it extends to the 86°F. isotherm, which means North Africa. During the last century it has spread much further northwards in north-west Europe, due, it is believed, to a gradual increase in mean annual temperatures.

Before man appeared on the scene the preferred habitat of the wood-pigeon was beech and oak woodland, which provided food, cover and nesting sites. Doubtless wood-pigeons inhabited other areas, as they do today, but their ability to survive in less favoured surroundings, such as conifer forests, was greatly improved with the commencement of man's agricultural activities. A European study, in 1956, showed thirty-four wood-pigeons per hundred hectares in oak and horn-beam forests, but only seven per hundred hectares in spruce. Even at the lower density the spruce dwellers sought their food in the surrounding countryside.

The gregarious inclination of pigeons is obvious to the observant countryman and has been turned to good account by shooting men in the technique of decoying on the feeding grounds. However, the social behaviour of wood-pigeons is considerably more complex than an instinct to flock together, and we owe a detailed assessment to Dr Murton. During the peak breeding season a pigeon can gather sufficient food in under an hour and then return to the nest to incubate or brood the young. Consequently, the maximum concentrations of birds in the feeding grounds are small. With the arrival of autumn, feeding grounds are fewer, food gathering takes longer and larger flocks become evident. Concentration also takes place in the roosts, as birds which had spread into hedgerows and spinneys to nest move back into the main woods.

Murton felt wood-pigeons were most integrated when they were most hungry, that is during the mornings, and tended to break up in the afternoons. This tendency, to return to the roost or sit in trees near the feeding area to preen, diminished as the shorter winter days arrived and food became scarcer. Marking birds showed that flocks were usually composed of the same birds and that they returned not only to the same field each day, but learnt which part of the field gave the best feeding. Obviously this is a general statement, for flocks will be broken up by disturbance, passing birds will join a feeding flock, agricultural operations or weather will change food sources and many other variations will occur; but the essential interesting point remains, that the behaviour of the birds is regulated and not haphazard.

Murton observed the response of passing birds to the flash of the white wing markings of alighting birds, a fact already known to sportsmen who have evolved various forms of wing flapping decoys.

In pursuit of the scientific dictum that all things have an explanation, Murton gave much thought to why pigeons flock. He discarded the theory that predators find it harder to take an individual when it is part of a flock in favour of arguing a feeding advantage. The reasoning is involved, but falls into two areas. Firstly, it would take a single bird a great deal of time to search an area and identify good feeding ground. However, with a gregarious species all the population is searching and once a few birds are successful the remainder rapidly join them. A good example occurs when spring drilling begins. For the first day or so only a few birds visit the newly sown fields but others quickly join them and large flocks develop.

The second reason for flocking is, to quote Murton, that 'given a specified amount of food and a population of birds requiring a known amount of food over a unit of time, it is easy to demonstrate that in the initial absence of competition more birds are forced to starve than if competition and mortality occur at all stages.' Put simply, this means that if the entire local population concentrates on a limited area of feeding then underfeeding, and eventually death, of some birds will begin at once, thereby leaving more food for the survivors. If the available food supply is inadequate to see the wood-pigeon population through the lean period of winter and early spring then the quicker the surplus dies the better, for they will have left more for the survivors. Without flocking the birds would spread and all would survive until the food supply was depleted, when more would die. As will emerge soon, this reasoning also affects the influence of shooting on pigeon populations.

It is the ill-fortune of the farming community that the feeding habits of the pigeon, prior to man's appearance, enabled it to take full advantage of the arrival of agriculture. Clover fields provide a more nutritious food than weed leaves in forest glades, stubble grain is a more reliable autumn source than acorns and beech nuts, and winter crops such as kale and sprouts are life-savers in severe weather. Dividing the year into the four quarters, January to March finds the wood-pigeon existing mainly on clover, although sanfoin is preferred if available. When the clover runs out, or the activities of sportsmen drives them from the leys, they will work old stubbles, seek weeds on pastures, or pick remnants from old sugar beet or potato fields. Ivy berries, seedling turnips and spring cabbage are local alternatives and, of course, in snow they are forced onto the high standing brassicae, although they leave these as soon as a thaw opens up the clover. Once spring cereal sowing begins, which can be as early as February for wheat, they work the newly-drilled fields, gleaning any unburied corn.

The April to June period begins with the final clean-up of the cereal fields. Murton calculated that once the density of exposed grain dropped below one in every five square feet the birds sought more productive feeding. A favourite alternative is charlock in sugar beet fields, and peas are also very popular. These are taken as leaf, and then both developing and ripe pods. I have memories of many good days of decoying over peas in the Balsham area of Cambridge, and many of the slain went to Dr Murton to be used in his studies. This is a leaner time for the pigeon than is generally appreciated, and they depend on pasture weeds to a surprising degree.

July to September provides an easy living of ripe or partly ripe cereal grains, beginning with green barley in early July and finishing with the stubbles. With the latter the wheat is favoured and the birds move to the barley stubbles only after the wheat is finished or ploughed. At this time wood-pigeons take considerably more animal food, for example snails and woodlice, supposedly to increase their protein intake during the peak of the

23. A small flock dropping into a clover ley.

24. In the spring, when natural food is scarce, buds are favoured.

breeding season. They also drink considerably more, although this may be due to milk production for their young. Incidentally, the method of drinking by the Columbiformes differs from all the other birds, who sip and raise the head to swallow, whereas the former drink continuously with lowered head.

The final period of October to December begins with last gleanings on the stubbles, which is prolonged on those which have been undersown with clover and not ploughed. Once the grain is finished, the birds return to clover and woodland feeding, including beech nut, acorns, hawthorn and elder berries.

The statistics given by Murton on feeding are fascinating. In mid-winter necessity forces the pigeon to spend 95% of the day feeding. The possession of a crop gives the pigeon the advantage over other birds; it effectively lengthens the day by enabling the pigeon to fly to roost with a full crop, but this requires intense feeding activity as daylight fades. On average they consume no less than 35,000 items per day with a dry weight of about 45 grammes. These are taken at about sixty items per minute during the morning but this feeding rate increases to one hundred items per minute in the late afternoon. To gather the day's food a pigeon covers about three-quarters of a mile, with a pace of 4.2 inches, and, moving up to 12 inches on either side of its route, searches about one-tenth of an acre. I must interpose that my own observations do not support a rate of one hundred items per minute, or even sixty, but Dr Murton and his colleagues 'measured the feeding rates of pigeons under a wide variety of conditions by making repeated standardised observations throughout the day' and are doubtless right.

The first steps in the annual round of breeding begins as early as February, but more usually in March, when a few of the male birds begin to establish a territory. At first these individuals feed and sleep with the main flocks, occupying their chosen territories only at dawn and dusk, but, as spring advances and more males seek personal territories, the period spent in their territory increases. This instinct is assisted by increasing food supplies which in turn give greater leisure; and by July almost all their time is spent on their 'home' ground. Sadly that pleasant and familiar sound of early spring, the 'coo-cooo-coo-coo-co', is not the endearing song of a pigeon to its mate but the territorial call of a male warning off intruders. Actual fighting occurs between competing birds, with both wing striking and pecking. Murton believes the familiar soaring flight, culminating in a stall and a wing-clap, is also a form of territorial warning. Personally I have reservations, having witnessed it many times in my own garden by birds who are not seen again.

Unmated females entering a defended territory provoke a bowing display in the male, in which the bird erects and fans the tail and then bows its head repeatedly. If the female is ready caressing begins, a process of mutual billing and preening, although this stage is often preceded by nest-calling, a mixture of bowing and calling, by the male, which often begins when he has identified a suitable nest-site but not found a mate.

The pair may either renovate an old nest or build a new one, but the resulting structure is sparse: little more than a thin platform of twigs. Copulation begins at this time, usually in the territory, frequently on a favourite branch, but rarely outside the territory. The female normally lays two eggs over two days and incubation is shared with the male, but not on an equal basis. The female sits for about eighteen hours of the twenty-four and the male takes over from roughly 10.00 hours to 16.00 hours. The basis of two eggs per female is fairly constant and more than two eggs in a nest usually arises from a second female. Equally, a single egg normally means predation.

The normal incubation period is seventeen days, after which, for the first three days of life, the young are fed solely on crop milk. This is a secretion from the crop wall, a cheese-like substance, varying in the proportions of its constituents (water 65–81%, protein 13.3–18.8%, fat 6.9–12.7% and ash 1.5%). The protein is essential, not just for body growth but the development of feathers, which contain a quarter of the protein in the bird. After the initial three days the young receive increasing quantities of the foods eaten by the adults until, between seven and nine days, the proportion of milk has dropped to just under 50%. Between ten to fourteen days milk only accounts for about 33% and thereafter 20%. Brooding is shared by both parents, in the same timetable as incubation, and the young leave the nest after about twenty-two days. By this time the parents have begun a fresh nesting-cycle and may even have a second nest with eggs. The young are fed for a week or more after leaving the nest.

While it is true that pigeon nests have been found in most months of the year, the common belief that the birds have a long breeding season is wrong. Murton's observations showed that only 30% of the wood-pigeon population in his study area tried to breed before July and the great majority bred between July and September. This follows the principle that animals breed when the supplies of suitable food for their young will be at their greatest. (I write these words on Skye, in early April, when the only birds incubating are ravens and golden eagles. Their young will hatch to coincide with the carrion arising from the effects of winter on other animals.) For pigeon nestlings the most nutritious food is ripe cereal grain and the statistic of survival illustrates this vividly. Prior to July only 1% of nestlings leave the nest and only 6% in July. In August and September the figure leaps dramatically to 70%, falls to 21% in October and to only 2% in November.

Over the centuries the population and distribution of the wood-pigeon has seen major changes in this country. In 1678 Francis Willughby wrote: 'These Birds in Winter-time company together, and fly in flocks; they build in trees, making their Nests of a few sticks and straws. They feed upon Acorns, and also upon Corn, and Ivy and Holly Berries.' This paints a familiar picture to us, but the difference was in numbers, not habits, as all the evidence suggests the bird was thinly spread and partly dependent on woodland feeding. The great explosion in numbers came with changes in farming methods, not just because this increased the food supplies but did so during the lean months when the pigeon population in excess of the available food dies off. From early in the seventeenth century new crops were grown and Hayes, in 1775, wrote in *A Natural History of British Birds*, that 'In winter it is generally found in turnip fields, especially those bordering woods.' As new farming methods spread so the wood-pigeon followed, including a large increase in both numbers and range in Scotland in the nineteenth century. As an example, *The Zoologist*, in 1843, carried a report by A. Hepburn that, 'It was extremely rare in East Lothian about the end of the last century, where it now swarms to a most injurious degree.'

Attractive though turnips may have been to winter-hungry pigeons, the great innovation was the arrival of winter clover leys, providing not just a highly nutritious food but one easily gathered. As a result, we now find pigeon numbers are frequently greatest in highly cultivated areas where their natural woodland habitat is very limited. This produces a bonus for the shooting man, as large numbers of wood-pigeons are forced to concentrate on relatively few roosts and roost flighting at the end of each game season frequently gives excellent results.

Dr Murton's study was conducted in just such an area, in Cambridgeshire, and, measured on the basis of wood-pigeons per 100 acres, he found an average July population of 63 birds, which increased through breeding to 154 in September and then dwindled to 70 in February. In 1952 James Fisher estimated there were 1¼ million wood-pigeons in Britain, a figure which even an observant layman would have thought too low. Murton, in 1965, suggested the population was not less than five million each July and rose to ten million each September.

Thirty-six out of every hundred adult wood-pigeons die each year, so to maintain the population each pair must produce 0.72 young. In practice they produce an average 2.1 young, and can achieve this even if as many as 80% of all eggs laid are predated.

Adult wild wood-pigeons attain an average age of thirty-eight months, and the emphasis is on adult as birds of a year or more have a higher life expectation than juveniles. This apparently unrealistic statement is based on the fact that wood-pigeons, and for that matter most wild animals, do not die of old age but through a variety of causes, the most important of which are starvation, disease and predation. Juveniles, lacking experience, are more susceptible and therefore suffer a higher death rate. When we next grumble over some trifling inconvenience of modern living it might put things in perspective to recall that, not very long ago in the time-span of the world, humans also knew nothing of old age.

One minor product of Murton's studies illustrates how apparently minor variations in weather can have literally life and death consequences for wild

25. *Few birds can out-fly the wood-pigeon.*

life. A juvenile wood-pigeon leaves the nest weighing about 300 grammes and if it is to survive through the winter must increase to about 500 grammes by early December. It cannot do this on green food and is dependent on grain. Given a dry harvest the machinery operates efficiently, little grain is spilled and the stubbles are ploughed quickly. Wet weather delays the harvest, ripe ears spill more grain, the stubbles remain and more juvenile wood-pigeons survive the winter.

Whether or not wood-pigeons migrate has been a hot topic of the correspondence pages of sporting magazines for years. Blaine (1852) certainly thought so: 'The greater part emigrate at the beginning of winter, and return in the spring (some deny this; we do not, but on the contrary believe it).' Murton disagrees, and backs his dissent with weighty scientific evidence. He does not, however, say there is no migration: merely that the numbers involved represent a relatively small proportion of the total. In general the pigeon is a sedentary bird and a study showed only 11% of the adult population moving more than twenty-five miles. There are many reports of observed migrations and the simple explanation for many of these is the flocking of the wood-pigeons of an area which occurs each autumn. Dispersed for breeding, and largely hidden by foliage, the numbers are not obvious, but airborne in one flock and doubled in numbers by the juveniles it is easy to form the impression of a vast band of pigeons on the move. In addition to the evidence produced by banding juveniles, Murton gives other arguments against regular migration, although speculating that British wood-pigeons possess a latent migratory instinct which only a few follow. M. K. Colquhoun, in 1951, argued that many Scottish wood-pigeons migrated south into England during the winter, basing this on a decrease in Scottish flocks and an increase in English. Additional confusion arises from the habit of some inland roosts of pigeons of flying out to sea only to return. Obviously anyone observing only the inland journey would presume this to be a migration from abroad.

In Norway, Sweden, Finland and north-west Russia the persistent winter snow cover forces the migration of all the wood-pigeons, but populations are not large and Murton makes the point that if the entire estimated one million pigeons in Scandinavia migrated to Britain it would only represent a modest percentage increase. In fact there is ample evidence that the main passage is south-west through Europe to the west coast of France, with some crossing the Pyrenees to the cork oak forests of north-west Spain. Most of the movement takes place in October and there is an observation for October 21, 1950 of wood-pigeons passing through the Col de Zizarrieta in the Pyrenees at a rate of 6,380 per hour.

The general conclusion on migration is that no large-scale movement exists from the Continent to this country, or vice versa, but that individual birds may make the crossing, or flocks may drift over in certain wind conditions.

Older shooting men will recall with nostalgia the days when the Ministry of Agriculture refunded 50% of the cost of cartridges purchased for pigeon shooting. This happy situation began in 1954, but was ended in 1965, largely due to the conclusions of Dr Murton.

As we have seen, the ultimate control on wood-pigeon populations is the supply of food, and shooting can actually increase rather than decrease the population. This is a surprising statement, but consider the facts. By the autumn there are more pigeons than the available food supply can carry through the hard months. If none are shot, more mouths feed on the same food supply which therefore runs low sooner. The more pigeons shot the more food is available for the survivors and the net result by spring is a higher wood-pigeon population. The retort that this argument did not save the American passenger pigeon does not compare like with like, for the British wood-pigeon could be wiped out if shooting pressure was high enough. The decline would begin when the number shot in a year exceeded the number bred. Beneath that we merely shoot birds which would have died of other causes. In practice economic and sporting considerations make it unlikely that the annual bag will ever approach the annual breeding total. Cartridge costs have risen at a much greater rate than the value of the dead pigeons and, more importantly, as pigeon numbers decline and sport diminishes, so the enthusiasm to pursue them fades.

The wood-pigeon is at greatest risk from predators before it leaves the nest and vast numbers of eggs and young are taken each year by jays, magpies, crows and grey squirrels. Even the occasional stoat will take advantage of a low nest. Once the period of helplessness is over, their division of time between tree tops and green fields, coupled with flocking, makes them a difficult prey.

There is no specific disease which troubles wood-pigeons as, for example, strongylosis does grouse. Tuberculosis is probably the most common complaint and A. McDiarmid concluded (in 1960) that between 2% and 4% are tubercular. Tuberculosis appears to be fairly common in birds and McDiarmid believes the wood-pigeon to be the principal host.

Forms of fungal disease have been found in wood-pigeons, but appear not to be a major problem. Virus diseases are also present, including ornithosis, which is a potential hazard to humans, sometimes causing death. One tragic example occurred among Faroese women in 1930 who handled infected fulmar petrels. According to a report in the *Lancet* (23 July, 1960), when fourteen pigeon fanciers were examined *only* (my italics) one was infected with ornithosis. Avian pox is another virus affliction, leading to obscene swellings in the pigeon's body. It is believed that symptoms which are dismissed as avian or pigeon pox are sometimes the protozoan disease, trihomoniasis.

The wood-pigeon has at least its share of parasites, including a variety of blood parasites and worms, of which the most common of the latter is the order Trichurata. The genus *Capillaria* is very common, and is a very thin worm, up to half an inch long. Externally, the parasites can be divided into those which live in the nest, for example the red mite, pigeon ticks and the bug, *Cimex columbarius*, and those preferring the more turbulent but prolific larder of the pigeon itself. Space does not permit, nor I suspect do my readers desire, a detailed list of the latter, but they include various lice, fleas and the dipteran fly. Readers are more likely to have encountered the latter as the unpleasant, and almost unsquashable, flat fly which is often found crawling over one's body, usually on the head, after handling recently shot grouse.

All in all, the wood-pigeon does not carry a greater burden of potential disease than any other living animal, including man. However, man has, in recent years, imposed a major threat on the pigeon by way of agricultural poisons. What had been a minor threat increased dramatically in 1956 when the large scale use of cereals dressed with chlorinated hydrocarbons began. It is the organochlorine group which is particularly fatal to animals and this includes dieldrin and DDT. This group is doubly menacing for some forms are both highly toxic and persistent, leading to deaths throughout the food chain. The effect on pigeons was dramatic and it was calculated that on one estate of less than 1,500 acres, nearly 7,000 wood-pigeons were poisoned in the spring of 1961. Fortunately for the pigeon, which is not loved by farmers, many other species also suffered and the use of the more dangerous forms of toxic insecticides has now been severely restricted.

Not all the feeding habits of wood-pigeons are harmful to agriculture. For example, if clover is not required during the winter, extensive feeding by pigeons will have no effect on the ultimate crop, and some weed eating from pastures is beneficial. This defence uttered, however, the pigeon is a major problem for farmers and many experiments have been carried out to discover a form of chemical repellent which will discourage the pest but not harm the product. Tests showed wood-pigeons have at least a simple sense of taste, but, not surprisingly, anything strong enough to discourage the pigeon would also have discouraged the customers. The ideal solution would be a selective poison which killed only wood-pigeons, but this is impractical as suitable baits will be taken by many other species. One solution, which has been explored ever since 1942, was narcotic chemicals which would put the animal to sleep for long enough for the operator to kill the harmful species and place the remainder in safety until they recovered. The first combination was tribromoethanol and peas, but the chemical was volatile and usually lost its power before being eaten by the pigeons. Eventually the combination developed to tic beans and alpha-chloralose, the former having gained favour because it was too large to be eaten by small birds. I well remember the shudder of anticipation that ran through the pigeon shooting community when extensive trials began in the early sixties. Having lost the rabbit to myxomatosis, were we now to lose the pigeon? The outcome demonstrated the gap that so often exists between theory and practice. It is one thing for scientists to select the right weather and crop, lay the bait, recover the sleeping (or, sometimes, dead bodies), nurse the innocent back to the wild and generally monitor the results. It is a very different matter for busy farmers, short of working hands and with many other urgent tasks, and even given time and labour a sudden fall of rain could render the bait harmless. Nor, even assuming a successful operation, was it necessarily economically worthwhile. The whole procedure would have to continue over a period and the cost of materials and labour could well exceed the value of the damage that *might* otherwise have been done to the crop. Given this practical drawback it is difficult to see a future for narcotic baits.

What of the future for the wood-pigeon? For the last decade or so there have been frequent suggestions by laymen that numbers are falling, and little scientific investigation to give authoritative guidance either way. One has to be very sceptical of lay statements, for the individual may be given to sweeping conclusions on little evidence and even if his assessments are sound they may only reflect local changes. Additionally, a letter to the sporting press reporting a shortage of this or that species will spawn a dozen or so further letters from those who agree, often in alarmist terms, and the belief takes root without weight being given to the many thousands who see no shortage and make no comment. However, enough sportsmen have been reporting a pigeon shortage for so many years that it is difficult to dismiss their views.

What little scientific evidence there is comes from the Game Conservancy in the the form of their National Game Census, which includes the number of pigeons shot over the observed area for more than twenty years. Put simply, it shows the bag in 1981 was roughly half that of 1961 and, all other things being equal, would prove a much reduced pigeon population. Equality, however, may be missing. For example, while driven game shots will cheerfully take part in roost flighting they rarely spend long hours in hides, decoying, and the men that did so in 1961, or their equivalents, may now spend more time polishing a car or watching the Saturday afternoon sport on television. Nor is pigeon shooting in the nineteen eighties as financially rewarding as in the sixties. In other words, if fewer men go pigeon shooting, fewer pigeons will be shot.

However, one statistic from the survey is significant: the total acreage of clover and oilseed rape grown on the study area fell over the twenty-year period to less than 50 per cent. From this emerges the logical conclusion that fewer pigeons were shot because the population was down and this fall occurred through a reduction in food supplies. It was, after all, changes in agricultural methods that put the pigeon population up and now the same cause has brought it down.

We need not, however, fear for the wood-pigeon. Numbers may fall, but I find it hard to ever see this wary bird as an endangered species.

14

The Rabbit

Writing in *British Game* in 1946, Vesey-Fitzgerald was critical of the rabbit, suggesting that it did not deserve 'the honour of a column in the game book'. His written judgement based this unkindness on the harm it did to agriculture, forestry and even game preserves, but game books assess not the hazards of farming but the sporting value of quarries and on this score the rabbit ranks high. Zig-zagging through the bramble or bounding across a ride it is ignored by the guns at a formal driven shoot only for reasons of safety. This occasion apart, the rabbit provides fine sport and, incidentally, has been the downfall of countless sporting dogs whose owners had hitherto believed well-trained.

Both rabbits and hares are grouped under the order *Lagomorpha* and this order is divided into two families. One, the *Ochotonidae*, or pikas, has only one genus, lacks an external tail and, living no nearer than Russia, will not be further mentioned. The second family, the *Leporidae*, has nine genera, of which eight relate to rabbits, one being the European rabbit *Oryctolagus cuniculus* Linnaeus 1758. This, in turn, is divided into six sub-species of which the British version, *Oryctolagus cuniculus cuniculus*, is the most widely spread, inhabiting the whole of central Europe, north of the Mediterranean region and west as far as Ireland. Successful artificial introductions have also been made to other areas of the world. The remaining five sub-species are located around the Mediterranean area, with Morocco having no less than three.

In the vernacular, and prior to the eighteenth century, only the young were known as rabbits, the adults being called coneys (cwningen in Welsh) and an area of densely populated burrows was variously referred to as a coneygarth, conyger or conigrie. Local names included warreners, for rabbits in an established warren, parkers for those in open, or park, countryside, hedgehogs for residents above ground in thickly wooded areas and sweethearts for pet rabbits in captivity.

The history of how and when the rabbit reached Britain gives scope for fascinating argument. Most writers favour the thirteenth century on the

146

grounds that there is no record of the rabbit in English literature prior to that period. There is a record of rabbits on the Scilly Isles in 1176 and references appear for Lundy Island in 1183, 1219 and 1274, when, in the later year, 2,000 rabbit skins were mentioned. Early in the fourteenth century rabbits became an important item at feasts, although as they commanded a high price they seem to have been relatively scarce.

If the thirteenth century, or thereabouts, is indeed the date of the rabbit's introduction then it would almost certainly have been brought in by the Normans and this theory is favoured by the majority of authors writing on the subject. Personally, I favour the second, but much less well supported, theory of a Roman introduction. We know from Pliny that their soldiers ferreted and also that they frequently shipped live rabbits from Spain to Roman markets for food. Would such an enterprising race have occupied Britain for 400 years and not imported rabbits for sport and food? Solid evidence comes from Marcus Terrentius Varro, who in his *Rerum Rusticarum* wrote, in 54 BC, that the Romans brought rabbits to Britain from Spain and reared them in *leporaria*. Some, surely, must have escaped, not least because there was no pressing reason to prevent them.

The argument for a Norman introduction rests entirely on a negative proposition—that no mention meant no existence, and this is inconclusive. In my book *Pugs and Drummers* I examined the possibility that the rabbit was here long before the Normans and the Romans. To state the case in detail would take far too long, but the essence of the argument is that while the rabbit must have been driven out by the last ice age (or more precisely by the Third Glacial Phase of the Last Glaciation) about 22,000 years ago, it could, theoretically at least, have recolonised from Europe before the melting ice caused the rise in sea levels which severed the land bridge to Europe, across what is now the Channel, about 5,000 BC. Certainly rabbits, if only in very few numbers, were in Britain before the last ice invasion, for fossil remains have been found from the Hoxian interglacial deposits at Swanscombe, Kent. Additionally, remains at Thatcham, Berkshire, have been radio-carbon dated at about 7,500 BC. This later discovery is more significant, for while any population existing in the interglacial would almost certainly have been driven from Britain by the advancing ice, the climate has only improved from 7,500 BC.

Even without the Thatcham evidence there was still a period of some three thousand years in which the Channel land bridge existed and climatic and vegetation conditions in Britain were suitable for rabbits. It is believed the land bridge was the main factor in the recolonisation of a thawed-out Britain by more than 95 per cent of our animals. Given that rabbits were, like our other animals, a living tide, ebbing and flowing before the ice, there is good reason to assume they were well established before the first Roman stepped ashore.

As a quarry the rabbit is on a par with the pigeon. It has no close season, does not attract visitors to an area, nor does it provide work for locals except in its extermination as distinct from sport. These negatives dispensed with, it ranks as one of the minor but consistently popular quarry species for the shooting man.

The pelt of a rabbit is not one, but three coats. The base coat is dense and soft and through this protrudes the longer coarser hairs of the main outer coat. This, again, is exceeded by a third coat of longer hairs but these are sparse. All three coats become denser in winter, and there is an annual moult which begins in March and, in the case of the undercoat, is not complete until the late autumn. Colouring varies locally, but the norm is grey-brown over the upper part, lightening underneath and turning to reddish-brown at the back of the neck. The throat and underpart of the tail are white, but the upper tail and the tips of the ears are blackish.

The feet are 'shod' with thick hair and the hindlegs are much longer and stronger than the forelegs. The latter provides one of the few ways of distinguishing between young and adult rabbits, for the epiphysial cartilage between the head and shaft of the tibia remains unfused until the age of approximately nine and a half months.

The average weight of a wild rabbit is 1.3–1.8 kg, with variations between areas due to available food supplies, with the females weighing slightly less than males. The stomach and intestines account for about 20 per cent of the weight and the weekly gain from four weeks of age varies between 40–60 g. The length of an adult's head and body runs up to 400 mm.

Being a gnawing animal, the rabbit is equipped with chisel-shaped incisor teeth, with two pairs in the upper jaw. It lacks canine teeth and there is a wide gap between the incisors and the cheek teeth. Each side of the upper jaw contains six cheek teeth and the lower jaw five, all being traverse edged to facilitate the grinding of vegetable matter. The incisors are rootless and grow throughout the life of the animal, occasionally producing grotesque 'tusks' where chance has prevented the natural wear caused by upper and lower incisors meeting.

Both the hearing and sight of the rabbit are good, the ears being large and the eyes placed well to the sides of the head. The long whiskers, being sensitive to touch, are useful to an animal living underground and moving outdoors mainly at night. There are four scent glands—on the chin, beside the eye and anus and around the rectum.

A study of the distribution of the rabbit in Britain over the centuries only provides a fragmented picture. Directly or indirectly there are numerous reports proving where, and when, rabbits existed, but these are incidental and incomplete. However, a useful guide for the late eighteenth century comes from the then Board of Agriculture reports, which show man-made rabbit warrens distributed throughout the country, with the exception only

26. Even at rest rabbits remain alert.

27. Wild rabbit of approximately three weeks.

of most of Wales. The larger warrens would enclose many acres of land and produce thousands of rabbits each year. They, and duck decoys, provided fresh meat to the towns and cities during the centuries when the lack of cold storage meant the source of supply had to be near the markets. Needless to say, where there were warrens there were escapees, so it is reasonable to assume rabbits were widely distributed but, by all accounts, not numerous.

At the beginning of the nineteenth century changes in farming practices encouraged land owners to destroy their warrens to put the ground to more profitable use and the wild population probably decreased. However, the decline was shortlived for two new developments favoured the rabbit. Firstly, an increasing human population brought more land under cultivation, giving the rabbit both more food and, with winter fodder crops, food when it was most needed. Secondly, shooting as a sport developed rapidly, particularly on the great sporting estates. The ranks of gamekeepers swelled and every creature harmful to pheasants and partridges, and, incidentally, rabbits, was pursued and their numbers reduced.

The rabbit population not so much flourished as exploded, and the literature of the period abounds with reports of their numbers, varying from the dry language of official reports to the desperate pleas of tenant farmers. One statistic provides a vivid example—in 1861, on one day and on one estate only, 3,333 rabbits were shot.

By the 1930s the rabbit population was estimated at around thirty million and the lack of control during the war years allowed further increases until, in the early 1950s, some authorities put the figure as high as one hundred million.

Given suitable habitat, rabbits can be found up to the tree line anywhere throughout Britain, although as it is agriculture which provides the most prolific feeding they are rarely dense away from man. Ideally, rabbits seek short grasses close to refuge and the old pattern of small pasture fields and hedgerows was perfect. Light, sandy soils are favourite, but burrows are found in chalk, shale, loam and even clay. Ease of digging will be a factor in their preference for sandy soils, but the greater influence is probably the drier burrows created by the better drainage. A normal hole has a diameter of about 15 cm except where enlarged into a chamber. No set plan is followed and the result is a twisting confusion which can be as deep as 3 m, but more usually is less than 1 m.

As a burrow grows in size to contain several families so it becomes a warren, and within this warren exists a complex and interesting social structure. Central to this is the oldest buck and doe, surrounded by their children and grandchildren and, as in our own society, there are the privileged and the not-so-favoured. The dominant pair live in the drier area of the warren, enjoy the best grazing and produce more and stronger young. They, in turn, gain better quarters, better mates, and ensure the dominance of the line. The less strong does live in the inferior quarters and if overcrowding begins may have to leave for new territories. Few of the young bucks are strong enough to win a mate in their first year and must either live in subordination to the superior bucks or leave the warren. It is from these emigrants that new warrens are formed and as these are established and the population grows so a new social structure of the dominant and subservient is formed.

Within the warren the bucks are possessive and aggressive, sometimes fighting to the death with a competing buck, while the does are peaceful and concerned with rearing. Rabbits are naturally clean, preening frequently with tongue and forepaws. Natural functions are performed outdoors with small elevations, such as molehills, being selected as permanent latrines. They are, of course, mainly nocturnal and most of the day, underground, is spent sleeping, emerging at dusk or earlier on sunny afternoons. Wind has no effect on their behaviour but rain is disliked and they emerge less, and for shorter periods, on wet nights.

R. M. Lockley, the author of *The Private Life of the Rabbit*, which in turn inspired Richard Adams' bestselling novel *Watership Down*, spent five years watching rabbit behaviour in a specially constructed warren and was emphatic that mating never took place below ground. As the very few reports of mating above ground occur at dusk, the great majority of mating activity must take place at night. Lockley observed very firm and permanent pairings between individual bucks and does, but this picture of fidelity is shattered by evidence from other observations, showing that virtually all does become pregnant no matter how much their numbers may exceed the bucks. Sexual behaviour above ground may be observed in daylight, varying from the buck chasing the doe; the buck laying his tail along his back to display his underside to the doe; simple affection such as licking and nuzzling; preliminary but rebuffed copulation; and, finally, enurination, where the buck emits a jet of urine at the doe.

Urine and faeces are also used to mark the territories of individual bucks, supplemented by a colourless liquid from the scent gland under the jaw. Although communication is mainly olfactory, alarm is signalled visually by flashing the tail during running. Vocally rabbits will grunt, growl, squeak and scream, the latter sound probably being used to indicate anger as well as terror. No research has been done on the hearing ability of the rabbit but commonsense observation suggests it is excellent.

Rabbits rarely move far from their burrows, usually staying within a radius of two hundred metres but doubling this where populations are low. Being timid, they range less widely on moonlit nights. Their journeys to the feeding areas follow well established runs, along which they leap rather than run. At slow speeds one foreleg is ahead of the other, but as speed increases the two limbs move together. Walking occurs only when feeding and even then only intermittently.

Ten rabbits eat roughly as much as one sheep, which makes the sheep roughly three times more efficient than the rabbit at converting grazing to meat. Granted the sheep has to be cared for throughout its life, but the labour costs of putting ten wild rabbits into the butcher's window are much more than the sheep.

In times of shortage rabbits will eat almost anything, but their preference is for young plants and, allowed access, they do great damage in young plantations. Given sufficient rabbits and time they will destroy woodlands, for as the old trees die the rabbits prevent natural regeneration. In the hills they eat heather and will gradually drive it back to higher levels. Practically all agricultural crops are attractive to them, including cereals, roots and pasture. With the latter, the cultivated species of grasses are slowly extinguished until mainly wild varieties with creeping habits remain.

Given a choice, which on normal farmland is usually the case, rabbits exhibit various dislikes. They will not eat rhododendrons, arum, lords and ladies, cowslip, primrose, burdock, comfrey, nettles, or sorrel. Honeysuckle, hawthorn, dogwood and azalea are also avoided, although possibly not to the same degree.

Rabbits are seen to feed vigorously at dawn and dusk, although there is some doubt as to how intensively they feed during the night. Lockley's observations showed that they remained out of the burrows at night but that feeding would probably be intermittent. Commonsense suggests a heavy meal at dusk, odd snacks throughout the night and a large breakfast to face a day underground. In fact, the ability of the rabbit to chew the cud by reingestion staves off hunger very successfully. When food is first taken it is formed into small, soft pellets within a membrane and containing about 56% bacteria, of which the protein content is 36% and the plant matter 11%. Several hours after eating, these small pellets are evacuated and then swallowed by the rabbit. In due course, and after more thorough digestion, the waste is again evacuated as the larger, harder, pellets with which we are familiar. Some observers believe reingestion is a device of nature to allow the rabbit to gather food rapidly, reducing the dangerous period of exposure and reingesting safely under cover. However, the majority see it merely as a more efficient use of food.

Finally, before leaving the rabbit's stomach and turning to its other main interest (Lockley once wrote, 'Humans are so rabbit'), there is the question of drinking. I have never observed a rabbit drink; no authority exists which states that they do and two specifically say they do not. Most of the food of the rabbit has a high water content and doubtless this suffices.

The number of animals preying on the rabbit, either to eat it or, in the case of humans, destroy it, is so formidable that any less productive species would have been eliminated years ago. It is a favourite sport of naturalists to calculate the number of offspring of a single pair of rabbits if undisturbed for four years and while the answers vary they range in millions rather than thousands.

Although rabbits will breed throughout the year, the main season is January to June and during the peak period 90% of does are pregnant at any given time. This is hardly surprising as a doe mates again within twelve hours of giving birth and produces the litter twenty-eight to thirty days later. Fertilisation is almost certain, for the eggs are released from the ovary not at regular intervals but shed in response to the act of mating. The average litter size is five or six and the female kittens can breed before they themselves are adults, in about eight weeks.

Nature, having given the rabbit this remarkable capacity to multiply, also provided a form of birth control which is regulated by circumstances as necessary. Not less than 60% of all litters conceived are neither born nor aborted but die in the uterus and the material forming the embryos is reabsorbed into the mother's body. Reabsorption also accounts for an average loss of 9 to 10% from all litters which proceed to birth. Scientists are, in the main, reluctant to advance a reason for reabsorption but Lockley felt it is due to stress caused by overcrowding. This is an appealing argument for, if true, it provides both a reason for triggering off the reabsorption and gives an excellent example of nature making provision for a widely ranging birthrate according to local need. The only other animal to share this capacity is the hare.

Towards the end of her period of pregnancy the doe makes a nest either by digging a separate 'stop' near to the warren, or making a short tunnel in the warren itself. This is lined with vegetation and fur plucked from her own breast. The litter, or kindle, is born without hair, sight or hearing and the doe conceals the entrance and leaves them to seek out her buck (or any buck, if one believes those observers with little regard for the morality of rabbits) and start the whole procedure anew. Doubt exists as to the precise development of the kittens in the nest but Sheail says the eyes open on the eleventh day, the ears on the twelfth and the kittens can stand on the thirteenth. At about three weeks they leave the nest weighing approximately 150 g.

Suckling takes place only about once every twenty-four hours and the young double their weight in the first week. After leaving the nest they graze outside, close by, and under the eye of their mother now well advanced in her next pregnancy. During the second month the young become increasingly independent, although the extent to which a relationship between young and mother persists in the long term is not clear. Lockley suggested a continuing relationship but other researchers were not convinced. Commonsense suggests this will depend on the size of the burrow or warren—in large, overcrowded warrens youngsters will be forced to leave to find both space and food, whereas in a small one-family burrow a few hours digging would suffice to enlarge the accommodation.

As with most other animals the number of young produced in a year by an adult female depends largely on the quality of food available. Watson, working in New Zealand, estimated that dominant females (that is to say strong does enjoying the better quarters and grazing), could average five young per litter and five litters per year, although the average was usually nearer twenty young than the theoretical twenty-five. In this country the average is believed to be just under ten.

In 1898 Harting, a highly respected naturalist of the period, wrote: 'What is certain is that we shall always have him (the rabbit) not only in a sufficiency but in superabundance.' For the next half century his words were entirely accurate: quietly, but very successfully, the rabbit filled its ecological niche until, in 1953, the arrival of myxomatosis brought disaster of such proportions as to make the Black Death plague of the fourteenth century seem relatively mild. The latter killed one third of the human population of Europe, but in many areas myxomatosis left only one rabbit in two hundred alive.

By coincidence it was in the same year, 1898, that Harting forecast the invulnerability of the rabbit, that myxomatosis was first reported in South America. The visual effects of the disease are most unpleasant. After an incubation period of five to seven days there is a watery discharge from the eyes. This thickens, the eyelids swell together and very shortly the animal is blinded. The bases of the ears and other parts of the body, particularly around the nose, chin, anus and genitals, may also swell. These swellings consist of a jelly-like tissue and, except for the survivors, death comes between eleven and eighteen days after infection.

Although the appearance of infected rabbits is appalling, many observers do not feel they suffer badly and my own experience confirms this. I have frequently watched badly afflicted, and totally blind, rabbits grazing and basking in the sun. Both animals and humans, when in pain, lose the desire to eat. Lockley even suggests they will attempt to mate when only a few hours from death.

Unsuccessful attempts were made to introduce myxomatosis into Australia prior to the last war, but in 1950 seven further liberations were made, six failing and the other proving remarkably successful. By chance, the latter attempt had been made in a wet area with a high mosquito population and, as was ultimately discovered, the myxomatosis virus can be spread by any blood-sucking or biting arthropod. The disease decimated the Australian rabbit population, killing many millions and attracting the thoughtful attention of European agriculturalists who saw it as a cheap and effective, albeit terrible, solution to their own rabbit problem. In June 1952 a retired physician obtained myxoma virus from Switzerland and inoculated two wild rabbits on his estate near Paris. By the end of 1953 the disease was rampant throughout not just France but Belgium, Luxembourg, Germany, Spain and the Netherlands.

It is possible, but highly unlikely, that the disease spread naturally. It is far more probable that the farmers of Europe grasped the chance to eliminate or

28. Caught in mid-leap.

29. Severe myxomatosis.

reduce the rabbit and transported infected animals across not just their countryside but national boundaries. Only this could explain why the disease spread in leaps across unaffected areas, rather than steadily like an advancing tide.

The first outbreak in Britain was confirmed on 13th October, 1953 at Bough Beech in Kent and within a fortnight it had reached East Sussex. November saw it in Essex and December, Suffolk. At this time, and based on the Australian experience, it was believed the vector was the mosquito and that, as this insect only over-winters as eggs or larvae, the disease might die out. Far from dying, myxomatosis lay low during the winter then, in the spring, galloped on to such widely spaced locations as Cornwall, Norfolk and Radnor. Research eventually showed that the vector in this country is the rabbit flea, which further proved the hand of man in spreading the disease.

However, a puzzle remained: why, as rabbit fleas are permanently resident on their hosts, did myxomatosis lie dormant in the winter only to spread rapidly in the spring? For the answer we have to thank the work of A. R. Mead-Briggs, who discovered that the breeding activities of the rabbit flea are considerably more calculated than hitherto suspected. Were the female flea to mate and lay her eggs on the rabbit indiscriminately, the chance of their survival would be small. The eggs would fall to the bare floor of the burrow and the larvae, once hatched, would have little chance of finding dried blood, their principal dietary component. Instead the female flea only mates on pregnant doe rabbits and, incredibly, times the mating until the stage when her own eggs can hatch into the nest of the newly-born kittens. In this ideal environment the flea larvae are themselves incapable of piercing the skin of the young rabbits, but feed on the faeces of their own parents, formed from partly digested blood. If, then, the flea breeds when the rabbit breeds, and this occurs principally in spring, we can see why myxomatosis spreads rapidly at this time.

Prior to myxomatosis the population structure of rabbits was very stable: although numbers might fluctuate, an area which was favoured would always hold rabbits. Now, although their reproductive ability remains high, continual fresh outbreaks of myxomatosis may cause extreme variations. Some low density local populations will decline and disappear altogether, only for in-comers to start a new colony which may prosper until once again crashing. By 1973, twenty years after the arrival of the disease, it was estimated that the rabbit population of the entire country was only about 5 per cent of pre-myxomatosis days. Now, in 1983, numbers are still well below pre-myxomatosis levels but annual national surveys from 1973 onwards have shown that since 1975 there has been a slow but continuing increase in the distribution of rabbits in Britain, particularly in east and south-east England.

A survey of juvenile recruitment into the adult population in 1979, in Wales, showed a ratio of 1.96 young of the year per adult rabbit. Although this was low compared with the potential increase in numbers, it was higher than the samples of 0.77 and 1.48 in 1971 and 1978.

Population studies in England and Wales from 1971 have shown relatively stable overwinter rabbit numbers, with no long-term increase; but summer rabbit numbers vary greatly between years, influenced by various factors. Rabbit control operations can at least halve the summer population, if carried out effectively in late winter; high predator levels can also reduce summer populations dramatically by removing most juveniles as quickly as they are produced.

The formation of Rabbit Clearance Societies was officially encouraged in 1958, in the aftermath of myxomatosis; the objective being to promote self-help among farmers/landowners and prevent a resurgence of the rabbit damage to crops of 1920–53. The movement had a measure of success but now only a few persistent societies remain. Changes in virulence of the myxoma virus and the development of innate resistance by the rabbit have led to an increase in the numbers and in crop damage. Direct reduction of numbers is effective only in the short-term and so must often be repeated; the most promising long-term approach may be by modification of habitat, but to be effective one must know which natural factors have most effect on numbers and how these can be altered by man.

Even spared from myxomatosis the life-span of the wild rabbit is determined not by how long it can live but how long it can survive the dangers of its environment. The work of H. B. Southern, over one breeding season, showed 36 does produced 280 young which emerged above ground. Of these no less than 252 failed to survive the season and 59 of the 70 adults also disappeared. Given protection in a pen a wild rabbit could expect to live not less than ten years, but in the harsh natural world eighteen months is about average. This poor performance is understandable when one considers that virtually every predator looks to the rabbit for sustenance. Foxes eat not just the adults but dig up the young. Wild and domestic cats, stoats, and (where present) golden eagles and polecats, take the adults. Buzzards, weasels and badgers feast off the young. Most of the owls, ravens, hooded and carrion crows, and black-backed gulls seize any chance offered. And man is always a threat, persecuting the rabbit for food, sport, or to protect his agricultural operations.

If this were not enough, the rabbit has at least its share of parasites. In addition to the flea, *spilopsyllus cuniculi*, previously discussed, it has two mites, a sucking louse and a sheep tick. Internally there are several parasites: tapeworms, liver flukes and several species of nematodes. In addition to myxomatosis the rabbit also suffers from the disease of coccidiosis, although this is normally only responsible for high mortality in high density areas and among young rabbits.

Considering all the factors ranged against this timid and defenceless animal, one can but admire its rugged survival.

PART III

WILDFOWL

Wildfowl

Fascinating though the various species of birds and animals we have considered so far have been, we move now to the wildfowl, whose lives have an extra dimension—the magic of long distance migration. Granted that woodcock migrate and some contented mallard live and die within a few square miles: these exceptions apart, wildfowl have a special appeal to one's imagination. Dimly, but just sufficiently to marvel, we can visualise the long, energy-draining, flight to the far north to breed: the vast, wild, unspoilt expanses of land and water briefly released from the grip of the northern frosts: the beauty of a brief summer there and the urgency to breed and retreat before the return of the ice: and the long passage south again, with many of the fowl heading for Britain. For many countries the winter sees the land largely denuded of birds, but we, in Britain, are enriched by the geographical good fortune of being a small island. The relatively warm sea waters make this country a haven for wildfowl frozen off the Continental areas to follow the flight of their ancestors for thousands of years to us.

On arrival modern wildfowl find both good and bad points when compared to their predecessors. To their detriment, there are substantially fewer areas of suitable wetlands, but they have the advantage of a more enlightened reception from the natives.

In the nineteenth century wildfowlers considered any bird encountered along the shoreline as fair game and the classic books on the sport give detailed instructions for shooting many birds long since protected. One of my favourite photographs shows Stanley Duncan, the co-founder of the Wildfowlers Association of Great Britain and Ireland, and as such regarded as a pioneer in correct behaviour, entering the old black hut at Patrington with a bundle of birds on his back which includes a heron. This would have been taken about 1908; if we move back about another century we are in the era of the famous Colonel Peter Hawker. Although we are indebted to the Colonel for a book and a diary which, together, give a vivid picture of shooting at that time, his concept of sportsmanship did not include much regard for his quarry. Success in bagging whichever species came his way—*whichever* species—was paramount, and considerations such as giving the quarry a sporting chance, or avoiding crippling where possible, were not allowed to interfere.

Those days are long past and the wildfowler of today has an excellent reputation in the field of conservation. It is also rare to meet a wildfowler who is not a good naturalist, for the conditions are so rugged, and success so comparatively rare, that no man would persevere were he not captivated by the atmosphere and the wild life encountered.

Of course not all wildfowl are found below the high water mark and it is interesting to look briefly at the habitat changes which have affected inland wildfowl, whether residents or migrants. Most writers on the subject have drawn attention to the enormous areas of wetland lost to wildfowl through drainage. The tendency is to regard this as a relatively modern problem; but in fact many of the writers of the second half of the nineteenth century were sounding the alarm and making gloomy forecasts for the future. However, while much has been lost there have been not inconsiderable gains. One, often unappreciated, asset is the extensive network of canals, built in the eighteenth and nineteenth centuries, and now fallen into disuse and disrepair. We naturalists must view the activities of the bands of amateur organisations, anxious to renovate and re-use them, with a distinct lack of enthusiasm.

Urban lakes, built to beautify cities, offer more than is often appreciated. Greater London alone has some two hundred acres of water, divided into forty lakes, and with a winter population of some two thousand mallard. Another unusual source of wildfowl habitat is permanent or semi-permanent floodwater gathering in subsidences caused by mining operations. One good example, Fairburn Ings in Yorkshire, has become a local Nature Reserve. The lagoons and drying-out fields of sewage farms make ideal habitat although, regrettably, the trend is now to construct the more compact chemical type of system which takes less land. Gravel pits are a prolific source of new wet areas and, as concrete is in continuing demand, there is every reason to expect existing gravel workings to be enlarged and new ones to be opened. In an average year something like 500 ha of wet gravel pits are excavated and roughly half of these will be flooded. Such massive alteration to the countryside has to be carefully policed and the various Planning Authorities do not give consent readily and, where they do, conditions are imposed to minimise the impact. Happily the gravel industry is taking its social responsibilities seriously, as witness the Wildfowl Research Centre at Great Linford in Buckinghamshire. This is constructed on the site of disused gravel workings and has been financed by the Amey Roadstone Corporation and is managed by the Game Conservancy.

Finally we have reservoirs which have grown in number to meet the needs of an increasing population and greater industrial demand. There are some 550 reservoirs in England and Wales, providing about 55 square miles of water. However the majority are of little use to wildfowl, being either too small, set at too high an altitude or in an exposed setting offering little shelter or food. Eliminating the unsuitable reduces the count to about one hundred and fifty reservoirs each of which may hold anything from two hundred and fifty duck to a thousand or more.

The life-style of wildfowl makes it much harder to estimate populations than with sedentary species, and, in particular, nest counts in the far north are impossible. However, the International Waterfowl Research Bureau now organises large scale winter counts in which the number of each species is counted, on a given day, to provide estimates of numbers and the main locations.

I must restrict my descriptions of wildfowl to those which form the principal quarries of the sportsman. Among the ducks these are the mallard, wigeon, teal and pintail; and of the geese the pink-footed, the whitefront and lesser whitefront, the greylag and the canada. The barnacle can be shot on Islay, in the Inner Hebrides, which is one of the world's most important wintering areas for this species. The brent goose is a protected species, but numbers have risen so substantially that it is now a nuisance not just to farmers but to other wildfowl. In the waters where it has become prolific it now takes much of the zosgrass which previously supported other species. There are good logical reasons for removing the brent from the protected list, but much of the support for conservation is based upon sentimentality rather than science and any attempt in this direction would doubtless raise a storm of protests.

In view of our unique position as hosts to a vast over-wintering population of wild fowl, coupled with this country's reputation for scientific research, it is not surprising that we have an institution devoted to wildfowl research which enjoys a world-wide reputation. This is the Wildfowl Trust, based at Slimbridge in Gloucester and grant-aided by the Nature Conservancy. Nor should one overlook the labours of smaller, but very professional, units, such as the previously mentioned Game Conservancy's Wildfowl Research Centre at Great Linford, or the Sevenoaks Experimental Wildfowl Reserve at Sevenoaks (created by the late Dr Jeffery Harrison and now so ably continued by his widow, Dr Pamela Harrison).

In the realm of pure conservation, wildfowl are well served by the chain of County Naturalists' Trusts or, as many are now called, County Trusts for Nature Conservation. These admirable voluntary bodies provide, either by acquisition or management, many good habitats. Nor must one overlook the major contribution of BASC—the British Association for Shooting and Conservation—which is the present-day form of the Wildfowlers Association. Through its various affiliated bodies, BASC has set up many coastal reserves, providing important sanctuaries.

By virtue of their mobility, wild fowl do not 'belong' to any one country, but Britain can reasonably claim to be playing a major part in maintaining these admirable birds.

30. The mallard is not given the credit it deserves for the beauty of its colouring and feathering.

31. Duck mallard—we take it for granted that all birds retract their 'undercarriage'.

The Anatini *(Dabbling Ducks)*

All the four species to be covered herein, mallard, wigeon, teal and pintail, are members of the *Anatini* tribe of the order *Anseriformes* and it will save repetition to deal with some common aspects under this general heading.

Dabbling or surface-feeding (which does not mean their food is necessarily on the surface) duck are all small to medium size wildfowl. Although the males are slightly larger, there is no marked difference between the size of the sexes. Both wings and tails are pointed, but while the tails are short the wings are long. Bills are of medium length and flattened to suit their mode of feeding. The legs are short and positioned centrally, so the stance places the body horizontally. All members take off and land on water with ease, particularly the teal which achieves near-vertical ascent. In the opposite direction they have a limited capacity to dive, which they do by using their wings.

Both sexes of most *anatini* have a bright speculum and are also alike in other aspects of plumage. In both male and female there is little difference between breeding and non-breeding plumage.

The preferred habitat of dabbling ducks is shallow, productive waters with rich vegetation along the margins. They avoid exposed marine waters and also faster rivers and streams, unless these contain quiet backwaters and pools. Ideally water should be standing or slow flowing, with thick, fringe vegetation and shallow margins rather than an immediate transition into deep water. The latter gives food and the former cover for nesting and the flightless stage of the post-breeding moult.

Most *Anatini* are omnivorous and feed by pumping water and mud through the bill, sieving out the food with the lamella. Some exist entirely by dabbling, taking seeds and invertebrates from shallow water, while others also forage on land. Although sometimes found singly, duck are naturally gregarious and are usually in pairs or flocks.

To breed they form monogamous pair-bonds, the relationship usually lasting for one season only with northern migratory duck but longer with residents. The short-term pair bonds normally commence in autumn or winter in the flocks and terminate when the female is incubating and the males begin to flock together again. As anyone who has observed park duck in the breeding season will have seen, the males—in spite of their firm pair-bonds—are highly promiscuous and rape is part of their life-style.

The courtship and mating procedures of the *Anatini* are complex and the importance of some aspects is not as yet fully understood. As preliminaries there are courtship-flights in which several males merely chase a female; three-bird flights, when a male chases the female of a pair who have trespassed into its activity centre; and rape-intent flights, which are a more advanced form of the courtship-flight. These activities are essentially communal and it is thought may have the role of dispersing pairs.

True courtship usually takes place on water and is of two main types. The first is a communal activity, sets with the males displaying to one or more females. This form of social display begins in the autumn, but as the winter progresses more and more of the participants have established pair-bonds. The displays by the males are elaborate, including both posture and voice, and some indication can be given by the descriptive names provided by ornithologists. These include upward-shake and wing-flap; lateral head-shake; head-flick; water-flick or grunt-whistle; head-up-tail-up; burp-display and down-up.

In due course the various couples leave the dance, as it were, and get on with the serious matter of pair-courtship. Some of the elements of communal courtship are repeated, but various new activities commence, including turn-back-of-head by the male and inciting by the female. Others are descriptively listed as bill-dip; full ceremonial-drinking and a variety of mock-preen displays. Mutual head-pumping precedes copulation, which usually takes place on water.

The calls of the female are louder than the male and include quacking. Those of the male are weaker but more variable, including rasping, wheezing, clucking, rattling and whistling.

Nesting is mainly on the ground, in thick cover and often well away from water. Occasionally cavities in trees will be used and, when provided, artificial nest-boxes are accepted readily. The female alone builds the nest, which is a shallow depression, lined with her down and rimmed with vegetation. Incubation is by the female only, who also cares for the young. The main defence against predators is the distraction display of the female who flaps awkwardly over land or water, feigning injury in the hope of luring the predator away from the young.

With the mallard, wigeon, teal and pintail, the shooting season commences on the 1st September and finishes on the 31st January inland and the 20th February below the high water mark.

15

The Mallard

Like so much that is familiar we take the mallard for granted. Were there just two hundred pairs left in the world we would extol its virtues. As it is, when the non-naturalist thinks of duck he thinks of mallard and it is perhaps in character that the model for Walt Disney's creation should have the unwieldy Latin name of *Anas platyrynchos*.

There exists ample evidence of the long residence of the mallard in Britain and two examples will suffice: their remains have been found together with bears, wolves and forest rhinos and also in the homes of Middle Stone Age hunters.

As the mallard is both the most abundant and widespread duck in Britain it forms a major quarry species, not least because it is also one of the most approachable. Wigeon, for example, roost and feed in open areas and must be ambushed on their flight lines, but mallard often frequent small, enclosed areas. Mallard are also the only duck reared for sport and although no formal records are maintained, now that BASC has discontinued its duck ringing scheme, the annual total reared must reach many thousands.

It is unlikely that any reader would fail to recognise a mallard, but a brief description must be given. It is large and heavily built—doubtless the reason why many years ago it was selected for domestication—with a long head and bill. The adult male has a mainly grey body, with a rusty breast and black and white stern. The head is bottle-green with a greenish-yellow bill and there is a white neck ring. The adult female is mainly brown with the feathering mottled and streaked with black and a dull orange bill. Both have a broad speculum of blue or purple, according to the light, edged at both front and rear by black and white.

Juveniles are similar to the adult female except that the male has a darker crown, nape and upperparts. Frequently the bill of the young male shows green before any plumage difference is noticeable.

The males start to moult between late May and early July, taking one month to complete the head and body. The females start when the young are two weeks old, finishing between mid-July and early August. Both sexes are flightless for a period of a month although, of course, at different times.

Mallard vary in length between 50–65 cm, of which the body represents about two-thirds; the wing-span is in the range of 81–98 cm. Males average larger than females. Weights are usually low in the winter, increasing to a peak in the spring and falling again in May and June. There is then another increase prior to the moult, which is lost in providing the energy for the new wing-growth. Finally fat is stored for the winter during the autumn. Average mid-winter weights are 1088 g for males and 944 g for females. By mid-summer these have risen to 1218 g and 1020 g respectively, a level which is approximately recovered again in the early autumn.

The mallard is found throughout the whole of the middle latitudes of the northern hemisphere, ranging from the Arctic tundra to sub-tropical zones. In Britain it nests in every county, on most of the islands, and up to, and even above, altitudes of 700 m. Reading the reports of populations in various countries it is refreshing to find that the vigorous and adaptable mallard is holding its own where so many species are failing. The winter population in north-west Europe is put at one-and-a-half million; a similar estimate is given for the Black Sea–Mediterranean; and one million for the Middle East. In all, the total population for the west Palaearctic is put at four to five million mallard.

Some question mark exists over the British population in summer, that is after the migrants have left. In 1940 James Fisher put the figure at 350,000 and, bearing in mind the creation of much artificial water-space since then and the numbers reared, I would not have expected a large fall in numbers. This reasoning is confirmed by a report in 1967 by Parslow that there was no evidence of a marked change. However, in 1970, Atkinson-Willes, who, as the editor of *Wildfowl in Great Britain*, is an authority, put the figure at 40,000 pairs which, even allowing for the unmated, would mean less than 100,000. The census figures for 1982 seem to favour the earlier estimates, for they suggest a peak winter population of 500,000, but with the possibility of a margin of error of up to 100,000 either way. If, as I state shortly, mallard only migrate in large numbers in severe weather, then a normal population of 80,000 or so seems far too low an estimate.

Although the mallard is very adaptable it still has preferences as to its habitat. It avoids open, exposed and fast flowing waters, seeking, instead, standing or gently flowing fresh water or coastal margins. It also seeks sheltered surroundings and shallow water for feeding. Within its catalogue of acceptance are included seasonal flood waters, sewage farms, canals, gravel pits, farm ponds, high altitude hill lochs and ornamental waters. Where it is left in peace, the mallard lives very happily alongside man, as witness the very large population in central London.

The mallard of south and west Europe are resident, apart from a tendency for the adults to move away from their breeding places for part of the year and for the young to disperse fairly widely in their first autumn. Severe weather will force a movement to the nearest open water, which usually means the coast, although occasionally sewage farms or power stations provide an alternative. Mallard from northern Europe are compelled to migrate by the onset of winter and some winter in Britain and Ireland. The majority of these European mallard come from the Netherlands, Germany and the countries around the Baltic, which is a lesser area than our wintering teal. Some doubt seems to exist over Icelandic mallard: *Wildfowl in Great Britain* states that 'There has been only one recovery, in Scotland, of a mallard ringed in Iceland'. *The Birds of the Western Palaearctic* assures us that 'Many Icelandic birds (mallard) winter in Britain and Ireland'.

Movement to wintering areas begins in August and numbers in south and west Europe reach their peak in November and December. Where weather permits the mallard move back to their breeding grounds in early February, but in the far north and east it may be early May before a thaw permits this.

Mallard are highly gregarious, living for most of the year in, and migrating in, large flocks. These, obviously, break up for breeding, but start to re-form with the males and those females who have failed to breed. The successful mothers avoid the flocks, staying with their broods until they break up.

Some pairs form from August onwards, although in migrant populations pairing may be delayed until the spring. Most residents are paired by October and all by February when the pairs are actively prospecting for nesting sites. With resident mallard the flocks disperse entirely in March, but with the migrants dispersal takes place very shortly after their arrival at the breeding grounds. Once established, the male defends the area around the female, although not with the same fervour and boundary exactitude as, for example, the grouse. When laying begins the male uses a waiting area fairly near the nest, but begins to range more widely as soon as incubation begins, gradually extending his wanderings until the pair-bond is broken.

Mallard roost communally, but their pattern of behaviour is very variable and depends on local conditions. In quiet areas mallard preen, oil and rest on land, often on sandbanks, islands and mud flats. Man-made loafing rafts are accepted willingly. Where there is much disturbance they rest on open water, but will always seek the more sheltered areas. As they are such a popular quarry the routine of mallard in many areas is to spend the day on some secure water, flighting to their feeding grounds at dusk and returning to roost at dawn.

The behaviour of mallard is far from the simple processes of eating and resting seen by the casual observer. There are complex behaviour patterns within the flocks; antagonistic behaviour routines between individuals and small groups; communal courtship between small flocks of both sexes; and pursuit-flights. Some of this behaviour is well understood, but much is still the subject of speculation. The end result is copulation, which takes place on water, from late September to May and peaking to several times per day in

February and March. Mating is preceded by mutual head-pumping, in which both male and female jerk the head down and then stretch it out. The female then stretches out her neck and head along the water, raises her tail and the male mounts.

In Britain the start of laying is partly dependent on temperatures, but can begin from mid-February onwards. In Iceland and other northern areas laying normally commences in mid-May. The nest is a shallow depression, with a lining of down and a rim of vegetation. A sample of 244 nests in south-west England showed 77 in thick ground cover, 58 in thin ground cover, 38 at the foot of a tree or post, 26 inside hollow trees, 14 in the crowns of pollarded willows and 11 in the open. The eggs are blunt oval, grey-green or buff, some 57 × 41 mm and weighing about 51 g. An average clutch contains nine to thirteen eggs, which take twenty-seven to twenty-eight days to incubate. A replacement clutch will be laid if the first is lost or even after the early loss of the young.

The young leave the nest some fourteen to twenty-one hours after hatching and are immediately self-feeding. The female is an excellent mother, brooding her young at night, caring for them well and defending the nest and young against predators. The young become independent about the time they fledge, which is fifty to sixty days after hatching, and normally breed at one year.

The mallard is noted for its willingness to eat almost anything and sportsmen concerned with flight ponds marvel at the manner with which such extreme offerings as rotten bananas and rabbit guts all disappear overnight. On water its range varies from sieving by pumping in and expelling water to obtain floating seeds and suchlike, to diving up to 2 m to obtain acorns. It will up-end in depths up to 48 cm for a maximum of eight seconds, although the norm is nearer five seconds. On land it will graze like geese, pluck leaves and shoots and bite and grub with its beak. To complete its repertoire it will even snatch insects from the air. The more one studies the mallard the more one understands the reasons for its success.

The list of food items is long. It ranges through a great variety of seeds, buds and leaves of aquatic and terrestrial plants; insects, molluscs, crustaceans, annelids, amphibians, fish, and small birds and mammals. Had mallard been substantially larger they would terrorise the world.

As with so many other species, the ducklings begin life by existing entirely on an animal diet. Work in the USA found ducklings being insect dependent up to nineteen to twenty-five days and, on water, not submerging their heads. From twenty-five days onwards they submerged their heads under water and gradually moved to a mainly vegetarian diet. Work by the Game Conservancy at Great Linford showed a link between a very high mortality rate of mallard ducklings and a reduced availability of their most important food, the midge *Diptera : Chironomidae*. In detailing their reasoning the Conservancy also

32. A healthy brood of mallard.

33. Mallard dropping in with undercarriages down.

points out that mallard in Iceland regulate their breeding season so that hatching coincides with the peak seasonal abundance of non-biting midges. The Conservancy is concerned that man-made wetlands, particularly gravel pits, lack an inflow of fresh water providing nutrients for the food chain involving insect life. They are, therefore, currently investigating a management technique involving placing barley straw in such waters to stimulate the rapid production of invertebrate fauna.

Ringing results in north-west Europe suggest an annual mortality of about 48% and a life expectancy of about 1.6 years. These are substantially better than in other areas; work in Finland suggested an annual mortality of 64% in the first year and 55% in subsequent years and in Sweden also showed 64% but 76% for juveniles. The oldest ringed bird was a remarkable 29 years and 1 month.

Managing mallard for sport can be misunderstood by some sportsmen. Mallard are not difficult to rear and the principle of putting back into the wild more than one takes out by shooting is both practical and laudable. The essential point to watch is that the young mallard have the minimum of human contact or they will rapidly become tame.

However, the wrong interpretation of 'management' is the creation of flight-ponds which, adequately fed, can attract large quantities of duck, not all of them producing the most testing of shots. There is nothing wrong with flight-ponds when used with discretion and normal sporting principles—it is simply a matter of degree.

As to the future, there appears no need to fear for the mallard.

16

The Wigeon

The wigeon is to the mallard what the grouse is to the pheasant—both the mallard and the pheasant are familiar and well-regarded but it is their relatives from the wilder habitats who capture one's imagination.

The wigeon has the Latin name *Anas Penelope*. For many years its common name was spelt widgeon and even today the latter version is quite common. In coastal areas it was frequently known as the poor man's pheasant, for it provided the bulk of the sport of the working man.

It has, of course, been either a resident or visitor to this country for countless years and fossil remains have been found ranging from the Late Ice Age to the Dark Ages.

The wigeon has long been a favourite quarry of the wildfowler, possibly the favourite, for mallard are too commonplace, teal offer less of a meal and other species are not so prolific.

The male wigeon is one of the most attractive of the ducks with its chestnut head and neck, topped by a yellowish forehead and crown. The breast is pink-brown and the upperparts and sides vermiculated grey. A belly and lower breast of white extend into a white patch at the rear of the flanks, where the whitish grey tail is surrounded by black. (In flight the white belly and extensive white areas on the forewing are striking.) The speculum is dark green: the bill grey-blue with a black tip: eyes brown and legs blue-grey to yellow-brown. In eclipse the male resembles the female but can be easily distinguished by the white forewings.

The female is brown on the upper breast and flanks and mainly white on the underparts. A tinge of pink is apparent in the brown of the head and neck, which are barred and spotted with black. The speculum can have a green gloss comparable to the male, but is normally much blacker. Similarly, the bill and legs are a duller grey-blue than the males.

Juveniles closely resemble the adult female, but by their first winter have grown plumage very similar to adults, except that the males do not normally gain the white forewings until the second winter.

Males have a length of about 51 cm and a wing-span of approximately

86 cm; the comparative measurements for females being 45 cm and 75 cm. Weights tend to vary quite substantially, peaking in the autumn at about 870 g for males and 710 g for females. There is a rapid drop once winter sets in, with one study showing the males averaging about 640 g and the females 560 g.

The distribution during the breeding season finds the majority of the world's wigeon spread over a vast area of northern Russia, Siberia and the shores of the Arctic. Others are spread through northern Sweden and Norway and all but the centre of Iceland. At the last estimate, in 1971, it was thought about 350 pairs bred in Britain, mainly in Scotland but some in northern England and a few in Wales.

To breed, the wigeon moves to the boreal and subarctic zones, overlapping slightly into temperate zones and the steppes. It has a preference for woodland rather than open tundra, and uses cover in both coniferous and deciduous woods for nesting.

For winter quarters the wigeon seeks shallow, sheltered coasts, with large expanses of tidal mud, salt-marsh and sand, which offer both feeding and security. It is a bird of open spaces and is rarely found in enclosed settings.

Although a few wigeon are residents in their chosen area, most migrate and large numbers over-winter in this country, the majority staying in Scotland and northern England with relatively few reaching the south or Ireland. Between 1948–9 and 1951–2 there was a decline in numbers, followed by a large increase in 1955. At the present time winter peak numbers for Britain and Ireland are about 200,000–250,000. Many others are spread through the North Sea countries, and the Iberian peninsula. In addition to the winter migration there is a moult migration when the males leave the breeding grounds for moulting areas where they flock with the immature non-breeders.

The beginning of the autumn migration varies with the latitude and the weather. Normally flocks gather in August and mass departures from the breeding areas begin in September, with most reaching their winter quarters in October and November. These dates are certainly accurate for the area I know well, the Thames Estuary; but there is always a noticeable influx if the Continent is hit by severe weather at any time during the winter. The northward movement begins in mid-March or early April, although mild winters will see earlier movement. Major north, north-east movements occur in the USSR during April, but the wigeon cannot complete their journey until the northern tundras thaw in the second half of May.

Wigeon are highly gregarious, a characteristic greatly to their disadvantage when punt-gunning was widely practised. Large winter flocks frequently rest in close proximity on the open sea or uncovered tidal banks. In areas where they suffer disturbance wigeon tend to rest during the day and feed at night, although activity is usually greatest at dusk and dawn. The pattern of activity is rarely fixed, but varies with tide, weather and other factors. For example,

34. Drake wigeon.

35. Drake wigeon displaying.

in the severe 1961–2 winter the wigeon in the area of the Isle of Sheppey had established a routine of grazing inland at night and roosting at sea during the day. As the weather grew harsher they reversed this routine and spent all the daylight hours seeking whatever grass could be seen above the snow on the freshwater marshes.

The male utters one of the loveliest calls of the marshes—the haunting, musical, two-syllable, whistling 'whee-oo'. The female's main contribution falls well short—a purring or grating growl, and she also lacks the ability to quack.

The wigeon will often fly several miles to feed and its diet is almost entirely vegetarian. On land it grazes, and on water takes most of its food from the surface. At one time the major food source of the wigeon was eel-grass, *Zostera*, but disease and other factors have greatly reduced the areas available. The list of plants, both marine and inland, taken by wigeon is very extensive and suggests that what is abundant is taken. In addition to leaves, stems, stolons, bulbils and rhizomes, seeds and algae are also eaten.

In the far north breeding is determined by the thaw, but in Britain the main laying time is May. The eggs are ovate and smooth, coloured cream or pale buff measuring 55 × 39 mm and weighing about 42 g. The clutch varies between six to twelve, but is usually eight to nine. One egg is laid per day and incubation takes twenty-four to twenty-five days. The young fledge in forty to forty-five days and become independent about then.

In 1975 it was estimated that the wigeon population of Europe and western Asia was about 1½ million. The mean mortality of birds ringed in north-west Europe has been 47% and the life expectancy has been forecast as 1.6 years. The oldest recovered ringed bird has therefore, at 18 years 3 months, been singularly fortunate.

In Britain man and severe weather are the main causes of death and the wigeon has little to fear in the way of natural predators. It is on the breeding grounds that it is vulnerable and a survey in Iceland showed 32.1% of nests failed to hatch due to predation and desertion, with the main culprits being raven and mink. In Scotland no less than 44% failed through predation.

The future of the wigeon is tied to the extent of human interference, primarily with its breeding grounds and secondly with its wintering quarters.

17

The Teal

The teal, *Anas crecca*, is arguably the most attractive and certainly the tastiest of all the ducks.

British mammals have had a far from easy time over the centuries, being forced to trek alternately north and south as the various ice ages made their various advances and retreats. The duck, however, had no such problems and merely changed their migration pattern to include this country once our climate warmed after each ice age. It is probable that most of the various species of duck alternately abandoned and recommenced visiting this country at much the same times and the fact that we cannot trace teal remains quite as far back as some other species does not reasonably make them an exception.

Teal remains have been identified in this country in Neolithic times, about 3,000 BC and in the Iron Age, about 250 BC, from the lake village at Glastonbury in Somerset. It is also mentioned many times in subsequent English literature and was obviously a common bird.

As large concentrations of teal only normally appear on the coast, it is no more than an incidental item for most inland sportsmen. However, for wildfowlers, and particularly in certain areas at certain times, it is sometimes the main quarry. On the principle that small birds always give a false impression of flying faster than larger birds, it is commonly held that mallard fly faster than teal. Lacking positive facts I cannot disprove the statement other than to say that when I lie in a creek on the north Kent coast and a party of teal flash over with a strong wind in their tails I find them as fast as anything within my experience.

For me the statement 'small is beautiful' rings true, and particularly so with the teal. It is a most exquisitely fashioned bird: small yet compact and powerful—a jet fighter to the mallard bomber. The head of the adult male is most distinctive; chestnut with a metallic green eye-patch running back to the nape and outlined in buff-white. The breast is rich cream with blackish spots, and the body grey with a horizontal white stripe above the wing, the whole ending in a black and yellow-buff stern. The speculum is metallic green and black. The adult female follows the normal pattern of being essentially brown with various dark markings and a white centre breast and belly. Identification is immediate as no other British duck is so small. The bill of the male is dark grey and that of the female is lighter grey and with pinkish-orange on the upper mandible.

The juvenile closely resembles the adult female but is darker and more uniform above, a distinction hard to apply unless both are to hand at the same time. However help in identification comes from the bill which is pink-horn in the juvenile.

Total length ranges between 34–38 cm, of which the body represents two-thirds, and the wing-span is 58–64 cm. As is usual with the ducks the weight varies with the season, the lowest point being January to March. At that time the males range between about 275–340 g and the females 240–310 g, but by the time the birds have settled in their summer quarters, and prior to breeding, the respective ranges increase to 320–400 g and 250–450 g.

Being largely migratory, the distribution of the teal throughout the western Palaearctic varies with the season. During the breeding season it covers north Russia, the Baltic states, Norway, Sweden, Finland, north Poland, north Germany, Denmark, Iceland, Britain, Ireland and also has minor representation elsewhere in Europe. In the autumn many fly south-west to winter in the North Sea, principally in the Netherlands and Britain. All but a few of the Icelandic birds winter in Britain, principally in Scotland.

Teal are very responsive to weather, and unlike some species who will stick to their wintering quarters to a dangerous degree, a cold snap will bring an immediate westward drift. In really severe winters some teal move to France and the Iberian peninsula and a few reach north Africa.

During the present century teal have nested in every county in Britain, but our resident population is fairly small: an estimated 1,000–1,500 pairs in 1970. Most of our nearest European neighbours are also at a low level with Belgium estimating 400 pairs, the Netherlands 750 pairs, West Germany 1,020 pairs and Denmark 200 pairs. These figures contrast sharply with Finland's 80,000 pairs.

There appears some dispute among the authorities on the behaviour of British breeding teal in winter. One source says they are resident the year round, while another states they move south with few remaining in Scotland and northern England. In 1963 the wintering population in England was thought to be in the region of 150,000 but by 1975 this was the figure suggested for the whole of north-west Europe's wintering population. The November 1982 census produced a wintering population estimate of 90,000–100,000. That for the Black Sea–Mediterranean region was put at 750,000 and in the west of the USSR 609,000 in not very severe winters.

Unlike the mallard the teal is not very tolerant of human activities and seeks isolated areas of water, preferably small and with shallow margins. It avoids waters that are deep, fast-running, or exposed to waves. Its preference is for plant-lined banks but it will accept estuaries, shallow coasts, and salt-marshes, particularly in winter when these may provide the only unfrozen area for feeding.

Watching teal fly, particularly at close quarters when the tearing noise of their wings through the air is unexpectedly loud, is an exhilarating experience. As they turn, dive, climb and circle in unison it is often difficult to conceive any purpose in either their route or their aerobatics and I am firmly of the view that, on occasions, they fly for the sheer joy of it.

Generally teal are gregarious, though tending to disperse to feed. Monogamous pair-bonds are formed in the flock, mainly in the winter, and lasting for the season only. Most pairs are formed between November and January and practically all by the end of March and, as usual, these break up once incubation begins. The male teal appears to have less territorial ambitions than most other species and little or no territorial defence has been observed.

Teal are mainly nocturnal feeders and spend most of the day roosting. Outside the breeding season they frequently roost, in groups, on open water or exposed tidal banks. However, in the area I know best there is extensive tide flighting, with birds dropping into the marsh as the rising tide lifts them off the mud banks.

The preliminaries of courting follow much the same pattern as the mallard and wigeon, except that the male teal are more hostile to one another. This vigorous male attitude is also directed towards the females with unfortunate consequences for it is not uncommon for several males to rape a female and, in the process, drown her. Although both sexes call frequently in the winter it is during the display period that they are most vocal. The principal call of the male is a melodious and penetrating whistle, of two syllables, and variously described as 'prip-prip' or, 'kirck-krick'. As is usual, the call of the female is entirely different: various forms of quacking, all higher pitched than the mallard. The repertoire of both is varied and comprehensive but their purposes follow the standard pattern.

The pre-copulatory display again follows the usual form of mutual head-pumping. Egg-laying begins in central Europe in mid-April, but rather earlier in Britain. Normally the nest is on the ground, in thick cover with overhanging vegetation and rarely far from water. As usual with ducks, the nest is a hollow, lined with down and rimmed with vegetation. The eggs are blunt, ovate and yellowish-white. They measure 45 × 33 mm and weigh about 29 g. A normal clutch contains between eight and eleven eggs and if this is lost a fresh clutch is laid. Incubation is by the female only and takes twenty-one to twenty-three days. The young are self-feeding, cared for by the hen and brooded by her at night. They are independent when fledged, which takes twenty-five to thirty days. In common with most ducklings their food in the early stages is mainly animal materials: Russian investigations have found percentages of 75%, 85% and 100% animal matter.

Once adult, teal live principally on seeds. The normal feeding technique is to abstract the seeds from the mud by walking slowly in shallow water and filtering with the bill. Alternatives are swimming with the head under water; up-ending; skimming and occasionally diving. One investigation found teal feed for 8 to 12.7 hours per day, essentially at night, but extending into the day if necessary. Other surveys found considerably more day feeding and it appears the feeding activity varies with the usual factors.

Most of the seeds taken are those of aquatic plants: sedges, bulrushes, pondweeds, wigeon-grass, milfoil, buttercup, dock, samphire, sea-aster, etc.—the list is extensive, as one would expect. Where available a wide range of animal material is taken.

The annual mortality in Europe is put at 47% for one- to two-year-olds. In Britain, and for all ages, male mortality is estimated as 49% and female 57%. In 1957 it was estimated (Boyd) that three-fifths of the male losses and half of the female were attributable to man (presumably by shooting). The oldest recovered ringed bird was 16 years, 10 months.

As with the other migratory duck, the future of the teal depends upon man not destroying its habitats.

18

The Pintail

I have placed the pintail (*Anas acuta*) last among the ducks because, as a result of a smaller population, it is the least frequently encountered. Indeed, depending on location, some readers could argue that other species should be included and the pintail left out. Perhaps this is so, but the pintail warrants its place simply because it is such a beautiful and graceful bird.

There is no reason to doubt that the pintail was among the myriads of duck which wintered in Britain when man was a very primitive being, but reports of pintail remains are hard to come by. The earliest I can trace was in Ireland, in Lagare, Co. Meath, in AD 750–950.

The status of the pintail as a quarry is low, not because it is in any way easier to bag than any other duck but simply because they are relatively few in number.

Pintail are large, slender duck who, by virtue of their thin necks and pointed tails have a particularly streamlined appearance in flight. The male has a very dark brown head and upper neck, a white neck stripe and underparts, a mainly black tail (with a creamy area in front of the underpart) and grey upperparts. The speculum is particularly handsome—metallic green glossed with bronze, shading to black at the rear, with a rich buff border in front and white behind. The male's bill is grey-blue with a black base, and the feet grey with black webs.

The female follows the usual relatively drab brown pattern of her sex among the other ducks, but is rather more pale and grey. The belly is whitish and the speculum less colourful. The bill is blue-grey and the feet green-grey. The juvenile resembles the female but is darker above and more heavily streaked and spotted below.

The length is of the order 51–66 cm, of which up to 10 cm is the pointed tail, and the wing-span 80–95 cm. The male is usually larger than the female. Weights are highest in early June, prior to moulting the wing feathers, and in the early autumn when building fat for the winter. At these times the male ranges from 900–1,200 g and the female 700–900 g. Winter weights are very variable.

The breeding distribution of the pintail is less extensive and more localised than the other species of duck we have previously considered. It is widely distributed throughout northern Russia and Finland, but is not usually found in the coastal areas of Norway and Sweden. Various breeding areas are dotted over central and west Europe but form only a small proportion of this land mass. Pintail breed in most of the coastal regions of Iceland.

In Britain the breeding population was estimated in 1970 as only 50 pairs, located principally in north and central Scotland, the Solway, the Wash and the north Kent coast. Most west European countries report only a very small breeding population, contrasting with Finland's 20,000 pairs and USSR's staggering 316,000 pairs in the western part alone.

It is estimated that approximately 50,000 pintail winter in north-west Europe and at least 250,000 in the Black Sea–Mediterranean region. The great majority of the Icelandic birds winter in Britain and Ireland. Those from north Russia as far east as Omsk, Fenno-Scandia and the Baltic migrate to the Netherlands and Britain. In this country the most favoured winter quarters is the Cambridgeshire Washes. The November 1982 census produced an estimate of 25,000–28,000.

Pintail share with teal a liking for shallow, still or slow moving waters. Where they differ is by displaying a strong preference for spacious, open environments, preferably lowland grassland or prairie. This trend continues in moulting, for rather than select an area of dense cover to hide the pintail selects open waters, sometimes treating the move as the first stage on its return migration.

It is a very shy and wary bird, inactive by day and a night feeder. In the air the pintail is a strong flier, with the un-duck like habit of sometimes moving in large flocks flying in V formation. On the ground it walks more gracefully than some others of its tribe.

The general behaviour pattern of the pintail follows that of the other ducks. It is, as usual, gregarious, although tending to stay in individual flocks of males and females until well into the autumn. The usual monogamous pair-bond is formed prior to the breeding season and, again as usual, this normally breaks once incubation begins, but not so positively. As the winter progresses the normal *Anatini* pattern is followed with flock and antagonistic behaviour, communal courtship and pursuit-flights, eventually culminating in copulation or rape.

The earliest egg-laying begins in late March or early April and in the far north is dependent on the thaw. Again at variance with the teal, the female pintail seeks a site with short cover and often on bare ground. The nest is hollow, lined always with down, but sometimes with a down/vegetation mix. The eggs are ovate, coloured yellowish-white to yellowish-green. They measure 55 × 39 mm and weigh 43 g. An average clutch will contain seven to nine eggs, which will take twenty-two to twenty-four days to incubate. If lost

36. Drake pintail drinking.

37. Drake and duck pintail.

it will be replaced. The female alone incubates, but the male pintail appears to frequent the nest area much more than is the practice with male mallard, wigeon and teal, even if only on occasions. The female broods the young in the early stages and also performs distraction-displays if necessary. Fledging takes forty to forty-five days, at which point the young become independent. Once again the ducklings are dependent on animal material in the early days. (A Russian investigation showed 80% invertebrates and a Canadian one 67%.)

The pintail is one of the less vocal ducks, and information on the voice is less positive. In general it is thought the vocabulary is similar to the mallard, although the male is credited with whistling like the teal.

It is thought the long neck of the pintail may be an adaptation for bottom feeding: certainly much of its feeding is done by up-ending and questing in the mud bottom at greater depths than other duck. The pintail is also a land feeder, using its beak to both pick up material and grub.

Both plant and animal material is taken, the lists showing no surprising variations from others of its tribe.

Few statistics are available on the population structure of the pintail. A forecast of mean annual adult mortality was made by Boyd in 1962, based on USSR recoveries, of 48%.

There is, of course, no question of managing the pintail for sport. Hopefully, with the growth of reserves in Britain in recent years, there will be an increase in our breeding population. However, this is an insignificant proportion of the world population and the future of the pintail, as with so many other duck, lies in the far north.

WIGEON

Anas penelope

The most common of all our winter visiting duck,
the wigeon shares with the grey partridge the twin
distinctions of being far more colourful in the hand
than at a distance and of being highly regarded by
knowledgeable observers.

TEAL

Anas crecca

The smallest of the European duck, the teal is
attractive, neat, talkative and a great aerial acrobat.

The Anserini *(Swans and true geese)*

Still in the order *Anseriformes*, and the family *Anatidae*, we have the tribe *Anserini*, which includes the pink-footed, white-front, greylag and Canadian geese.

The *Anserini* include the largest wildfowl, and among these there are two main genera of geese: *Anser*, the 'grey' geese, with nine species which include the major quarries of the wildfowler, and *Branta*, the 'black' geese with five species.

As we have seen with the ducks, Britain and Ireland provide winter havens for many species breeding in the northern areas which become untenable in winter and the same rhythm of migration applies to the great majority of the geese. There is every reason to suppose this pattern has existed into the dim recesses of time and what evidence we can trace confirms this.

Going back some 500,000 to 600,000 years, to Lower Pleistocene times, there is evidence of a goose, species unknown, from the classic fossil beds of East Anglia. Moving on some 50,000 years, a very small step in the world's history, and to the Forest Bed of Norfolk, a greylag has been identified. And leaping another 100,000 years to Mindel glacial times, when the weather was cooler and reindeer had joined the early forest elephants, mammoths, hippopotami and rhinoceroses roaming Britain, there were brent geese on the estuaries. As recently as the Middle Pleistocene, that is between 400,000 and 160,000 years ago, more greylag fossils are reported. Man had yet to enter the Stone Age.

The various species of geese share common characteristics and these can be conveniently listed here. They graze; and their bills are constructed for this task by the lamella taking the form of horny 'teeth' along the edge of the upper mandible. Their preference is for the Holarctic: that is the cool or cold regions, although stopping at the fringes of the ice and snow. They live by eating both aquatic and terrestrial vegetation, with the exception of the brent goose, and choose the margins of the sea rather than deep water. Where possible they concentrate on grassland or other low vegetation, avoiding wooded areas, deserts and mountains. In Britain they make extensive use of cultivated farmlands, particularly in Scotland, northern England, and other areas which are open and spacious.

There is considerable dispute over the harm geese may, or may not, cause to agricultural crops. The truth is that, depending upon what they graze and when, they can be both harmful and beneficial.

Grazing grass leys in the autumn, when gleaning stubbles for spilt grain, is good for the grass as a cropped single seed then develops several stems. Grazing a pasture in the early spring, which the farmer has almost certainly previously top dressed to provide an 'early bite' for his ewes or beef stores, is unquestionably harmful. Such grazing will retard growth and may weaken the plant. Even where it does not, the food value is denied to the farmer's stock. The only solution is to use scaring devices but these often have the negative effect of sending the geese to a neighbour's fields.

The action of cleaning stubbles of grain, and various weed seeds is helpful and a similar service is performed when geese clean old potato fields as the missed potatoes could carry diseases through to the following year.

Geese often graze winter wheat, causing the less charitable farmers to assume they are digging up the grain. However there is no evidence of this and studies have shown no reduction in the ultimate crop unless grazing occurs in temporary standing water. In fact too much leaf growth in the autumn is regarded as undesirable and it is quite common to graze this off with ewes.

On the debit side, greylags and pink-feet can damage spring sown barley and oats if unseasonal warm weather causes early growth.

The content of wild goose manure is comparable to other animal manures and it is sometimes suggested that the goose droppings compensate for any damage done. However, research has shown that even as high a density as one dropping to the square foot will only provide about 2% of the nitrogen requirement of the average wheat crop.

A fair assessment is that, taken over the country as a whole, the amount of damage caused by geese is infinitesimal, particularly when compared to other bird problems such as the wood-pigeon. However, this is of little consolation to the unfortunate few upon whom the geese concentrate at the wrong time.

They are strong fliers, vigilant and wary. The old wildfowlers credited geese with considerable reasoning powers and would often attribute greater depth than was justified to simple, routine acts. Prior to flight geese usually call vociferously and indulge in lateral head-shaking in the case of the grey geese and head-tossing in the black.

Breeding takes place on a loosely colonial basis, that is a number of pairs spread over a site which is traditional and selected for its quietness. Geese have the admirable characteristic of mating for life and having strong family ties, not only between parents and young but the young themselves. Given this fidelity there is no communal courtship among the geese. Pre-copulatory display consists of mutual head-dipping with the female eventually taking up a prone position. Copulation takes place on water, except for two species which do not concern us. Geese have loud voices which, to our pleasure, they use freely and, unlike the ducks, there is little difference between the calls of the sexes. All species hiss when threatened, a habit most readers will have observed with swans which are, of course, members of the same tribe.

As with all arctic breeding birds, the laying period is highly synchronised to take advantage of the brief but productive summer. Geese nest on the ground, usually not far from water, and using down for lining. The clutch normally varies between four and seven eggs, which are white, creamy-white or pale green. Incubation takes twenty-four to thirty days and although the male takes no part in incubation he is usually in constant attendance, mounting guard near the nest and covering the eggs when the female is absent. The female alone broods the young but both watch over them and are highly aggressive in the face of predators. Nature arranges matters so that the pair wing-moult at different times, always leaving one parent able to fly to better protect the young. Not only do the young usually stay with their parents through the first winter and sometimes the spring migration but they sometimes reunite at the end of subsequent breeding seasons.

Given these qualities of loyalty and affection it is understandable that when wild geese are reduced to captivity, usually as a result of being wounded, they form a close bond with men. They are a most lovable group of birds and we are fortunate that so many winter in this country. The sight and sound of large skeins of geese, at dusk or dawn, against a winter sky is breathtaking. Many wildfowlers, of whom I am one, start with a near-fanatical desire to bag geese but soon mellow into contented observers.

38. *Pinkfeet and whitefront geese.*

19

The Pink-footed Goose

I have a special affection for the pink-foot for there was a time, with Shep White's old house still standing, when I lived rough on the sea wall of the Wash in their pursuit. Whenever I hear the romantic call of flighting geese my mind leaps back to the great, grey, expanses of mud, sand and marsh grasses: to the smell of frying bacon and eggs, to stubbly chins, hopes, ambitions, plans and the permanent cold. Few geese were bagged either by my friends and I or any other of the socially mixed and somewhat frightening band who plodded out onto, and back from, the mud at every dawn and dusk, but in sharing the surroundings and the weather we developed an affinity with those magnificent birds.

Economically the pink-footed goose has some small influence for men travel considerable distances to wildfowl in their wintering areas. At one time professional guides earned their living by acting as the shooting equivalent of the salmon fishers' 'ghillie' but few of this species now survive. This is not because wildfowlers no longer need their services but because the work was dirty, cold and required unsociable hours. With increased standards of living, few are prepared to guide on a permanent basis. I am unable to explain to readers who have never contracted wildfowling fever how some are enthusiastic about wildfowl for sport whereas others will not even consider it for money.

The pink-footed goose (*Anser Brachyrhynchus*) is smaller than the greylag goose, the latter, I believe, being the origin of the farmyard goose. There is no obvious difference in appearance between the sexes, both being pinkish-grey with a dark, round head and foreneck, together with a pale forewing. Both neck and bill are relatively short, the latter coloured pink with some brown extending from the base. The eye is dark brown and, obviously, the legs and feet are pink, sometimes so dark as to become near purple.

The juvenile is darker with less pink and grey and more mottled. The distinguishing features of the pink-foot as against the other grey geese are the shorter neck, resulting in a more general appearance of compactness: and the contrast between the dark head and the greyer body and forewing.

The length of an adult ranges between 60–75 cm and the wing-span between 135–170 cm. Weights, in the autumn in Britain, average about 2,770 g for the males and 2,520 g for the females.

The pink-foot breeds in Greenland, Iceland and Spitzbergen, and winters in Britain, Denmark, Germany and the Netherlands. The Greenland and Icelandic birds winter in Britain and they rarely mix with the Spitzbergen geese who winter on the Continent. In recent years there has been a contraction in their winter range in this country with more geese electing to winter in Scotland. This trend is particularly marked in Ireland which now sees very few over-wintering pink-feet. The likely explanation is changing farming practices which mean the geese now have ample food in the Scottish lowlands. Overshooting may have also been a contributory factor in some of the English coastal areas, particularly the Wash and the Solway. Certainly geese have virtually disappeared from the north Norfolk coast in the once famous fowling areas of Wells and Blakeney. The story goes that a prime cause was the habit of anti-aircraft gunners using them for practice in the last war, but the shooting literature of the 1930s shows the decline had begun before 1939.

During the first half of September the Greenland population crosses to Iceland, joining the bulk of that country's breeding stock, mainly in the interior. Once the first snows cover the Icelandic feeding grounds, usually in the first half of October, the main emigration to Britain begins, and is almost complete by the end of October. Most of the autumn birds arrive over the north and north-east coasts of Scotland but when the return commences in April a major contingent choose a route up the west coast and over the Hebrides. Fortuitously I write of the pink-foot in mid-April and on the Isle of Skye. At this precise moment a gale from the west is slashing hailstones against the cottage window, but when the storm dies, and milder weather returns, each day will see small skeins of geese driving steadily northwards and calling sparingly. At the peak, and on the rare days in the Hebrides in April that betoken spring, there will be a procession of skeins the day through, appearing to east or west of the Cuillins, following the coast-line and eventually disappearing to the north.

In this country, and on the coast, they roost on the estuarine flats of mud or sand, but when feeding well inland they use large areas of freshwater. On their breeding grounds the geese have strong attachments to particular areas, although the reasons are not always understood, and on these areas nest at densities of more than 130 nests to the square kilometre. In Iceland there is an inconsistency of choice of nest-sites, with some geese selecting inaccessible river gorge areas and others relatively flat, exposed ground. A possible explanation is that the latter are in upland areas which are only habitable for a brief spell in the summer and predators may not readily penetrate this far. Many of the breeding areas experience a rapid change in conditions, commencing with snow and ice cover which thaws to shallow water and then to boggy grassland with ample plant material for food.

In Greenland laying is delayed until late May and in Spitzbergen a week or so later. In Iceland laying begins in early May and the nest sites are frequently re-used, eventually developing a permanent rim. (Some are estimated to be at least forty years old.) Contrary to the hollow utilised by most birds, the pink-foot builds a mound of vegetation with a hollow cup having a diameter of 30–40 cm. Much down is used and during incubation the female may incorporate droppings. The eggs measure 78 × 52 mm and weigh about 132 g. There is no record of replacement clutches being laid if the first is lost. The eggshells are left in the nest and eaten by the female when she returns in the spring. The young are self-feeding and brooded by the female. The degree of parental care is shown by a report that many pairs at the nest made threat postures towards a low-flying helicopter. Fledging takes fifty-six days.

In the breeding area pink-feet eat a wide variety of tundra plants, this applies also to the young, who appear not to be reliant upon animal material as in so many other species. There is some evidence that the goslings take more herbs and *Equisetum* than adults. In Britain practically all the feeding takes place on farmland and the diet is largely determined by what is offered by local agriculture. However, over the long term geese will move their areas to those offering the most attractive foods and I personally believe the practice of ploughing in the stubbles immediately after harvest was, at least in part, responsible for the drop in numbers in the Wash area. Throughout their stay in Britain the geese eat grass, but their preference is for cereal grains and potatoes. Leaves of rape, roots of carrots and other brassics are also taken.

Normally geese feed during the daytime, flighting out to their roosting area well before the duck flight and not returning in the morning until the return flight of the duck is over. However, in moonlight the geese will often feed through the night, with small parties returning to the roost area from time to time to bathe. If, on a night with thick cloud but a strong moon, the cloud clears, the geese will begin to talk and often fly off to the feeding areas shortly after.

In contrast to so many species discussed in this book, the population history is favourable. In the early 1950s the main breeding colony in Iceland contained 2,500–4,000 pairs: by 1970 this had risen to 10,700 pairs and by 1974 8,000 pairs. Our wintering population has increased from about 30,000 birds in 1950 to some 76,000 in 1966. There was a dramatic increase to 89,000 in 1974, but numbers fell back to about 70,000 subsequently. However, by the autumn of 1980 the annual census of the Wildfowl Trust recorded 95,000 which fell back by autumn 1981, as a result of an indifferent breeding season, to about 90,000. The November 1982 census was little changed at 89,000. When one considers the large numbers of pink-foot which once wintered on the Wash and the north Norfolk coast, the percentage split of the winter population locations shows the dramatic change in the recent times. They are north Scotland 14.7, east central Scotland 30.7, south-east Scotland 30.0, south-west Scotland 3.7, north England 20.3 and east England 0.6. The increase is put down to a lower adult mortality rate, increased winter food supplies and more statutory refuges on the wintering grounds.

During the period 1950–69 the proportion of young Icelandic bred birds wintering in Britain varied from 11% to 49% with an average of 25.6%. Those in the age range 4–16 months suffer a mean annual mortality of 42%, but once adult this declines to 21.5%. The life expectancy of an adult is 3.3 years and the oldest ringed bird 21 years 5 months.

A major threat to the pink-feet arose in the early 1970s when the Icelanders contemplated a major hydro-electric scheme which would have flooded, or otherwise disturbed, important breeding areas. In the event it was found not to be cost effective, but the threat remains and a substantial rise in the cost of alternative energy supplies could lead to the scheme's resurrection.

39. Pinkfoot goose grazing.

20

The Greylag Goose

Anser Anser is the largest and also the most studied of the grey geese. As a quarry species it probably ranks in importance with the pink-footed goose.

Compared to its relatives it is larger, thick-necked, big-headed and has a large bill. The sexes are alike, although the male is bigger. In general terms it resembles the other grey geese, but one immediate distinguishing feature is the pale forewing, which is very obvious in flight. The bill is triangular in shape, and coloured pale orange with a pink tinge behind a white nail. The legs are flesh coloured.

The greylag can be separated from the other grey geese by an appearance of heaviness, both on the ground and in flight, its bulk, uniform paleness of colouring, lighter forewing, pink legs, and large bill and head.

Juveniles can be distinguished by their more mottled plumage which also lacks the sharp definitions of the adult bird.

The greylag is 75–90 cm long, and has a wing-span of 147–80 cm. The weight follows a predictable cycle with the birds arriving lean in October, with males averaging 3,454 g and females 3,039 g, gaining weight until December when the respective values become 3,793 g and 3,170 g, losing weight in the hard months to 3,509 g and 3,108 g, and increasing again in the summer to 3,455 g and 3,237 g.

At one time the greylag probably bred over the whole of Europe but, while the range remains extensive, there are large areas where no breeding occurs due to pressure from man. There have been numerous introductions in recent years, including Sweden where it was in danger of extinction, and in various parts of England. Our only natural resident population numbers some 1,000–2,000 and is centred on Loch Drudibeg in South Uist in the Outer Hebrides. All in all, the position of resident greylags in Britain is fairly healthy and part of the credit must go to the British Association for Conservation and Shooting.

Iceland has one of the major populations and this increased from some 3,500 pairs in 1960 to about 18,600 pairs in 1973. In the USSR, on the other hand, there was a major decline to some 50,000–60,000 birds by 1967.

Outside these two countries no breeding area claims more than 2,000 pairs, except Norway where a rather vague 1971 report said, 'some thousands of pairs'.

The breeding populations of north-west Europe migrate through the Netherlands, where a few decide to remain, to Spain. Britain is in the happy position of receiving the whole of the Icelandic breeders, who arrive in the second half of October or the early part of November. On arrival they bunch in large flocks, until splitting and dispersing to their preferred wintering grounds. These are concentrated in Scotland and northern England and migratory greylag are virtually never found south of Cumberland and Northumberland. The total numbers wintering in Britain and Ireland increased from about 26,000 in 1960 to 76,000 in 1973 and 68,000 in 1974. This excellent trend continued until 1981 when the annual autumn census, by the Wildfowl Trust, recorded 96,000. Unfortunately the November 1982 census showed a significant fall to about 80,000, probably through a hard winter loss. The 1981 census also showed the percentage locations of the populations and I include the 1979 percentages for the various areas in brackets. North Scotland 56.2 (40.5), east central Scotland 22.3 (41.1), south-east Scotland 7.5 (6.6), south-west Scotland 8.4 (6.8), north England 5.6 (5.0). These figures show how volatile the population is from year to year.

The greylag is more tolerant in its preferences for habitat than the other grey geese, accepting boreal and temperate habitats as well as arctic tundra. However, this apparent passport to a wider range of areas than other grey geese is limited by its insistence on a combination of suitable grasslands and water. To gain security for nesting, the greylag seeks extensive areas of open, fresh water with dense vegetation and, ideally, small islands. In winter it often seeks milder climates than other geese and shares with many humans a preference for passing the hard months in the Mediterranean. Here again it looks for large expanses of open water.

The behaviour pattern of the greylag follows that of the other grey geese in all major respects. After the young are born the families stay together until the next breeding season, but on leaving most of the young form casual groups with other juveniles and unpaired adults. The remainder are solitary until pairing, but approximately half of all young have contact with their parents in the second year, often rejoining them if there are no succeeding young.

The voice is more complex than most geese with a wide variety of cackling and honking calls. One which will be familiar to many readers is the distance-call, used by flocks in flight and answered by birds on the ground. It is described as a high-pitched, sonorous cackling of 'gnong-ong-ong', and is also used by a solitary goose seeking a lost partner. Other calls are listed as contact-call, locomotion-call, pre-flight call, distress-call, copulation-call, nest-alarm, and so on.

In Britain the first eggs are laid at the end of March or early April, but in Iceland laying is delayed until the end of April. The nest site is often less open than with the pink-foot and a Czechoslovakian survey found 59.3% of 463 nests to be in reed beds and 19.7% in pollarded willows. The nests are rarely more than 10 m from water and the exceptions are on islands. A sample of British eggs were 85 × 58 mm and weighed 149 g. Contrary to the pink-foot a replacement clutch is laid if the first is lost. Fledging takes fifty to sixty days and the young mature at three years, although occasionally two.

Plant-material provides all the food of the greylag, mostly taken by grazing on land, but sometimes while floating on water. The vegetation includes roots, tubers, green leaves, flower heads and stems, but greylag tend to avoid hard material. It will pull up the stems of plants in soft mud to eat the roots. The greylag has a preference for young green material in summer and the underground storage organs in winter.

Our Icelandic greylag, in Britain, eat mainly grass, but also cereal grains, potatoes, carrots, turnips, sugar beet and the leaves of rape. The advantages and disadvantages to the farming community have already been discussed.

The mean annual mortality of Icelandic adults was calculated, from ringed birds, as 23% and the adult life expectancy 3.8 years. A study in Denmark gave a substantially lower expectancy of 2.6 years. The oldest ringed bird was 17 years, 4 months.

As with the pink-foot, the future of the greylag in Britain is dependent upon the maintenance of its Icelandic breeding grounds.

21

The White-fronted Goose

The restricted wintering areas in Britain of the white-fronted goose make it a relatively minor quarry species, but locally it can be important.

It is larger and longer than the pink-footed goose, smaller than the greylag and, in all but exceptional cases, larger than the lesser white-front. In general appearance the white-front resembles the other grey geese but it has the strong distinguishing feature of a buff-brown chest strongly barred and blotched with black. The upper grey-brown flanks also have a noticeable edging of white. The bill is pink, with a white nail and some adjoining orange tingeing, and the legs and feet are orange.

Both male and female are alike, although the male is usually larger. Juveniles lack the black bars underneath and the white forehead.

Lengths range between 65–78 cm (of which the body is 43–50 cm) and wing-spans 130–165 cm. Weights in England, in winter, averaged 2,450 g for males and 2,180 g for females. Juveniles averaged 2,150 g.

There are two distinct races of white-fronts wintering in Britain. *Anser albifrons albifrons* breeds on the islands of Novaya Zemlya, Vaygach and Kolguer, off the north Russian coast, and on the tundra of the Siberian mainland. Most of these birds winter in Germany and the Netherlands, but some reach us and winter in England and Wales, principally at Slimbridge (the headquarters of the Wildfowl Trust), the Montgomery-Salop border and Hampshire. This race is often a late arrival as it leaves its breeding grounds in September for the Gulf of Finland where it remains in large numbers until December before moving on to its proper winter quarters. This appears to be a fairly recent change in behaviour, for in 1963 *Wildfowl in Britain* observed that, 'whereas considerable numbers used to be in England in December and the winter peak occurred in January or early February, in the last few years the biggest arrivals have been delayed until February, with a peak at the end of that month or early in March'.

The second race is *Anser albifrons flavirostris* which breeds in west Greenland and winters entirely in Britain and Ireland, mainly the latter. The principal wintering areas in Britain are Kirkcudbright, the mainland islands

40. White-front geese overhead.

41. White-fronts alarmed.

of Argyll and the Outer Hebrides. The southward movement begins in late August but the main migration is in September and early October, some stopping off in Iceland and others making the journey to us in one stage only. The return commences in mid-April with almost all going first to Iceland and reaching west Greenland from the second week of May onwards.

For the breeding season in the tundra the white-front seeks low-lying shrubby ground, close to water, and with undulations to provide nest sites with a good view. In these surroundings it establishes a daily routine between the feeding, resting, bathing and nesting areas. The Greenland race breeds on a plateau at a height of 700 m. In their case egg-laying begins in early June and, as with the pinks, old nests are frequently re-used. The design and construction of the nest follows the same pattern and, although both sexes build, the female does most of the work. The eggs measure 79 × 53 mm and weigh 114 g, which figures are surprising in that they are lower than for the pink-foot which is a smaller goose.

The social pattern and behaviour of the white-front closely follows that of the other grey geese. The voice of the male is pitched higher than the female, and both sexes' voices are higher pitched than their relatives. Diet also follows the norm for the grey geese, although it appears to feed closer to the roost than some species and if undisturbed will actually roost on the feeding grounds. An English survey showed that in the short winter days white-fronts spent over 90% of the day feeding. It will also feed at night, particularly when there is moonlight.

It is estimated that the USSR population, west of the River Khatanga, is in the order of 100,000–150,000 birds. The numbers of this Russian race wintering in the North Sea–Baltic increased substantially between the early 1960s and 1973, rising from about 30,000 to 130,000. In this country we currently have a mid-winter peak in January and February varying between about 5,000 and 4,500.

I cannot trace a breeding population estimate for the Greenland white-fronts, but the first ever attempt at a British census was made in November 1982. This revealed some 7,000–7,500 in Scotland and it was thought about the same numbers in Ireland. There were a few only in Wales but it was thought the total population would be around 15,000.

The mean annual mortality is about 34% and the life expectancy 2.4 years. The oldest ringed bird was 13 years, 8 months.

22

The Canada Goose

This is not the most popular goose in Britain, either with the farming community or with many shooting men as it falls well short of offering the testing sport of the grey geese. The latter criticism is, in part, due to their habit of flying at fairly low heights, but an additional factor is that Canada geese are often either treated as ornamental waterfowl or left in peace. As a result, it is hardly surprising they are not wary and vigilant, testing the experience and skill of sportsmen. To put a parallel case, when swans were a legitimate quarry the man who bagged a particularly large one would have his success reported in the local paper and, as a result, the wild swans of those days were a very different breed to the present generation. However, whatever we may think of it, *Branta canadensis* is well established in Britain and its numbers are likely to grow rather than decrease.

Although we tend to think of the Canada goose as a fairly recent introduction, it was first brought to this country in the seventeenth century and has subsequently been introduced elsewhere in north-west Europe. As suggested in the preceding paragraph, it is not a highly sought-after quarry, but a commonsense estimate of the annual bag warrants its inclusion herein.

There is little chance of mistaking a Canada goose, except along the coast, for it is the only black goose to be found inland. In appearance it is a fairly large goose, mainly grey-brown with a black head and neck, white throat-patch, white lower belly, and upper and under tail-coverts, and dark flight feathers and tail. It has a long neck, and large feet and bill. There are no seasonal differences, no differences between the sexes, and the juveniles are indistinguishable by the first winter. The barnacle is the nearest goose in appearance but is smaller, shorter-necked, and has a white face, black breast and grey, instead of brown, plumage.

A complete moult occurs after breeding is complete, during which it is flightless for three to four weeks.

Sizes vary considerably with different populations, but in Europe the length varies between 90–100 cm, of which the body is less than two thirds, and the wing-span between 160–175 cm. The male is larger and much

42. Canada goose.

heavier. Average British weights, in June, were 4,880 g for males and 4,390 g for females.

Introduced populations exist in Sweden, Norway, Finland and West Germany, and birds occasionally appear in other countries. In Britain the bulk of the population is found in England, although pockets are dotted across the Lowlands and central Scotland and two areas of Ireland. By the late 1960s the total was estimated at about 10,500. This had increased to 19,400 when the last census was taken in 1976, and at that time the population was estimated to be increasing at about 8% per annum. Increased pressure by man may have reduced this growth slightly and the likelihood is that the current level is not less than 30,000.

As the name implies, the Canada goose originates from North America where it is spread across the entire Continent. There most of the races of the Canada goose are migratory, but in Britain it is a resident with a preference for lowland waters. One authority states that it favours ornamental waters but I suspect it is not so much the scenic merit as the peaceful environment which is the main attraction. It has a preference for waters sheltered by tree stands and with nearby fields for grazing. Deep, rocky and exposed waters are avoided.

As with the grey goose, the Canada forms life-long monogamous pair-bonds and, generally, its pattern of behaviour follows that of its relatives already described, although with a tendency to be more antagonistic with its fellows. Given this characteristic it is hardly surprising that the male is anything but tender to the female during copulation, grasping the female by the back of the neck and sometimes forcing her entire body under water.

The voice is rather more resonant than with the greys, and is used to produce a variety of honking calls. Both the range and purpose of the calls closely resemble those of the grey geese. A similar resemblance is found with food, as the Canada lives primarily on plant material. Most of this is taken by grazing on land, but it sometimes feeds in the water, either by dipping the head or up-ending. My own experience, with a flock who resolutely refuse to leave our fishing lake where they insist on flighting in with great splashings just as an evening rise of trout is developing, is that they are perfectly happy grazing meadow grass. This they take from the water's edge, only moving into the meadow as the fringe ground is cropped.

Egg laying starts in the second half of March, but the main period is the first half of April. The site is close to water and on islands if these are available. (In my personal experience a nest is never sited on the mainland if island space is present.) Shelter is sought, usually a bush, but bracken or heather will suffice. The nest is a low pile of twigs, leaves, grass or reeds and is re-used in successive years. It is lined with down, has a height of 20 cm and a diameter varying between 50–75 cm. The eggs are oval, matt or cream, measuring 86 × 58 mm and weighing 220 g. A normal clutch is five to six and a replacement clutch is laid after a clutch loss. Incubation, by the hen alone, takes twenty-eight to thirty days and the resultant young are self-feeding. As usual with the geese both parents care for and protect the young. Fledging takes forty to forty-eight days and the young stay with their parents until the start of the next breeding season.

The mean mortality of English adults has been calculated at 22% and the life expectancy three to nine years. The oldest ringed bird was 23 years, 5 months.

As the environment in which the Canada goose has lived successfully for many years is unlikely to change, there is no reason to fear for its future. Indeed, as numbers have risen slowly, the trend will probably continue.

Conversion Tables

LENGTH

cm	inches
1	0.4
2	0.8
3	1.2
4	1.6
5	2.0
6	2.4
7	2.8
8	3.2
9	3.5
10	3.9
20	7.9
30	11.8
40	15.7
50	19.7
60	23.6
70	27.6
80	31.5
90	35.4
100	39.4

km	miles
1	0.6
2	1.2
3	1.9
4	2.5
5	3.1
6	3.7
7	4.3
8	5.0
9	5.6
10	6.2
20	12.4
30	18.6
40	24.9
50	31.1
60	37.2
70	43.4
80	49.7
90	55.9
100	62.1

AREA

ha	acres
1	2.5
2	5.0
3	7.4
4	9.9
5	12.4
6	14.8
7	17.3
8	19.8
9	22.2
10	24.7
20	49.4
30	74.1
40	98.8
50	123.6
60	148.2
70	173.0
80	197.7
90	222.3
100	247.1

MASS (WEIGHT)

kg	pounds
1	2.2
2	4.4
3	6.6
4	8.8
5	11.0
6	13.2
7	15.4
8	17.6
9	19.8
10	22.0
20	44.1
30	66.1
40	88.2
50	110.2
60	132.3
70	154.3
80	176.4
90	198.4
100	220.5

Bibliography

Barnes, R. F. W., Tapper, S. C. and Williams J.
The Use of Pastures by Brown Hares
The Game Conservancy, Fordingbridge, n.d.

Bagfield N. G. and R. Hewson
'Automatic Monitoring of Trail Use by Mountain Hares'
Journal of Wildlife Management, 39, i, January 1975

Birds of the Western Palaearctic, The
Chief Editor: Stanley Cramp
Oxford University Press, London 1977, 1980

Book of British Mammals (RSPCA)
Edited by Leofric Boyle. Collins, London 1981

British Sporting Birds
Edited by F. B. Kirkman and H. S. Hutchinson
T. C. & E. C. Jack Ltd., London 1936

Chitty, D.
'The natural selection of self-regulatory behaviour in animal populations'
Proceedings of the Ecological Society of Australia 2, 1967, 51–78

Coles, C. L.
Game Conservation in a Changing Countryside
Museum Press, London 1968

Corbet, G. B. and Southern, H. N.
The Handbook of British Mammals (second edition)
Blackwell Scientific Publications, Oxford 1964

Dixon, Charles
The Game Birds and Wild Fowl of the British Islands
Chapman and Hall, London 1893

Duncan, James
'Louping-ill virus'
Game Conservancy Annual Review, 1980

Duncan, J. S. and others
'Ticks, Louping-ill and Red Grouse on moors in Speyside'
Journal of Wild Life Management, 1978

Ecology and Management of European Hare Populations
Edited by Z. Pielowski and Z. Pucek
Polish Hunting Association, 1976

Evans, G. E. and Thompson, D.
The Leaping Hare
Faber and Faber, London 1972

Fisher, James
The Shell Bird Book
Ebury Press and Michael Joseph, London 1966

Flux, John E. C.
'Life History of the Mountain Hare in North-East Scotland'
Journal of Zoology, London, 161, 1970

Fuller, R. J. and Youngman, R. E.
'The Utilisation of farmland by Golden Plovers wintering in Southern England'
Bird Study, March 1979, 26, i

Fur, Feather and Fin Series:—
The Pheasant, 1895
The Wildfowl, 1912
The Partridge, 1893
Snipe and Woodcock, 1904
Longmans, Green & Co., London

Game Conservancy, The
Annual Review, 1974, 1975, 1978, 1980, 1982

Game Conservancy, The
The Hare Project, 1980, 1981

Gladstone, H. S.
Record Bags and Shooting Records
H. F. & S. Witherby, London 1922

Green, Dr R. E.
Population Ecology of Alectoria rufa
The Game Conservancy, 1982

Grouse in Health and in Disease, The
(Being the final report of the Committee of Inquiry on Grouse Disease)
Smith, Elder & Co., London 1911

Grouse (Proceedings of the Second International Symposium on Grouse)
Editor Dr T. W. I. Lovel
The World Pheasant Association, 1982

Harrison, Matthew L.
British Mammals
Collins, London 1952

Hewson, R.
'Browsing by Mountain Hares'
Journal of Zoology, London 182, 1977

Hewson, R.
'Food Selection by Brown Hares'
Journal of Applied Ecology, December 1977

Hewson, R.
'Grazing by Mountain Hares'
Journal of Applied Ecology, 13, December 1976, 657–666

Hewson, R.
'Population study of Mountain Hares in North-East Scotland from 1956–1969'
Journal of Animal Ecology, June 1976, 395–414

Hudson, P. and Tapper, S.
'Grouse Populations—do they cycle?'
Game Conservancy Annual Review, 1979

Hudson, P., 1980
'The production of Red Grouse in 1980'
Game Conservancy Annual Review, 1980

Jakcs, Λ. D. and Watson, Λ.
'Winter Whitening of Scottish Mountain Hares'
Journal of Zoology, London, 176, 1975

Lever, Christopher
The Naturalized Animals of the British Isles
Hutchinson, London 1977

Lockley, R. M.
The Private Life of the Rabbit
Andre Deutsch, London 1964

Macdonald, D. G. F.
Grouse Disease—its cause and remedies
W. H. Allen & Co., London 1883

Mackenzie, J. M. D.
'Fluctuations in the number of British tetraonids'
Journal of Animal Ecology, 21, 128–53

Marchington, John
Pugs and Drummers
Faber and Faber, London 1978

Maxwell, Aymer
Pheasants and Covert Shooting
Adam and Charles Black, London 1935

Mead-Briggs, A. R.
'The reproductive biology of the rabbit flea *spilopsyllus cuniculi* (Dale) and the dependence of this species upon the breeding of its host'
Journal of Experimental Biology, 41, 1964, 371–402

Millais, J. G.
Game Birds and Shooting Sketches
Henry Sotheran, London 1894

Miller, G. R.
'Burning of heather moorland for red grouse'
Bulletin Ecologique, 11, 1980, 725–33

Moran, P. A. P.
'The statistical analysis of game-bird records'
Journal of Animal Ecology, 21, 154–8 and 23, 35–7

Moss, R., Watson and Parr
Maternal nutrition and breeding in red grouse
Institute of Terrestrial Ecology, 1975

Murton, R. K.
The Wood-Pigeon (New Naturalist series)
Collins, London 1965

North of England Grouse Research Project
Reports, 1979–82

Parker, Eric
Game Birds, Beasts and Fishes
(The Lonsdale Library)
Seeley Service, London 1935

Potts, G. R., Dr
'Sheep, sheep ticks, grouse and hill farming'
Game Conservancy Annual Review, 1979

Potts, G. R., Dr
The Effects of Modern Agriculture, Nest Predation, and Game Management on the Population Ecology of Partridges
The Game Conservancy, Fordingbridge, n.d.

Prater, A. J.
Estuary Birds of Britain & Ireland
T. & A. D. Poyser, Calton 1961

Price, Lloyd
Rabbits for Profit and Rabbits for Powder
H. Cox, London 1884

Ratcliffe, D. A.
'Observations on the Breeding of the Golden Plover in Great Britain'
Bird Study, 23, ii, June 1976

Sheail, John
Rabbits and their History
David & Charles, Newton Abbot, 1971

Tapper, S. C., Green, R. E. and Rands, M. R. W.
Effects of Mammalian Predators on Partridge Populations
The Game Conservancy, Fordingbridge, n.d.

Tapper, Stephen, and Parsons, Nicola
Changing status of the Brown Hare in Britain
The Game Conservancy, Fordingbridge, n.d.

Thompson, H. V. and Warden, Alastair N.
The Rabbit (New Naturalist Series)
Collins, London 1956

Vesey-Fitzgerald, B.
The Vanishing Wildlife of Britain
MacGibbon & Kee, London 1969

Vesey-Fitzgerald, B.
British Game (New Naturalist Series)
Collins, London 1946

Wallace, R.
Heather and Moor Burning
Oliver and Boyd, Edinburgh 1917

Watson, A. and Miller, G. R.
Grouse Management
The Game Conservancy, Fordingbridge 1976

Watson, A. and Moss, R.
'Advances in our understanding of population dynamics of red grouse'
Ardex, 1980

Watson, A. and Moss, R.
Population cycles in the Tetraonidae
Institute of Terrestrial Ecology, 1979

Wildfowl in Great Britain
Edited by G. L. Atkinson-Willes
Her Majesty's Stationery Office, London 1963

Wilson, G. R.
'Diseases in Red Grouse'
Game Conservancy Annual Review, 1977

Woodland Grouse Symposium, 1978
Edited by Dr T. W. I. Lovel
The World Pheasant Association, 1979

Index

Compiled by Mrs P. M. McDougall

Page numbers printed in italics indicate illustrations

Adams, Richard, *Watership Down*, 151

Africa, winter migrants, 105, 108; wood-pigeon, 134

agriculture, effect of modern methods on wild life, 12, 27, 30, 34, 36, 38, 120, 123; and wood-pigeon, 135, 136, *137*, 140, 144, 145; and geese, 186, 195

Alexander, H. V., and woodcock, 97, 98

America, over-shooting pigeon, 130, 143; Ducks Unlimited, 130

Anatini (dabbling ducks), characteristics, 165–6

Anserini (swans and true geese), characteristics, 185–203

Asia, wild life, hare, 114; pheasant, 50, 51; ptarmigan, 65; scolopacid birds, 89; snipe, 102; woodcock, 91

Australia, introduction of hares, 114, 117; myxomatosis, 154, 156

Barrington, R. M., woodcock migration, 92–3

Breadalbane, Lord, and capercaillie, 80

Britain, host to wintering wild fowl, 161, 163, 185, 190, 192, 194, 195; capercaillie, 79–80; ducks, 174, 178, 182; geese, migrant, 185, 190, 192, 194, 195; resident, 191–2, 193, 200, 201; golden plover, 108; grouse, 12, 71; hare, 111–12, *113*, 114, 121, 122, 126; partridge, 28, 29, 30, 40; pheasant, 58; ptarmigan, 67; rabbit flea vector, 156; snipe, 102; woodcock, 89, 91, 92; *see also* England; England and Wales; Scotland; Wales

British Association for Shooting and Conservation (BASC), 2, 163, 167, 193

Brodie, I., and capercaillie in Scotland, 80–1

Browne, Sir Thomas, and red-legged partridge, 39

Buckinghamshire, Great Linford Wildfowl Research Centre, 162, 163; duckling mortality and midge availability, 170, 172

Burt, Edward, and capercaillie, 79

Buxton, Sir Thomas Fowell, 80

Canada, hare breeding habits, 117

capercaillie (*Tetrao urogallus*), 62, 69, 71; appearance, 81–2; behavioural patterns, 73, 82–4; calls, 83; decline and re-introduction, 79, 80, 85, 86; distribution, 80–1, 85; feeding habits, 82, 84; in flight, 82; management technique, 85–6; mortality rate, 85; population trends, 85; quarry ranking, 27, 81; shooting season, 81

Chambers, Ephraim, and red-legged partridge, 39

Channel Islands, red-legged partridge, 39, 41

Chapman, Abel, sportsman/naturalist, 2

Charadriiformes Order, 89, 107

Charles II, King, and red-legged partridge, 40

Chitty, D., aggression in red grouse, 22

Cobbold, Dr T. S., and strongyle organism, 24–5

Colchis, origin of common pheasant, 48

Cole, Charles, 3

Columbiformes Order, 130, 138

County Trusts for Nature Conservation, 163

curlew, 89; protected species, 2

Daniel, William B., and red-legged partridge, 40

diseases, grouse, and population dynamism 20–1, 23–4; louping-ill, 25; hare, 114, 123, 129, 157; pheasant, 59, 61; rabbit (myxomatosis), 154, 156; wood-pigeon, 143

dotterel, 110
doves, varieties, 130
ducks (*Anseriformes*), common behavioural
    patterns, 165–6; shooting season, 166
    Mallard (*Anas platyrynchos*), 161, 163;
        appearance and physical characteristics,
        164, 167–8; behavioural patterns,
        168–70, *171*, 172; in flight, *164*, *171*,
        177; flight ponds, 172; quarry ranking,
        167, 173; winter population, Greater
        London, 162, 168
    Pintail (*Anas acuta*) 163; appearance, 181,
        183; behavioural patterns, 182, 184; in
        flight, 182; quarry ranking, 181
    Teal (*Anas crecca*), appearance, 177–8;
        behavioural patterns, 169, 177–9; call,
        179; distribution, 178; feeding, 179, 180;
        in flight, 89, 165, 177, 179; quarry
        ranking, 177
    Wigeon (*Anas Penelope*), 163, 167;
        appearance, 173, *175*; behavioural
        patterns, 174, 176; call, 176; in flight,
        173; predation, 176; quarry ranking,
        167, 173
Duncan, Stanley, and wildfowl, 161

Egypt, ancient, and pigeons, 131
England, grey partridge, 29; red-legged
    partridge introduction, 39–40, 43; the
    pheasant, 46, 55, 57; extinction of
    ptarmigan, 65; woodcock migration, 92;
    teal wintering population, 178
England and Wales, grouse moor acreage, 8;
    louping-ill disease, 25; grey partridge in
    decline, 27; habitat, 29–30;
    disappearance of black grouse, 72; rabbit
    population, 157; reservoir habitats,
    162–3; wintering geese, 196, 199
Europe, rabies decimation of fox population,
    58; black grouse in snow, 75; effect of
    hares on cultivated plants, 116; duck
    mortality, 172, 176; wild life,
    capercaillie, 82, 84, 85, 86; ducks, 169,
    172, 176, 178, 182; geese, 190, 194, 195,
    196; golden plover, 107, 108; grouse, 12,
    72, 75, 77; hares, 114, 116, 117, 121,
    123; partridge, 28, 29, 30–1, 32, 37, 40,
    41; pheasant, 51, 57; ptarmigan, 65;
    rabbits, 141; snipe, 102, 105, 106; teal,
    178; woodcock, 90, 91, 92; wood-
    pigeon, 142

Fairburn Ings Nature Reserve, 162
farming, *see* agriculture
Fife, Earl of, Mar Lodge estate, 80
First World War, and game shooting world,
    27, 49

Fisher, James, 7–8, 140; mallard population,
    168
flocking, black grouse, 73; wood-pigeon,
    135–6, 142
Flux, John, study of mountain hare, 126,
    127, 128
forestry, 46, 51, 70, 76, 80, 86
fossil remains, British, 79, 111, 167, 173,
    177, 185

Galliformes, Order, 27, 39, 46, 62, 71, 79
Game Conservancy, 2–3; insects in grouse
    chick diet, 16; red grouse research, 23,
    24; vaccination of sheep against ticks,
    25; predation losses in nesting hen
    partridge, 32, 34, 38; pheasant research,
    57, 58–9; woodcock research, 89;
    National Game Census, 89, 91, 123, 145;
    'The Hare Project', 114–15, 116, 120,
    123; *Grouse Management*, 9; heather-
    burning instructions, 26
gamekeepers, and grouse predation, 25;
    increase in pre-First World War, 27; and
    driven partridge, 30; and partridge
    predators, 32; use of traps, 32, 34; and
    partridge and pheasant foods, 35;
    protection of game birds, 150
Glasshouse Crops Research Institute, insect
    predators on aphids, 37
Goose (*Anseriformes*), 185
    Barnacle, 200
    Brenta ('black'), 185; common behavioural
        patterns, 185–7; call, 186, 187; in flight,
        186; fossil beds, 185; migration rhythm,
        185, 187
    Canada (*Brenta canadensis*), 163, 185;
        appearance, 200–201, *202*; behavioural
        patterns, 201, 203; calls, 201;
        distribution, 200, 201; quarry ranking,
        200
    Greylag (*Amer Anser*), 163, 185, 189;
        appearance, 193; behavioural patterns,
        193–4, 195; calls, 194; food, 195;
        migration route, 194; quarry ranking,
        193; mortality, 203
    Pink-footed (*Anser Brachyrhynchus*), 163;
        appearance, 189–90; breeding
        distribution, 190, 191; damage by, 186;
        migration route, 190; population history,
        190–2
    Whitefront (*Anser albifrons albifrons*), 163,
        185; appearance, 196, *197*, *198*;
        behavioural patterns, 198; call, 198; in
        flight, *197*; history, 79; quarry ranking,
        196; wintering in Britain, 1, 196, 198,
        199; in Russia, 196

Lesser Whitefront (*Anser albifrons flavirostris*), wintering in Britain, 196, 198

Gould, John, and Japanese pheasant, 49

Green, Dr R. E., and red-leg partridge, 43; double clutching, 44

Grouse, black (*Tetrao tetrix*), 27, 144; appearance, 71–2; behavioural patterns, 73–5; calls, 74; in decline, 72, 76; family, 62, 69, 71, 72; in flight, 72; plant food, 75; 'lekking' arena, 73–5; quarry ranking, 71; predation, 77; shooting season, 71; weather and chick survival, 77

Grouse, red (*Lagopus lagopus scoticus*), appearance, 8–9, *10*, 11, *18*; behavioural patterns, 13–15, 19–20; calls and flight songs, 15, 20; chick survival, 16–19, 25; in flight, 8, *10*, *18*, 66; food supply, 12, 15–16, 17, 22, 66; habitat, 7, 12–13; population dynamism, 12, 14, 15–16, 20–2, 26; predators, 14, 22; quarry ranking, 7, 8, 27, 62, 89; shooting season, 8, 20, 62; territorial aggression, 14–15, 22; sex and age tests, 11

grouse moors, 8, 14; rentals, 8; list of shootings, 8; acreage, 8; spring stock variations, 14; heather and bed rock quality, 17; heather burning, 25–6; threatened by sheep, 26

Handbook of British Birds, extinction of capercaillie, 80

Hare, brown (*Lepus capensis*), appearance, 112, *113*, *119*; behavioural patterns, 114–18, *119*, 120; diseases, 114, 122, 123; leveret survival and dispersal, 114, 118, *119*, 120; licence to kill (1100), 48; predation, 115, 120, 122–3; quarry ranking, 111–12, 123–4; radio tracking, 115–16; shooting restrictions, 111, 112; snow burrows, 75

Hare, mountain (*Lepus timidus*), 112; appearance, 125–6; behavioural patterns, 126–8, camouflage in snow, 126; low economic/quarry ranking, 125; predators, 128–9

Harriers, hen, 110

Harrison, Drs Jeffrey and Pamela, 163

Hawaii, pheasants, 51

Hawker, Col. Peter, 2, 131; concept of sportsmanship, 161–2

heather; food and shelter for grouse, 12–13, 14, 84; availability in Britain and Ireland, 16; dependence on management, 17; and chick survival, 17; winter browning, 17; burning against

ticks, 25; ptarmigan and, 66; hare food, 127

hedgerows, replaced by barbed wire, 30; egg-laying and nesting cover, 32, 33, 37, 43, 57

Hewson, Raymond, hare feeding habits, 116, 127

Hiraethog, Gruffydd, pheasants in Merionethshire, 48

Hirons, Dr Graham, study of woodcock, 89, 93, 95, 96, 97, 99

Hudson, Dr Peter, grouse ecologist, 23

Iceland, geese, 190, 191, 193, 194, 195; golden plover, 107, 108, 109; migrant mallard, 169, 172; ptarmigan, 67, 68; teal, 178; wigeon, 174

insecticides, toxic, and chick survival, 36; and hares, 123; wood-pigeon deaths, 144

insects, chick dependence, 1, 16, 19, 34, 36, 67, 76, 84, 170; preferred species, 34–5, 36

Institute of Terrestrial Ecology, 16, 22, 23

International Waterfowl Research Bureau, winter counts, 163

Ireland, capercaillie, 70; ducks, 169, 174, 178, 181; grey partridge protection, 27, 30; heather acreage, and availability, 8, 16, 17; decrease in keepering, 27; pheasants, 48; wintering species, 108, 125, 126, 128, 194; woodcock migrants, 92–3

Japan, mountain hare, 126; pheasant, 51; ptarmigan, 65

Jeffries, Richard, and shooting syndicates, 49

Lagomorpha Order, 111, 125, 146

Latham, John, and capercaillie, 79–80

Leaping Hare, The, 111

Leeds, second Duke of, and red-legged partridges, 40

Lesley, John, Bishop of Ross, pheasants in Scotland, 48

literature, sporting, 1, 2, 21, 131

Lockley, R. M., *Private Life of the Rabbit*, 151, 152, 153, 154

Lowe, Dr P. R., and Pheasants in Roman Britain, 46, 48

Macdonald, Dr Davis, and fox/pheasant relationship, 58

Macdonald, Duncan, moor rents, 8; discredits scientists, 21; on Cobbold, 24–5

MacKenzie, J. M. D. and Moran, P. A. P., analysis of grouse bag numbers, 21

Malmesbury Abbey, licence to kill hares and pheasants, 48
management techniques, brown hare, 123–4; capercaillie, 85–6; ducks, 172; grey partridge, 37–8; grouse, 25, 77; pheasant, 57, 61
Millais, J. G., *Game Birds and Shooting Sketches*, 21, 63, 67, 72
Moryson, Fynes, on pheasants in Ireland, 48
Murton, Dr R. K., and collared dove, 130; and wood-pigeon, 132, 134, 135–6, 138, 140, 142, 143

National Environmental Research Council, 43
New Zealand, hares, 114, 117; pheasant, 51; rabbit, 154
Niewold, F. J. J., black grouse in decline, 77
North America, geese, 190, 196, 198, 199, 201; hare introduction, 114; pheasants, 51; ptarmigan, 68; woodcock, 91, 96; relationship with earthworm, 95; remains, 89
North of England Grouse Project, 22–4
North Sea, teal, 178; whitefront goose, 199
Norway and Sweden, *see* Scandinavia

Old Statistical Account of Scotland, The, 'last' capercaillie, 80

Partridge, shooting methods, walking up and driving, 28; record bags, 28; dependence on reared birds, 28–9; shooting season, 29; chick survival, 34–7, *42*, 44–5
   Grey (*Perdix perdix*), appearance, *28*, 29; behavioural patterns, 30–1; calls, 31; in flight, 30, *33*; food supply, 27, 31–2, 34–5; habitat, 29–30; dependence on insects, 1, 34–5, 44–5; effect of insecticides, 36–7; suggested management technique, 37–8; population dynamism, 27, 30, 38; quarry popularity, 27, 30, 39; predation, 32
   Red-legged (*Alectoris rufa*), appearance, 41, *42*; breeding biology, 43–4; calls, 41; chick behaviour, 44–5; compared with the grey, 39, 40, 41, 44–5; food, 44, 45; habitat, 41, 43; introduction into Britain, 39–40; quarry ranking, 40–1; predation, 44; sporting management, 45
Pennant, Thomas, and Chinese ring-necked pheasant, 49
Peregrines, predators, 110
pests, grouse, 23–4, 143
Phasianidae family, 27, 39, 46
Pheasant (*Phasianus colchicus torquatus*), 27; appearance, *47*, 50, 56, *60*; behavioural patterns, 52–5, 57; call variety, 53–4, 54–5, 57; egg-laying and incubation, 55, 57; in flight, 51; food supply, 51, 53, 57; habitat, 50–1; early history, 46, 48; nesting, 51, 52, 53, 55, 57; predation, 58; quarry status, 7, 49; shooting season, 49; survival of reared birds, 57–8; socio/economic effects on countryside, 46, *47*, 49–50; the syndicate, 49; variations, 46, 49
Picozzi, N., and woodland grouse, 69, 76
Plover, golden (*Pluvialis apricaria*), appearance, 107–8; calls, 109; distribution, 107, 108–9; food supply, 109, 110; habitat, 108, 109; predation, 109; wintering areas, 108
poaching, 53, 63
pollution, acid air, 85; rubbish dump predators, 85
Potts, Dr Richard, and Game Conservancy, 23, 43, 89
predation, and red grouse decline, 22, 25; and driven game shooting, 27; and incubating hen partridge, 32; control by keepering, 32; use of traps, 32, 34; and partridge chick survival, 34; created by rubbish dumps, 85; wild life adaptation, 120
predators: avian, 14, 15, 58–9, 122, 128, 143, 157; cats, 14, 32, 38, 128, 157; fox, 14, 25, 32, 38, 57, 58, 122–3, 128, 157; stoats, 14, 32, 34, 38, 59, 128, 143, 157

Rabbit (European *Oryctologus cuniculus*), behavioural patterns, 127, 150–2; breeding procedures, 153–4, 157; distribution, 146, 148, 150; ferreting, 131, 147; introduction to Britain, 39, 146–7; myxomatosis, 122, 154, *155*, 156; physical characteristics, 112, 148, *149*, *155*; population structure, 156–7; quarry status, 146, 148, 150; warrens, man-made, 148, 150
Rabbit Clearance Societies, 157
radio telemetry, use of in woodcock study, 89, 93, 95, 96, 97; and hare behaviour, 115
Ratcliffe, D. A., breeding golden plover, 108
Report of the Grouse Disease Committee, 9, 16

St John, Charles, sporting writer, 131
Sandpipers, 89
Savory, John, crop content of grouse chicks, 16
science, and natural world, 1, 21, 69
Scolopacidae Order, 100

Scotland, grouse moor acreage, 8;
population, 12; variation in heather
quality, 17; eagle predators, 128–9;
capercaillie, 80, 85, 86; ducks, 174, 178,
182; geese, 186, 190, 192, 193, 194, 196,
198, 201; golden plover, 107, 108, 109;
grouse, 8, 12, 72, 73; hares, 112, 114,
117, 125, 126, 128; partridge, 27, 29, 30;
pheasant, 48; ptarmigan, 65, 66, 68;
snipe, 102; woodcock, 92; wood-pigeon,
140
Second International Symposium on Grouse,
1981, 80–1
Sevenoaks Experimental Wildfowl Reserve,
163
Shaw, De Visme, and woodcock, 91, 92, 94
sheep, a threat to grouse, 26; ticks, 25, 157
Silchester, Reading, Romano-British midden,
46, 48
Snipe, common (*Gallinago gallinago*), 89;
appearance, 101–2, *103*; behavioural
patterns, 102, 104, 105–6; distribution,
102, 106; drumming flights, 100, 101,
102, 104; essential habitat, 101, 102,
106; migrants, 104–5; underground
feeding, 105
Snipe, jack 101; protected species, 2
Snipe, Great, 101–2
Scandinavia (Arctic; Baltic States; Norway
and Sweden), capercaillie, 80, 82, 85;
duck, 182; geese, 190, 191, 193; grouse,
72, 73; partridge, 29; pheasant, 51;
snipe, 102; woodcock, 90, 91, 92; wood-
pigeon, 134, 142
Snow bunting, 110
swans, legitimate quarry, 200

Tapper, S. and Parsons, N., and hare
population, 114
Tetraonidae family, 21, 22, 62, 71, 77
Thompson, Nethersole, bird population and
climatic changes, 110
tree-planting, for pheasants, 51; useless
'factories', 51, 70; Sitka spruce, 80, 81,
82, 84; 'grannies', 82, 86; and
woodcock, 98

Upton, Nicholas, rearing pheasants, 48
USSR, grouse population, 12; partridge
mortality, 37; pheasant habitat, 50;
black grouse, 72, 73; woodcock, 90, 91,
92; hare breeding habits, 117; wood-
pigeon migration, 142; ducks, 174, 178,
182; geese, 193, 196, 199

Van Oss, Richard, 3

Vesey-Fitzgerald, B., 2, 48, 115, 146; and
ptarmigan, 65, 67

Wales, grouse moors, 8; heather quality, 17;
mountain hare introduction, 126
Watson, Dr Adam, grouse research, 14, 17;
ptarmigan chick flight, 67; capercaillie
chick diet, 84
Watson, A. and Miller, G. R., and grouse, 9,
25
Watson, A. and Moss, R., *Population Cycles
in Tetraonidae*, 22–3
weather, wild life and snow, 15–16, 31, 126;
and heather quality, 17; and population
fluctuations, 22, 24; and partridge night
roosting, 31; and partridge survival, 37,
44; ptarmigan migration, 67–8; and hare
population, 120–1; and feeding, 127–8;
and wild life survival, 140, 142
weeds, and partridge chick survival, 35–6;
losses due to herbicides, 44
Wegge, Per, capercaillie in decline, 85;
rubbish dumps predators, 85
Wild Life and Countryside Act, 1981,
protected birds, 101
Wild Life in Great Britain, 168, 169, 196
Wildfowl Trust, Slimbridge, 163, 191, 194,
196
Wildfowlers Association of Great Britain and
Ireland, 161, 162
Willoughby, F. and Ray, J., on the red-leg,
39; wood-pigeon flocking, 139
Wilson, Edward, A., 21
Woodcock (*Scolophax rusticola L.*),
appearance, 90, 91; behavioural
patterns, 89, 90, 93, 95; backward facing
brain, 89, 90; calls (roding), 95–6; chick
obscurity, 94, 96; in competition with
pheasant, 98; and earthworm density,
92, 94, 95, 96, 98; food range, 94–5;
preferred habitat, 91–2, 97–8; migration
habits, 91, 92, 93, 101; nesting and egg-
laying, 95–6; quarry ranking, 89–90;
roding flight, 91, 93–4, *94*, 95; effect of
shooting on numbers, 98–9
wood-pigeon (*Columba palumbus L.*),
appearance, 132, *133*; breeding round,
138–9, 140; alleged Continental
invaders, 134, 142; diseases and
parasites, 143–4; in flight, *141*; habitat,
134–5, 140; migration speculation, 142;
pre-history remains, 130–1; influence of
shooting on population, 136, 140, 143,
145; status with shooting man, 131–2;
social behaviour, 135–6, *137*, 138, 142
World Pheasant Association, 69, 78; and
grouse, 83; and capercaillie, 85